Harvard Economic Studies, Volume 139

The studies in this series are published under the direction of the Department of Economics of Harvard University.
The Department does not assume responsibility for the views expressed.

The Land Question and the Irish Economy, 1870–1903

Barbara Lewis Solow

Harvard University Press
Cambridge, Massachusetts, 1971

Acknowledgments

My debt to Professor Alexander Gerschenkron of Harvard University is very great. I would neither have undertaken nor continued in this work without his assistance and encouragement. I am indebted to his wisdom as well as to his knowledge. Parts of this frail vessel were launched in the shark-infested waters of his graduate seminar in economic history at Harvard.

I discovered early that from my husband and his colleagues in the Economics Department at M.I.T. I had insensibly acquired a set of academic standards so exalted as to be, for all practical purposes, completely paralyzing. It was only my husband's monumental indifference to the Irish land question that gave me courage to begin. During the course of this work he exhibited qualities of tact and diplomacy that neither of us suspected he possessed. I am sure he must be very grateful to me for bringing their existence to his attention.

Professor Oliver MacDonagh of University College Cork kindly read parts of the manuscript and gave me indispensable aid at an earlier stage. Professor Robert W. Fogel and Professor George J. Stigler, both of the University of Chicago, and Professor Maurice Lévy-Leboyer of the University of Paris at Nanterre also made helpful comments. I am also indebted to Mrs. Elizabeth W. Carlhian for guidance in matters of agricultural techniques. I am beginning to wish I had accepted all the advice offered so I could blame these eminent scholars for the errors that remain; however I did not and cannot.

Acknowledgment is made to the estate of the Sixth Marquis of Lansdowne for permission to quote from *Glanerought and the Petty-Fitz-Maurices* and to *The Economic History Review* for permission to quote from S. H.

Cousens, "The Regional Variations in Population Changes in Ireland 1861–1881."

Finally I am grateful to Mrs. Inez Crandall for bestowing the same care on the typing of the manuscript that she has bestowed on many, perhaps more substantial, works in economics.

Contents

TABLES

FIGURES

FIGURES

*The Land Question
and the Irish Economy,
1870–1903*

1.
Introduction

Now we will proceed to other like defects,
amongst which there is one generall
inconvenience, which raigneth almost
throughout all Ireland; that is, the Lords
of land and freeholders doe not there use
to set out their land in farme, or for tearme
of years, to their tenants, but onely from
yeare to yeare, and some during pleasure,
neither indeed will the Irish tenant or
husbandman otherwise take his land, then
so long as he list himself. The reason
hereof in the tenant is, for that the land-
lords there use most shamefully to racke
their tennants, exacting of them what he
pleaseth. So that the poor husbandman
either dare not binde himselfe to him for
longer tearme, or thinketh, by his continuall
liberty of change, to keep his landlord the
rather in awe from wronging of him.

Edmund Spenser (1596)

The view that the land tenure system provides the explanation for Ireland's poverty-stricken past has an ancient and honorable history. What can we say of a diagnosis of Irish economic development that is repeated again and again from the time of Elizabeth to the time of Victoria? Have we a monument to the immemorial wrongs of the Irish people? Or should we look more closely at the logic of the argument, try to assess its validity and relevance, and consider the causes and consequences of attributing principally to the tenure system the course of Irish economic development? The latter is the aim of the present inquiry.

The land tenure explanation of Irish economic problems did not dominate the field from the first. The explanations put forth during the first half of the nineteenth century may be grouped under three heads. The first was associated with the conceptual framework of the English classical economists. If the land area of a country is fixed and population increases, diminishing returns to labor will set in and rents will become a progressively larger share of the product. If population is increasing along Malthusian lines, land of a given quality will be worked by more labor, at lower wages, and with higher rents than in an economy without such population pressure. This theory stood behind those who pointed to overpopulation and excessive subdivision as the root of the Irish problem. The policies appropriate to this diagnosis were emigration and reclamation of wasteland, both of which would alter the land/labor relation, and these solutions had important advocates in pre-Famine Ireland.

Although capital plays a smaller role in the economic formulation, it certainly was in the minds of those who applied the scheme to Ireland. Indeed, the successful organization of English agriculture into large farms and capitalist farmers, with accompanying expenditures on buildings and improved technique, provided a contrast to Ireland that was hard to escape. If by emigration or other means the population could be controlled, capital must be free to move in and take advantage of profit opportunities. This meant that institutional barriers to the movement of capital must be removed, and the cry for free trade in land was taken up by those who believed impediments to capital mobility were important. In Ireland two major legislative acts embodied this policy: the Encumbered Estates Act, which allowed embarrassed landlords to sell estates that had previously been bound up in legal entanglements; and the Deasy Act of 1860, which removed the final traces of feudal relation between landlord and tenant at law and introduced important simplifications to land law.

A second approach to the Irish problem, which might be called the underdeveloped country explanation, was not articulated as a theory but may be attributed to those who emphasized the need for social overhead capital. This emphasis was more prominent before the triumph of laissez-faire ideas, but many people continued to look at Ireland in this way throughout the century. In the early years, perhaps it dominated. Thus there were Reports of Royal Commissioners on Bog Drainage in 1810, 1810–1811, and 1813–1814. The Select Committee on the Poor and Disease in 1819 recommended, along with drainage, flood control measures and improved communications in the mountains and fishing districts. The 1823 Select Committee on the Poor recommended the extension of the linen trade to the South, encouraging fisheries, improving harbors, and opening mountain roads. This committee supported the drainage recommendations of the 1819 committee and did not shrink from advocating the use of public funds. In the years before the Famine, there was a continuing stream of reports on fisheries, roads and bridges, the linen trade, Shannon navigation, and other proposed improvements.

These policies were not seriously tried. Ireland has not often been a popular subject at Westminster. Nor is it clear that, if the expenditures had been made, the state had yet developed the kind of administrative apparatus necessary to ensure their success. In any case it would be asking a lot of a government whose own best path to economic progress lay in hacking away at a crippling legacy of state interference to institute for part of its people a program based on just such "interference." Nevertheless, however far from realistic political implementation, the perception existed of Ireland as an underdeveloped country for whom the best hope was public expenditure on drainage, flood control, communications, education, rural industries, and the like.

Parallel to these views on the causes and cures of the Irish problem, increasing attention was paid to the land tenure system. In 1835 Sharman Crawford, then M.P. for Dundalk, moved for leave to bring in a bill to amend the law of landlord and tenant in Ireland. This bill embodied a modest demand for tenants upon eviction to be compensated for the improvements they had made on their holdings. It was an important moment in the history of the Irish land question. Before we pursue the argument of Sharman Crawford and of those who believed the system of land tenure lay at the root of Irish economic difficulties, let us take a closer look at the existing land law in Ireland.

The English law of tenure deals with the relationship of lord to tenant as it developed in medieval England. That relationship ceased to have practical meaning in the modern world, but English law nevertheless proceeds from the old feudal pattern. In a world where the right to occupy and cultivate land was bought and sold like any other marketable object, the law remained encumbered with a baggage of feudal concepts. One way to perceive the English law is to contrast it with a code that had not been trammeled by such a burden. This expository device was adopted in a small volume published in 1880 by Alexander Richey, Deputy Regius Professor of Law at the University of Dublin, and his explanation is closely followed here.[1]

Roman law, free from the feudal system, began with a clear idea of absolute ownership—*dominium*—over land as well as chattels. In English feudal law, nobody owned land (unless the king): the basic relation was between lord and tenant. The tenant held land of his lord (who indeed held it of someone else, until we reach the king) in return for services; if the services were unfulfilled, the tenant had no right to occupy the land. Ownership had no place in such a system; the right of possession (*seisin*) is the central concept, and all the real actions of medieval times were based on the right of *seisin*.

When the French jurists came to think about the hiring of land, they were free to proceed directly with the concept of a contract in which the lessor transfers to the lessee the ownership of the premises. Now, no contract expresses all the rights and obligations that flow from the terms of the agreement—this would be impractical—and they are annexed to it by law. That which is annexed is based on a presumed contract between honest and intelligent men, and the abstract contract devised by French civil lawyers became the model for subsequent legislation that was embodied in the Code Napoleon. It is this legal system that Richey contrasts with Irish land law.

The letting of agricultural land, in the standard French treatise of Richey's time, was viewed as a contract creating reciprocal rights and duties: the lessor put the lessee into possession and guaranteed quiet possession; the tenant must pay rent, treat the premises in a husbandlike fashion, and surrender them in the condition in which he had received them. The nature of rent was at variance with English ideas. In some respects the contract was considered to partake of the nature of a sale, as well as of a hiring, and in this way the concept of fraud crept in. If a landlord induced a tenant to offer an exorbitant price, evidence of fraud could be brought, and the contract would be unenforceable. The nature of rent was moreover also affected by its history in feudal France. Originally the lessor had paid the landlord a fixed proportion of the gross product. When this was commuted to a money payment, two equitable rules were made: (1) that the landlord should be taken to have convenanted that the annual produce would exceed the rent, and (2) that if the crop failed by an unforeseen cause, the lessor should share the loss with the lessee. These provisions are spelled out in detail in the Code Napoleon. If the tenant failed to perform his obligations, his interest in the holding was determined—not summarily, however, but consequent upon the judgment of a court. If the landlord brought an action not merely for the payment of rent but also for ejectment for nonpayment, the French law held that, whatever the judgment, if the tenant paid the rent and costs at any time before the execution of the judgment and reentry of the landlord, the tenant could have the action dismissed and remain on the farm. If he failed to pay before this time, he had no further opportunity to redeem, and the landlord was entitled to recover the farm in the same state in which it was let. In this case, and in this case alone, where the landlord determined the tenancy before its full term, the tenant was entitled to the value of his improvements.

Thus the Roman Law of landlord and tenant as codified by the French system, a system commanding much admiration for its clarity, logic, and equity. The reciprocal rights and duties of landlord and tenant emerged naturally from the contract of hiring, whereby the tenant took possession of the landlord's property. No such legal structure was possible in England. The tenant does not take possession of the landlord's property in this way at all; he is considered to have acquired an estate in the land in an agreement antecedent to any contract of hiring. From early medieval times those interests that entitled tenants to *seisin* of the land were called estates, a word related to the tenant's status:

originally only free men could have a freehold estate; villeins were entitled to a copyhold estate. An estate that descends to heirs is an estate in fee, either entailed or in fee simple; an estate that determines on the death of the grantee is a life estate. In English law no one owns the land; a man owns an estate in the land that entitles him, not to ownership in the land, but to *seisin*.

The English (or Irish) landlord then is generally "seised of X for an estate in fee simple (or in fee tail)." What relation does he then have to his tenants? The letting of agricultural land may be of one of three types: tenancies at will, yearly tenancies, or tenancies for terms of years. Tenancies for terms of years (or for lives) were invariably created by a formal document that set out the terms of the covenant explicitly. Tenancies at will amount to bare permission to occupy land during the pleasure of the lessor, and could be determined by either party at will. Such tenancies were rare in England and Ireland. By far the commonest Irish tenure, amounting in the mid-nineteenth century to perhaps 70 or 75 percent of the tenancies, was the yearly tenancy. In the case of lettings of an unspecified type or term, the law made the presumption that a yearly tenancy existed, because it was the one in ordinary use. This tenancy, which apparently first arose in the sixteenth century, was for an indefinite period, although determinable by either party on six months' notice and expiring upon the anniversary of its commencement. Although the yearly tenancy sounds precarious, such tenancies in fact existed for generations and were regarded by tenants as a perpetual interest. Richey observes that "at an early period of the Common Law it would probably have developed into a perpetual customary tenure, as was the case of the copyhold tenure in England." [2]

In the absence of express agreement, what were the rights

and obligations of landlord and tenant in English law compared with the French law? English landlords were not required to guarantee title, or to keep the premises in repair, or to provide the tenant with what the French call a "possession utile." The tenant was bound to pay the rent and to give up possession at the termination of the letting, but he was not bound to treat the premises in a husbandlike fashion or to give them up in as good condition as he received them. The tenant's treatment of the premises is governed not by the mere fact of being a tenant but by the English common law doctrine of waste, waste being an act whereby the value of the estate is reduced, entitling the owner of the estate to an injunction or an action for damages. The law distinguishes voluntary waste, which involves doing positive harm such as pulling down fences, and permissive waste, which implies allowing the premises to deteriorate. A tenant for life is liable for voluntary waste only, and it is Hargreaves's opinion that "it is at least doubtful whether a lessee for years is in a worse position." [3]

The relevance of the doctrine of waste lies in its application to the law of fixtures. The concept of fixtures is not especially related to the law of leases but governs the wider question of what constitutes realty. The law of fixtures commences with the presumption that whatsoever is annexed to the land becomes part of the land, and whatsoever is not annexed to land is not part of the land. If a lessee for years annexes his chattel to the land it becomes realty; it is no longer his but a part of the land; its removal constitutes an act of waste. The strictness of this law was from an early period relaxed in the case of trade or business fixtures, but it was decided in 1802 (*Elwes* v. *Mawe*) that agricultural fixtures were not trade fixtures. The consequence was that an agricultural tenant for years who by his investment permanently increased the value of the property had no right of compensation at the end of his tenancy.

In the French system we saw that failure to pay rent necessarily determined the tenancy; in the English system this was not so. How then may rent be recovered? First, by an ordinary personal action for debt. Second, by the proceeding of distress. Distress originally was the means of enforcing the performance of feudal obligations, by seizing the chattels on the demised premises and holding them until the obligation was fulfilled. It is an ancient remedy and is one of the last survivals of regulated self-help in English law.[4] Once the remedy was applicable to money rent instead of services, the landlord acquired the right to sell the distrained goods and retain his arrears from the proceeds. Inevitably, in any proceeding of self-help the tenant would require much protection; accordingly, such a vast body of case and statute law grew up around the proceeding that landlords in Ireland were at length reluctant to adopt it, because failure to observe any of these surrounding legal technicalities would expose them to heavy damages. Moreover, neither debt nor distress would provide an adequate remedy to a landlord who had granted a long lease: if the tenant will not pay and has no goods upon which to distrain, the landlord may find himself kept out of possession for a long time. To avoid this contingency, leases generally were drawn with the proviso that the landlord should have the right of reentry if the rent were in arrears. Thus, although failure to pay rent did not automatically determine the lease, it did allow landlord reentry, and landlord reentry determined the lease. The action of ejectment, an action to recover possession of land, thus could only be brought when a reentry clause was contained in the lease. In Ireland prior to 1851 the right to bring an ejectment for nonpayment of rent was limited to holders of written leases (irrespective of whether the reentry proviso was explicit); the landlord in the usual case of yearly tenancies could not eject for nonpayment of rent but had to proceed directly to serve a notice to quit. The elapsed time between the original nonpayment and the earliest possible moment of repossession was such that a landlord would lose two and a half years' rent before he could recover possession. To remedy this situation, the landlords were given the right to bring an ejectment in Civil Bill Courts upon nonpayment of a year's rent in the case of holdings not held under written lease at a rent of less than £50 per year. The Courts of Equity viewed the ejectment proceeding strictly in the light of securing payment for rent, and consequently the landlord was compelled to reinstate the tenant if, within a reasonable time, he paid arrears and costs.[5]

This was the law that regulated the relation of landlord to tenant in Ireland before 1870. "Of all the fatal gifts which we bestowed on our unhappy possession [the worst] was the English system of owning land," [6] intoned Froude, an historian with some claim to being the most scurrilous libeler the Irish people ever knew. The argument that the system of land tenure prevented economic development rests firmly upon the undoubted fact that tenants who made investments that permanently enhanced the value of their holdings had no right to compensation at the termination of the tenancy. A clear investment disincentive existed. In an economy in which the landlord traditionally provided fixed capital, capital accumulation could progress satisfactorily under these laws. This was thought to be the English case. Alternatively, economies in which landlords do not provide fixed capital can evolve by historical tradition some customary arrangements under which the landlords are bound to compensate outgoing tenants for their improvements. Such customs would be enforceable at law as implied terms of the tenancy agreement. In the province of Ulster in northern Ireland a set of customs existed that, according to this line of argument, amounted to the same thing.

Ulster custom comprised two aspects: first, landlords undertook never to evict a rent-paying tenant; second, tenants were deemed to have acquired certain rights on their farms which, upon departure, they could sell to the incoming tenant. The presumption was that tenants would be compensated through this payment for any permanent investment they had undertaken; thus, wherever Ulster custom was observed, tenant investment incentives were firmly established. The logic of Sharman Crawford's bill was, then, that wherever landlords did not invest and tenant right did not exist, the land law as it stood was a bar to capital accumulation and a deterrent to economic development and ought to be amended. If it is not, there will be no capital accumulation, or else the fruits of capital accumulation will be appropriated by the landlords through their powers of eviction or of rent-setting, and the tenant class will remain impoverished. This is the argument.

The parliamentary history of the Irish land question for many years consisted principally of Sharman Crawford's patient persistence in the face of continued rebuffs. One important concession he secured. In 1843 Sir Robert Peel agreed to appoint a Royal Commission to inquire into the occupation of land in Ireland. This was the Devon Commission, the first of those great parliamentary inquiries from whose voluminous pages emerges much of the economic history of Ireland. The Report of the Devon Commission "[tended] to prove," at least in the eyes of some, "that the source of all Ireland's misfortunes and poverty was the fatal system of land-tenure existing in the country." [7] Although the Devon Commission itself did not go quite so far, the view is not unfair. The report concluded that "although it is certainly desirable that the fair remuneration to which a tenant is entitled for his outlay of capital or of labour, in permanent improvements, should be secured to him by voluntary agreement rather than by compulsion by law; yet, upon a review of all the evidence furnished to us upon the subject, we believe that some legislative measure will be found necessary . . . We are convinced that, in the present state of feelings in Ireland, no single measure can be better calculated to allay discontent, and to promote substantial improvement throughout the country." [8] Lord Stanley in parliamentary debate on the Devon Report agreed that nothing "went so much to the root of the social condition of the people of Ireland as the providing greater security to the industrious tenant of some compensation for the permanent, or almost permanent, improvements effected by him during his occupation of the land." [9]

This on the eve of the Famine! Since the last quarter of the eighteenth century, the population of Ireland had perhaps doubled, unaccompanied by any industrial revolution. By 1851 half the English population was in towns; in 1841 perhaps a fifth of the Irish population was in towns— towns moreover of decaying, not expanding, industry. The increasing population was more and more densely packed into minute holdings and kept alive only by cultivation of the potato with its prodigious yield per acre. As population kept growing the only real alternatives for the Irish tenant were increasing subdivision—by which eventually his holding would be unable to support his family—and emigration. It is difficult to believe that any tenure system man could devise would have materially altered the tragic course of Irish history in the 1840's. But the notion was firmly established that defects in the system of land tenure lay at the root of Ireland's economic difficulties, and the cure of these difficulties lay in reform of the land law. This was to be inscribed upon the banner of the Irish parliamentary party under Sir Gavan Duffy and under Isaac Butt: land tenure is the trouble; a reform of the land laws is the cure.

The view survives to the present day, not only as part of "what every schoolboy knows," but in the minds of the best historians specializing in the Victorian era. It is almost an unquestioned assumption. "The key to the Irish problem," writes Robert Blake in his recent biography of Disraeli, "was the unsatisfactory system of land tenure." [10] "The English . . . had imposed landlords on Ireland who were too often at best no more than a worthless encumbrance on Irish life and a drain on Irish resources," writes Dr. Kitson Clark. "Partly as a result of this Irish land tenures were a museum for all that can be intolerable in land tenures and probably prevented the proper cultivation of the soil." [11]

In what follows, my aim will not be to berate distinguished historians for error. Rather, I shall argue that the important determinants of Irish economic development are to be found elsewhere. From the premise that the land law contained investment disincentives, we can draw no conclusions about actual historical development without an examination of the concrete economic situation. Such an examination for post-Famine Ireland will reveal a pattern of tenure customs in which eviction was rare, rents were moderate, and tenant investment incentives were established. We shall see that a more important question for economic development posed by the actual tenure customs concerned, in fact, landlord incentives to invest. Nevertheless, we shall argue, the Irish economy made impressive progress in the decades after the Famine, and we shall investigate the sources and pattern of this progress. But if the land law did not restrain economic development, the belief that it did will turn out to be of central importance in Irish history. For this belief led to important legislative acts, and the working of these acts, in the context of the actual economic developments of the late nineteenth century, resulted in the eventual transfer of the land from the landlords to the tenants.

In the course of evaluating the validity and importance of the land tenure theory of Irish economic development, we shall be compelled to sketch out an alternative interpretation of that development. This is a task so large—involving almost a rewriting of the post-Famine economic history of Ireland—that it is manifestly impossible to do it adequately in a work of this kind. Still it is an urgent task, and somehow, somewhere, a beginning must be made.

2.
Mr. Gladstone and the
Land Act of 1870

He had a tendency to persuade himself,
quite unconsciously, that the course he
desired to take was a course which the
public interest required. His acuteness soon
found reasons for that course; the warmth
of his emotions enforced the reasons. It
was a dangerous tendency, but it does
not impeach his honesty of purpose.

Bryce

Even contemporary observers felt that the death of Palmerston marked a new era in English history. The social and economic developments of the mid-Victorian period made the continued aristocratic control of Parliament a conspicuous anachronism. There had been no lack of reformist social ideas in the Palmerston era, but Parliament had declined to translate them into legislation. Both political parties lay under the control of the traditional governing class, the landowners.

Palmerston died in October 1865; Lord John Russell announced his retirement from the leadership of the Liberal Party at Christmas, 1867; Lord Derby resigned in February 1868. The leading characters of the mid-Victorian period were gone from the scene, and new leaders were to appear. The Dissenting middle-class tradesmen and artisans whose numbers and wealth were so disproportionate to their political influence were waiting in the wings to come on. These groups had to make their bid for political power from an extraparliamentary base, and the Dissenting religious bodies were well suited to be the basis of the challenge. Chapel provided leadership, continuity, and a measure of financial solidity; the revival of Dissenting religious feeling in the 1850's and 1860's not only in England, but importantly in Scotland and Wales, provided a new enthusiasm and fervor; and the Anti-Corn-Law League provided a model for mobilizing extraparliamentary pressures to gain specific reforms.[1] The mid-century thus saw the establishment of leagues or societies specifically devoted to furthering the principal political aims of the middle-class Dissenters: reform, temperance, education, and disestablishment. Disraeli's splendid audacity brought the Tories credit for the first step in the new direction with the Reform Bill of 1867; but it remained for Gladstone, a man with both aristocratic connections and popular sympathies, to push through the accumulated reforms that had been left undone in the years of the mid-century.

This, briefly, was the political situation in England on the afternoon of December 1, 1868, when Mr. Gladstone, in his shirt sleeves, was pacifying his spirit by his celebrated pastime of cutting down beeches at Hawarden. Evelyn Ashley, standing by holding the woodsman's coat, has described how the news came that Mr. Gladstone would shortly be sent for by the Queen to form his first government. "After a few minutes the blows ceased, and Mr. Gladstone resting on the handle of his axe, looked up and with deep earnestness in his voice and with great intensity in his face, exclaimed, 'My mission is to pacify Ireland.' "[2] His first step, the resolutions on disestablishment of the Irish church, had been announced in the Disraeli ministry, and now the new Prime Minister was in a position to continue his program.

The Ireland that Mr. Gladstone proposed to pacify had just completed one of the most prosperous and peaceful decades in perhaps all her long history. Economically, there was no break in the upward trend in prices and production. Great progress had been made in technology and transportation. Politically, the vacuum formed by the collapse of the Independent Irish Party had been filled by the National Association. Their program aimed at an alliance with the English Liberals and was mild by later standards: maintenance of the Union, disestablishment of the Irish church, denominational education, and a minimal demand for compensation for improvements in regard to the land question. There was not a great deal to pacify here.

It was the Fenian Brotherhood that brought Ireland to the attention of the English in the late 1860's. James Stephens had founded the Irish Revolutionary Brotherhood (whose American branch was called the Fenian Brotherhood) in Dublin on March 17, 1858. He did so with American encouragement and American funds. By and large the Irish support of the Brotherhood came from shopmen, servant boys, and farm laborers; the church and the middle classes were opposed, and the movement lacked broad support among the great mass of tenant farmers in Ireland.[3] The Fenian uprising in Ireland on March 5 and 6, 1867, was easily crushed; the earlier "diversionary" raids on Canada by the Fenians in America had been quickly dispersed. But, in September 1867, two Fenian prisoners were rescued from a police van in Manchester, and a policeman was killed in the melée. Three months later a Fenian exploded a barrel of gunpowder outside a London prison, where fellow-conspirators were held, this time killing several people.

English public opinion was thoroughly aroused. The isolated occurrence of these acts of terrorism, rather than any economic or political change in the condition of Ireland, made Ireland the question of the day.

In this political setting Mr. Gladstone undertook to frame his Irish program. No one would ever accuse Mr. Gladstone of framing his policy solely with an eye to those powerful forces—those Dissenting middle-class tradesmen and artisans—whose delayed appearance on the stage is perhaps the principal political event of the time. But it is striking how well his Irish program did fit in with the predilections of these people, now more powerful than ever after the Reform Bill of 1867: they were in large measure Dissenters; they had a strong interest in disestablishment; they were especially liable to emotional appeals; and if they lacked interest in the Irish tenant farmer, they were certainly not going to be disposed to defend the landlord class, the very class whose political power they were seeking to limit. The appropriate observation is Labouchere's: "I do not mind Mr. Gladstone always having an ace up his sleeve, but I do object to his always saying that Providence put it there." [4]

In 1868 the Irish question indeed seemed to be a sound political stroke; while Mr. Gladstone may have felt that Providence had put the card in his sleeve, he knew very well that it was an ace and not a lower card. "Our mode of warfare cannot but be influenced by the troops we lead," he wrote to Bishop Hinds about the Irish church bill. "Our three *corps d'armée,* I may almost say, have been Scotch presbyterians, English and Welsh nonconformists and Irish Roman catholics. . . . The English clergy as a body have done their worst against us and have hit us hard, as I know personally, in the counties. Yet we represent the national force, tested by a majority of considerably over a hundred voices. It is hazardous in these times to tamper with such a force." [5] It was the composition of Mr. Gladstone's army and events from America that molded his Irish policy rather than any stirrings or promptings from changing domestic conditions in Ireland.

However problematical Mr. Gladstone's unconscious motivations, the development of his views on the land question can be traced in detail in a series of remarkable memoranda he wrote in the autumn of 1869 and in his correspondence with his closest associates in framing the bill.[6] The old Whig diagnosis could provide no promising leads for public policy. If the trouble had been overpopulation and uneconomic holdings, the mid-century had evidently witnessed emigration and consolidation, and the policy of free trade in land had been conscientiously tried. The contemporary Whig position was defended by Robert Lowe, then Chancellor of the Exchequer, in speeches and letters of considerable brilliance.

Lowe had given a clear statement of his position the previous spring (1868) in the March 10 House of Commons debate on Maguire's motion for a committee on the state of Ireland. He had begun by denying the existence of a crisis in Ireland. He viewed the Fenians as an extremist group composed of disbanded American soldiers, and he warned that reform of Irish land (or church or education) was not going to stop Fenian outrages, since these were not the Fenian grievances. Lowe did not exaggerate Irish economic progress, observing that an economy based wholly on agriculture would necessarily progress unevenly, but he argued that progress was occurring. Small holdings he viewed as ruinous, and compensation for improvement as futile ("no tenant so small can effect any real improvement"). His policies were the old Whig policies of emigration and capital investment, but he hoped that investment would be directed toward industrializing Ireland and diversifying her economy. He felt that capital would be forthcoming were it not for the outrages, and he described Ireland as caught in a vicious cycle of poverty and outrages. But Lowe's conclusion for public policy was that lamest of all policies, "Restore confidence." A missionary could hardly inscribe that on a banner.

It is a paradox that Mr. Gladstone, who did more than anyone else to translate the conclusions of classical economics into public policy, had a natural habit of mind so unlike an economist's.[7] No one who has worked over the literature on the Irish land question can have anything but admiration for Mr. Gladstone's considerable intellectual achievement in analyzing the purely economic aspects of the problem, and no one will want to criticize him for the deep compassion he felt for the very real sufferings of the Irish tenants; but his thinking intertwined moral and political and economic considerations so firmly that he was not able to keep the strands separate in his own mind. Confusion resulted. Both the moral and emotional bent of Gladstone's mind and the opportunities of the political situation gave him the answer to Irish economic problems before he even asked an economic question.

Of his many memoranda on the Land Bill, that of December 11, 1869, prepared for presentation to his cabinet, but evidently never delivered, gives the most revealing picture of Mr. Gladstone's approach to the problem.[8]

He did not begin by asking about Ireland's economic development and what sorts of policies might assist it. He thought in terms of the "relief of Ireland's ancient wrongs," perhaps even of atoning for the English conquest: "We are about to legislate for the redress of wrong as well as for the general benefit." He assumed without question that poverty was the result of exploitation, and he looked upon the tenant as a victim and the landlord as a potential wrong-doer whose power must be restrained. He wanted to do justice to the Irish tenant and to confer a "boon" upon him. Thus, the granting of land tenure reform seemed to be an honorable and equitable gesture for the English to make; Mr. Gladstone did not arrive at land tenure reform, however, by asking what was the most promising cure of poverty in Ireland.

In Irish legislation, as on other occasions in his career, Mr. Gladstone's energy and fervor could only be aroused on a moral, almost a religious, issue. The argument that land legislation should be undertaken for Ireland because England had grievously wronged her over the centuries is a *moral* argument. Lord Salisbury was fond of remarking, "As Peel would say, there are three courses of action open to us." The working of Peel's (and Salisbury's) kind of mind was different from Gladstone's. They tended to ana-lyze a problem into constituent parts and to select from the available instruments of public policy that one (or that set) which would provide the best solution. Gladstone, to whom political problems tended to be moral issues, found it harder to be so coolly flexible. The timing of the policy might be subject to qualification and to political realities, but for the answer itself there was less room for compro-mise.[9]

If Mr. Gladstone began by feeling that England owed something to Ireland, he was naturally led to ask what the Irish wanted. The Irish political demand was for some kind of fixity of tenure, and this was where Gladstone began. Only later, almost as an afterthought, did he begin to con-sider the economic arguments for fixity of tenure. The Irish tenant deserved some fixity of tenure, partly for historical reasons, partly because he wanted it, and partly because it would encourage him to invest in his land (also, because it was believed that this would keep him quiet). In view of the richness of empirical data on Ireland available at the time, it is surprising that so little economic analysis and field work preceded the drafting of the Land Act of 1870.

What Mr. Gladstone proposed to give the Irish tenant, then, was fixity of tenure: "though not fixity, yet security, or as it has been well called by the Duke of Argyll, stability in his tenure." [10] In the course of the autumn of 1869, Mr. Gladstone became convinced that the legalization of Ulster custom in the North and its simulation in the South were the legislative means to this end. By the time he wrote his December 11 memorandum he could assume he had carried his cabinet thus far. It was widely felt that the prosperity of Ulster and the relative ease of tenant-landlord relations there were somehow a result of Ulster custom, and that Ulster custom endowed the tenant with some measure of fixity of tenure in some not precisely defined way. Although imperfectly understood, it was generally agreed that Ulster custom "worked." It had the considerable political advantages, as Mr. Gladstone observed, of being familiar and intelligible, local to Ireland, and not likely to be shipped across the Channel to the consternation of English landlords. The problem of legalizing the custom where it already existed was relatively simple; how, though, could it be extended to the South? In wrestling with this Mr. Gladstone worked hard and impressively to analyze the economic meaning of Ulster custom, but, as we shall see subsequently, he never succeeded in taking the final steps.

Without fully understanding Ulster custom, then, Mr. Gladstone pushed on with it as the basis of his Act. He had been told that fixity of tenure was already the rule in the

North of Ireland and the practice in the South. He knew that the largest problem lay with the smallest tenants, whose improvements were probably worthless. He had been told that, on the one hand, tenant-right payments crippled incoming tenants and robbed them of adequate working capital; on the other hand, in some cases tenant right was valueless; and, in any case, tenant right could be extinguished by a rise in rent. Nevertheless, in a memorandum of December 14, written after an exchange of views with his Chief Secretary Chichester Fortescue, the main principles of what would become the Land Act of 1870 were set forth: (1) establish tenant right judicially, (2) reverse the presumption that improvements were made by the landlord rather than the tenant (i.e., improvements are tenant property), and (3) where there is no Ulster custom, introduce a compensation for disturbance to an evicted tenant, according to a fixed scale.

We have tried to indicate how Mr. Gladstone was led on moral and political grounds to formulate land tenure legislation and to believe that an approximation of Ulster custom was the best legislation to adopt. This "cure" for Irish economic difficulties he worked over in great detail; the difficulties themselves he neither investigated, analyzed, nor described. That lack of tenure was the cause of Irish poverty was assumed. No diagnosis was made. No alternative economic program was discussed. In Dr. Steele's dissertation we can see how Mr. Gladstone's superior energy and intellect swept a doubting and reluctant cabinet to his foreordained conclusions.

The Duke of Argyll protested that "concessions to political necessity" and "a just solution to the Irish land problem" were quite separate things.[11] Gladstone, he said, yielded to political exigencies and then constructed arguments to justify himself. Lord Clarendon considered the first draft of the bill merely "an attempt to bribe the tenant into obedience to the laws by subsidizing him out of the pocket of his landlord." [12] But it was Lowe who summarized the point neatly: "No one," said Lowe, "has better reasoning faculties than Gladstone, but he economizes them in the formation of his opinions and uses them mainly in their defense." [13]

ULSTER CUSTOM

The underlying concept of the Land Act of 1870 is that the Irish "land question" would be solved by legalizing Ulster custom in the North and by extending some approximation of the custom, or some of its benefits, to the South. It is remarkable how little was known about Ulster custom and how confidently it was expected to provide a solution; perhaps the ignorance explains the confidence. The only serious attempt to accumulate information on the Ulster custom dated back to the Devon Report; it should have been obvious that any pre-Famine investigation of Irish conditions was by 1869 at best verging on irrelevance.

Analysis of the Custom

The common description of Ulster custom is that it insured fixity of tenure at fair rents and allowed an outgoing tenant free sale of his interest in his holding, or, in other words, the three F's: fixity of tenure, fair rents, and free sale. The first article of the custom was that landlords undertook never to evict a rent-paying tenant. This meant not only that the landlord was powerless to consolidate his holdings but even, on some estates, that he could not take his land into his own hands. But it was never the case that Ulster landlords had no power to increase rent, and Ulster rents moved in some measure with the rise and fall of prices and land values. What was specified was that rents must be "fair"; if the two interested parties did not agree, rents were referred to some outside arbitration. Frequently, a landlord set his rents by calling in a firm that specialized in valuation work; the landlord and the tenant would then abide by the valuer's decision.

With these elements of the custom at hand, we can try to analyze abstractly what they imply. Let us begin by asking why a rational landlord would evict a rent-paying tenant. (We may assume that the landlord was satisfied with the rent at the commencement of the tenancy; otherwise he would not have agreed to it.) He would do so (1) if he thought he could earn more money by putting the land to an alternative use, or (2) if another farmer made a higher bid for the land. In principle it will be a matter of indifference to a landlord (1) whether he evicts an incumbent tenant and increases his revenue by transferring the land to another use or another tenant, or (2) whether he raises the rent of the incumbent tenant by the amount of the increased potentiality of the land. Suppose then that he seeks to raise the rent of the present tenant. We know that Ulster custom permits him to ask for "reasonable" rent increases. If the tenant is unable or unwilling to pay the increased rent and the rent is not judged "unfair" or "unreasonable," then the tenant will certainly lose his farm. It turns out that he has not got fixity of tenure at all. The crux of the matter is the judgment of the reasonableness of the rent increase. Fixity of tenure where rent is free to vary is fixity in a very restricted sense; a long lease is more protection. A landlord could get around the fixity of tenure by raising rents sufficiently. Nothing can be said a priori on the subject of guaranteed fixity of tenure; it turns on the question of rent. There is nothing *in the institutional arrangement* called Ulster custom that guarantees a fixity of tenure, and whether Ulster tenants (or Southern tenants) had fixity of tenure is an empirical question. If we want to see whether Irish tenants were undisturbed in their tenure, we shall have to examine the statistics on eviction, and it will be illegitimate to draw conclusions from the prevalence of Ulster custom.

The other aspect of Ulster custom is free sale, or what is conveniently called tenant right. When an outgoing tenant leaves his farm, he sells this tenant right to his successor. What does the incoming tenant purchase when he buys the tenant right? We can divide the answer into two conceptually separate components. First, he is paying the outgoing tenant for the value of unexhausted improvements that remain on the farm. At common law these improvements are the property of the landlord, but it was mutually beneficial to landlord and tenant to consider them tenant property.

But this is only one aspect of tenant right, and not the controversial aspect. Liberal English public opinion was by 1869 fairly willing to go as far as compensation for improvements. So were many Irish landlords. The second aspect of tenant right is the "something beyond" compensation for improvements that Mr. Gladstone wanted to grant. Many people who assented to the claim of compensation for improvements were reluctant to grant the further kind of claim. It is denoted frequently by the concept of "co-proprietorship," and accompanied by romantic historical arguments about tenant's rights to some partial ownership of the land, over and above the improvements. It was just this aspect of tenant right that roused landlord talk of expropriation and invasion of property rights. That these were two sides of the same coin was neatly put by Palmerston in his famous remark, "Tenant right is landlord wrong." It is particularly important to isolate this aspect of tenant right and analyze it.

It was frequently observed that large payments for tenant right changed hands in cases in which no improvements had been made at all. For convenience let us call this "pure tenant right." Let us consider such a case (equally, we could suppose improvements had been made, valued, and paid for). The incoming tenant is now paying for the right of occupying the land, a right that attaches to the previous tenant and which he is permitted to dispose of. Now, the right to occupation of land is nothing more or less than a lease, either explicit or implied, so let us conceptualize the situation by saying that the incoming tenant is buying up the unexpired lease of the outgoing tenant.[14] Let us go back a moment. Suppose I hold a lease on my house for £50 per month. Suppose this to be the equilibrium price that rules in the market, the price that equates supply and demand. Let me now propose to leave my house and put my lease out to auction. If £50 is an equilibrium price, no one will offer me a penny for my lease; he can rent a house anywhere for £50. It is only if the house is rented for less than market value that the lease will fetch any sum whatsoever on the open market. In fact, what the lease will fetch will be the capitalized value of the amount by which the farm is underrented. This aspect of tenant right is expressly implied in the landlord's willingness to accept less than market value for his land.* If the landlord raises his rent to a competitive

---

* That this was understood by some in nineteenth-century Ireland is illustrated by the testimony of John LaTouche, a Kildare landlord. LaTouche's testimony is given in *Report of the Commission of Inquiry into the Working of the Landlord and Tenant (Ireland) Act 1870, and the Amending Acts, with the Evidence, Appendices, and Index, P.P.* 1881 (c. 2779) XVIII, XIX. This will henceforth be referred to as the Bessborough Commission, from the name of the chairman. Citations will be given by the number of the query.

Here the questioner is Baron Dowse. At the time of the Commission (1880), LaTouche had been managing his own estates in Kildare and elsewhere for thirty-three years. The LaTouches were an old family of Huguenot origin.

"Do I understand Mr. LaTouche to deny that the tenant has any

level, he extinguishes the value of the pure tenant right entirely. (Indeed, it was a common Ulster saying that a shilling on the rent is a pound off the tenant right.) And if the outgoing tenant sells his tenant right for what it will bring at auction, he is playing the rack-renting landlord to the in-

---

estate in the land at all except his claim for improvements?—Yes.

"You do not give him any estate in it at all?—No, I do not.

"And you will not allow him to sell because he has nothing to sell? —Nothing to sell. I think the difference between what a landlord has let his land at, and what he might have obtained for his land from another tenant, ought to be the landlord's, and I don't think that the landlords in general have their land let at the highest rent they could obtain for it. I was offered double the rent a few months ago for a farm that I let at exactly one-half the rent I was offered for it. Suppose the tenant I let it to for half its market value, suppose he chose to sell what, under the Ulster tenant-right custom, would be his interest, then, because I was kind and indulgent, and let my land not at the highest rent I could obtain for it, but at a moderate rent, the tenant takes advantage of that to make the difference his property.

"Why did you do that? In that particular case was it because you thought the tenant you were letting the farm to was a better man than the other?—No.

"Then why? Was it because you thought the man offered too much? —Well, he did not [*sic*] offer too much, but that was not altogether the reason. One of them was a person I had known for some years, and I would rather have those that I have known holding farms about me than a stranger coming in" (Bessborough Commision, 951–955).

In subsequent questioning, William Shaw endeavored to establish that it was only on small farms that such underrenting obtained: "You would not let a farm of 300 acres, I suppose, on the same terms?—I could quote many instances on my own estate where I could have obtained a very much higher rent than what I let my land at." This suggests that both questioner and witness agreed there was underrenting on small holdings, but it was never established for large holdings, and Mr. Shaw's incredulity went unchallenged.

Cf. also the definition of tenant right given by Charles Uniacke Townshend, an important land agent with over thirty years' experience in a dozen counties, including five in Ulster: "Now the Ulster tenant-right custom means some kind of saleable interest which they would not possess if a farm was not worth more than they are paying for it" (ibid., 1641).

coming tenant. It is a wonder that such outgoing tenants were not denounced for avarice.*

In the memorandum of December 11, 1869, Mr. Gladstone wrestled with the meaning of that part of the tenant right payment not related to compensation for improvements, the pure tenant right. If it were a payment for the anticipated profits of an implied lease, then a man evicted after one year's tenancy ought to receive a greater payment than a man evicted after a tenancy of twenty-five years, he reasoned. But this kind of payment, Gladstone saw, bore no relation to the injury inflicted by eviction. The "mischief of eviction," he wrote, "depends upon the difficulty of getting another farm. This difficulty increases with the increase of demand for land, decreases with the decrease in its excess, and disappears as soon as the demand for land reaches a point at which it stands in just relation to the supply." At such a time the damages for eviction would be a small sum, analogous perhaps to severance pay. Mr. Gladstone characterized tenant right over and above the value of improvements as "the sign and concomitant of an imperfect state of things," and felt that, if tenant right were adopted, it would later on fade away, as the supply of farms increased or the

* Somerset Ward, a land agent for Lord Bangor in County Down, testified to this effect before the Bessborough Commission: "I gather from your evidence that you are opposed to allowing free sale of tenant-right to the highest bidder.—Very much opposed to it. I think it is against the interests of the tenantry because it is in fact rack-renting the incoming tenant. If the landlord charges but a low rent for the land, it makes no difference to the incoming tenant if free sale is permitted, because the price exacted for the tenant-right owing to the competition of one man bidding against another, has the effect of rack-renting the incoming man" (Bessborough Commission, 7109).

Cf. also the testimony of R. U. Penrose Fitzgerald, a Cork landlord: "If the tenant is to have a free right to sell . . . you simply hand over to the outgoing tenant the right to rack-rent the incoming tenant" (ibid., 29551).

demand lessened. What Gladstone realized quite explicitly is that, in a state of perfect competitive equilibrium, pure tenant right will not exist. In equilibrium the demand for land will equal the supply of land. But what equates the demand and supply of land? Obviously, the *price* of land, that is, the rent. So long as rents do not rise to this level, there will be a market for pure tenant right. If Mr. Gladstone had been able to see the last step, he would have been spared considerable puzzling. Did the pure tenant right represent anticipated profits? Did it somehow reflect the excess of demand over supply? Should an outgoing tenant receive the amount he had paid? What if it were, as it undeniably was in some cases, a "preposterous excess"? Should the outgoing tenant receive the market value of the tenant right? Mr. Gladstone puzzled to the end about these questions and never solved them. When Chichester Fortescue urged him to consider how rent variation affected tenant-right payments, he did not see the light, and he went ahead with the legislation without solving the questions he had himself posed in his December 11 memorandum.

What are the consequences of the Ulster custom? Having analyzed the custom abstractly, it will be convenient to answer this question under separate heads. First, what can we say briefly about its role in the economic development of Ulster? Second, what are the consequences of not evicting a rent-paying tenant? Third, what are the consequences of the sale of tenant right, distinguishing the payment for unexhausted improvements from the payment for pure tenant right?

Ulster Custom and Ulster Prosperity

The prosperity of Ulster as compared with the South has frequently been attributed to the existence of Ulster custom,[15] but the explanatory value of the custom in this connection turns out to be a slender reed indeed. In the first place there is no evidence of greater prosperity in Ulster until some two centuries after the custom was introduced. "Take the road to Markethill [Co. Armagh]," wrote Arthur Young on his Irish tour. "I am now got into the linen country and the worst husbandry I have met with." [16] In Antrim, "the linen manufacture spreads over the whole country; consequently the farms are very small, being nothing but patches for the convenience of weavers." [17] In the North, he found, where the linen manufacture had spread, the tenants "no more deserve the name of farmers than the occupiers of a cabbage garden." [18]

The picture of a thriving Ulster agriculture, accumulating capital under the beneficent Ulster custom and investing it in improved techniques, does not belong to the eighteenth century, when Ulster was covered with tiny holdings of weavers so impoverished that they needed the yields of primitive agriculture to bring their pitifully small earnings from weaving up to subsistence level.[19] That these weavers should have accumulated enough capital in their condition to finance the growth of the linen industry and eventually the Industrial Revolution in Ulster is not credible. For the rise of the linen industry we shall probably do better to look to the Huguenots who came to the North in the early decades of the eighteenth century, with capital, skills, technology (especially in bleaching), and a knowledge of the marketing and trading methods of the more advanced countries of Western Europe. It is true that the linen industry was *based* upon the weaver-farmer, without whose willingness to provide woven cloth at a less-than-living wage the industry could not have developed. My feeling is that in the South, in the plains of the Midlands, the dairylands of Limerick, and the corn counties of the Southeast, a tenant would have been ill-advised to turn to weaving; it promised him no riches. In one sense it can be viewed almost as an accident that the Industrial Revolution eventually flourished among the descendants of the Ulster weavers, and providential that most of Ulster's soil was too poor to support permanent grass without careful management by methods unknown in the eighteenth century.[20] The prosperity of Ulster agriculture rose with the departure of the weaver from the countryside; indeed, Ulster prosperity finally came about in the way that Arthur Young advised prematurely: "But if instead of the manufacture having diffused itself as absolutely to banish farming, it had been confined to towns, which it might very easily have been, the very contrary effect would have taken place, and all those vast advantages to agriculture would have flowed, which flourishing manufactures in other countries occasion . . . The manufacturers would have been confined to their own business and the farmers to theirs. That both trades would have flourished the better for this, the minutes of the journey very generally show." What Arthur Young failed to see, and what Gill has shown so well, is that the early organization was a necessary prerequisite for the later.[21]

No Eviction of a Rent-paying Tenant

The first article of Ulster custom, "no eviction of a rent-paying tenant," was credited with endowing Ulster tenants with fixity of tenure. (We have seen that only a restraint on the rent-setting mechanism can guarantee any real fixity of tenure.) The historical evidence that rent-paying tenants were not evicted is very strong; it is not limited to Ulster; it was the custom of the South as well.[22] This was well understood in Ireland. All the discussion about "assimilating the law to the actual conditions that prevail" rests upon the observation that landlords nowhere felt free to evict. For this to make sense at all, it must mean that in general land-lords neither instituted ejectment proceedings at law with a view to clearing away tenants, nor that they raised rents to such levels that tenants were unable to pay them and per-force could no longer remain "rent-paying tenants."

A landlord who does not evict rent-paying tenants when it is profitable for him to do so is a landlord who is not acting as an economic maximizer. "Fair rent" really only means noncompetition rent; "rack rent" means competition rent.* And the notion that only a heartless exploiter would

---

* This was also perfectly well understood in nineteenth-century Ire-land. Consider the following question, which Lord Bessborough ad-dressed to a witness: "You don't mean what the land would let for if put up to competition, but the fair rent—what you would call the fair letting value?" (Bessborough Commission, 864).

Charles Uniacke Townshend testified before the Bessborough Com-mission as follows: "Competition means putting a farm up for letting, offers being taken, and possibly the highest bidder accepted. I have never done it. I do not know of its being done; but I do know of valuators being employed to value land, and a settlement come to with the tenants on an estate; and on that same estate I have known a case where a farm got up from the tenant, and when offers were taken—and not the highest accepted nor nearly the highest—the rent taken from the incoming ten-ant would be 50 percent over that of the adjoining tenant, whose rents were raised under the valuation. That is in the case where the lands were taken up . . . What I hold is that the rents in Ireland are not competi-tion rents" (ibid., 33958). Uniacke Townshend guessed that "upwards of 500,000 tenants" paid rents below competition rents (ibid., 33964).

Thomas Baldwin, superintendent of the Agricultural Department of National Education in Ireland, states that rent in Ireland is generally not the competitive rent: "The rent of everyday life is a totally different thing from the rent of science; the rent of science is a scientific abstrac-tion. Rent in Belgium, for example, is what the tenant gives to the land-lord for the use of his land.

"It is the competition rent?—The competition rent: and if I should live long enough I hope to see Ireland able to bear the effects of that rent. At the present moment you have to deal with an abnormal state of things . . . I would prefer to see Ireland, I must say, very much as Belgium is, that every man should be free to make a contract with his

go so far as to charge a competitive rent underscores the fact that the socially acceptable custom was to charge a lower rent. The landlord who exacted a competitive rent was the target of the blunderbuss; a farmer who outbid another was the subject of ostracism or worse; the history of agrarian disturbances back to the eighteenth century shows that an important aim of the secret societies was artificially to restrain the demand for land and thus keep rents below the competitive level. Another way of expressing this would be to say that a level of rent that would equate supply and demand would disintegrate the social fabric; the Irish tenant transmitted this message to his landlord in unmistakable terms.

These concepts, which are elementary to the economist, were hardly clear to the Irish tenant. Let us see where the confusion lay. A competitive rent is arrived at by the free play of demand and supply. But there is no guarantee that rents so arrived at will bring a man a subsistence income out of any given farm. The latter point is really at the back of the notion of a fair rent. What can we say about the competitive rent arrived at by the free play of demand and supply? No potential tenant can be expected to offer a rent so high as to leave him less than the return he can get for his labor elsewhere in the economy, assuming that there is residual employment accessible to him. Call that return the

---

neighbor for the use of his land and everything else. Ireland is not fit to do that now . . .

"Some people think that the present condition of Ireland is owing to the doctrine of Adam Smith and Mr. Lowe: you don't think that?—I do not indeed. I find in every civilized country, wherever you have rent, wherever you have landlord and tenant, there is competition rent. I take Belgium as an example. The people are prosperous and contented. There is nothing in Belgium as bad as the action of the landlord in Connemara already mentioned; but, taking Ireland as a whole, the small tenants in East and West Flanders are more rack-rented than the mass here" (ibid., 32379, 32387).

going wage. Conversely, no tenant can hope for long to pay a rent that will leave him significantly more than the going wage; because other potential tenants who are in fact earning only the going wage can be expected to bid up the rent (unless they are constrained from doing so in ways we have described, by coercion or custom). Thus, barring that qualification, the competitive rent on any farm will leave the successful tenant approximately the going wage in the economy.

However, there is no guarantee, at any moment, that the going wage will be above "the subsistence level." An economy may be so unproductive that it can not generate a going wage higher than the—biological or conventional—level of subsistence for its current population. In the longer run, one would expect population to fall in such an economy and the going wage to rise to the subsistence level. That is what Malthus was all about.

The Irish tenant always complained that his rent was high. If we assume that by this he meant something more than that he was a poor man, we can assume that he meant it was high relative to the net product of the land, either leaving him less than the going rate of return for his labor or even less than a subsistence wage. By this measure, rents were indeed high; in fact, it is easily established that they were *higher* for small holdings than for large holdings, holdings being of equal fertility. But rents were nevertheless *lower* than what the free play of supply and demand would set on the small holdings, while for large holdings rents were probably equal to the competitive rent set by supply and demand. Thus, rents may be high or low relative to the competitive equilibrium rent, and rents may be high or low relative to the net return the tenant can obtain from the land; in perfect equilibrium, rents will be set by supply and demand such that a farmer will be able to obtain the going rate of return for his labor, but this rate of return may or may not be above subsistence level.

Tenant Right: Payment for the Unexhausted Improvements

The land laws that operated in Ireland, giving the landlord title to any improvements that remained on the holding upon determination of a tenancy, contained a clear disincentive to the tenant to invest and a clear case of inequitable treatment for the investing tenant who quit his holding. Provision for compensation to the tenant for the unexhausted value of his improvements would remedy these defects in the land laws. The influence of the existing land law on the course of economic development is far from being a closed case, however, and it is wrong to conclude from the fact that the landlords had the power to appropriate the value of tenant investment that they actually did so. If rents are stable and evictions rare, in fact the tenants' incentive to invest will be reestablished.

The notion that landlords would habitually act in such a way as to prevent profitable investment in their lands is on the face of it not wholly credible, but it was certainly widely believed. We should expect any landlord who permitted a tenant to undertake profitable investment on his property to see not only increased income for the tenant but also increased value for his own property. It is hard to believe that a rational landowner would prefer unimproved to improved lands, or poor tenants to well-to-do tenants. Even if the law were working to the mutual disadvantage of landlord and tenant, we should reasonably expect them to come to some leasing agreements or work out some customary arrangements that would enable them to proceed on the mutually advantageous course. There is one kind of person, however, who may be interested in maximizing the short-run financial proceeds of a landed estate, without regard to deterioration or the long-run value of the estate. This is the middleman, who holds from the landlord on a lease at fixed rent and sublets to the occupiers. The maximizing of present monetary income is primary to the middleman, and it would not be surprising that where middlemen flourished, rents were raised so high as to prohibit the exploitation of profitable investment opportunities.* The middleman system, described as disappearing in the days of Arthur Young, as declining in the aftermath of the French wars, and as rare in the Devon Report, still showed a few lingering cases in the era of the Bessborough Commission.

When Lord Shelburne succeeded to the family estates in Kerry in 1761, the "middlemen were fully occupied in rack-renting their undertenants and in quarreling amongst themselves." [23] Shelburne made his first visit to Kerry in 1764, of which no record remains; but in 1770 he addressed a petition for troops to the Lord Lieutenant, who happened to be his friend, George Townshend. "The country is wild and unimproved," he wrote, "either by Tillage, Manufactures or Arts; and abounds with Mountains and Morasses which afford a secure retreat to numbers of the Inhabitants who frequently disturb the Peace and transgress the Laws of their Country . . . [the inhabitants] frequently meet in large Associations and Cabals under different Leaders, and swearing fidelity to each other, and threatening instant Death to those who refuse to unite with them, they commit the most violent outrages, in defiance of law and Government, and to the prevention of all improvement and reformation, by terrifying Men of different principles (who might introduce the Protestant religion, attachment to Gov-

---

* The middleman's attitude toward tenant investment will depend on the length of tenure of his lease, his possibilities for renegotiating rents of his subtenants, and the length of time before the investment becomes profitable.

ernment, obedience to the Laws, Acts and industry) from settling among them or by ruining such as have attempted it . . . The Country though wild is very capable of improvement." [24] There can be little doubt that the King's writ did not run everywhere in Kerry (or in West Cork, or Connemara) in the late eighteenth century.

On the subsequent visit to Kerry (1775), Lord Shelburne "order'd the land out of lease to be divided into 4 Sorts; the first which was *fit for Building,* I directed to be divided into small lots, and given forever Rent free, to incline wealthy people to come into the Country, and build, and employ the natives; the 2d which was the *Improv'd Land* I directed to be divided into Lots of 20 acres each to accommodate those which should build in the Town, and to be let to them at a reasonable Rent; the 3d which is the *Improveable Ground* or ground which is not, but may be with tolerable perseverance made good, I directed to be divided into Lots of 8 acres each, and to be given to the poor Tenants, upon condition of their living upon it & improving it, Rent free for 21 years—the 4th which is the *Bog and Rock* I reserve to myself, that it may be always kept in common." [25]

There is no need to attach historical importance to what Lord Shelburne may have jotted down in an idle moment, but it does show how anxious and willing he was to encourage improvement and how unlikely he would have been to rack-rent an improving tenant. The story of the middlemen and agents on Shelburne's Kerry estate is, however, a dreary succession of tales of dishonesty, neglect, and incompetence, although Lord Shelburne continued for a time his enthusiasm for improvements of all kinds, even sending his second son to Edinburgh to observe the thriving Scotch agricultural methods. It must have been difficult for Shelburne to continue his interest in providing leases, and in building roads, schools, bridges, and towns (all of which he did) when his plans, first frustrated by agents and middlemen, were finally crowned by the Rebellion of 1798.[26]

If we put the end of the middleman system sometime between 1815, when it began to decline sharply, and 1845, by which date it had effectually disappeared, we find historical support for our a priori expectation. "Certainly many, perhaps most, landlords eagerly desired a more solid and skilful tenancy, men who would pay their rents more steadily, and who would be less likely to become dependent on rate payers," concludes Connell, writing about the period between 1815 and 1845. "There was a fairly general desire amongst landlords to 'improve' their estates, to get tenants with more capital who would treat the soil with greater consideration than the peasant." [27]

Throughout the nineteenth century, Irish landlords commonly provided slate and timber to all tenants who wanted to construct buildings and sometimes paid tenants a sum for each foot of drainage the tenants undertook. Landlords pleaded for the adoption of manures and green crops; some landlords brought Scottish "grieves" to instruct their tenantry in better agricultural methods. William Bence Jones, a Cork landlord whose experience dated from pre-Famine times to the days of the Land League, is only one example of a man who implored his tenantry to improve and stood ready to assist. In his peppery memoirs he writes with some exasperation, "The number of landlords who are such idiots as to refuse their assent to real improvements that would better secure their rent, and at some time after add to it, is so small as to make no practical difference to the country . . . It is a mere delusion that farmers in Ireland are burning to carry out useful improvements and are kept back by landlords. It is earnestly to be wished the fact was so, for the remedy would then be easy." [28]

From all this we can perhaps strictly conclude no more than that the admitted defect in the land law cannot be expected to lead automatically to suboptimal investment. The amendment in the laws, which will without question improve the logic of the legal structure and make for equity at law, will have an effect on economic development which cannot be predicted a priori but must be determined by reference to historical fact. When evictions are rare and rents are fairly stable, a tenant will certainly have an incentive to invest, for the returns to the investment will accrue to him.

Tenant Right

The usual advantages claimed for tenant right are that the outgoing tenant is paid something for his property in the holding and that the landlord is guaranteed payment for arrears out of the proceeds of the tenant-right sale.* The gain of the outgoing tenant, however, will not simply be the proceeds of the sale of tenant right. The tenant right also cost him something to acquire. Landlords indirectly pointed this out when they complained that incoming tenants were crippled by tenant-right payments and often lacked sufficient working capital to farm properly. The real point is that, if the degree of underrenting remains the same from the date of the purchase of tenant right to its sale, the sale of the right will bring the tenant exactly what he paid for it. He will be no better and no worse off on that account. He *will* be better off if the land increases in value and the landlord

* The view of tenant right as a guarantee against defaulting tenants makes the institution equivalent to requiring a sort of deposit on the rent. It is difficult to attribute serious economic consequences to such arrangements. To quote Bence Jones again (p. 57), the absence of tenant right in his neighborhood merely "means that County Cork landlords have not been in the habit of making incoming tenants pay up the arrears of those who failed."

does not raise the rent accordingly. The Ulster tenant's real rent is the sum of what he pays to his landlord plus the interest on his tenant-right purchase. If tenant-right prices are set by auction, Ulster tenants are paying fully competitive rents; if they are set in some other way, less than competitive rents. What has happened is that landlords and tenants are acting jointly as landlords, and the return to land as a factor of production is being divided between them. The "underrenting" of the landlord is being compensated for by the tenant. Although at first glance this might seem like a pure gift to the tenant and no source of difficulty, certain adverse side effects may well arise. If there is uncertainty about the terms of the partnership, about its extent and duration, about the rights and duties of the respective partners, the efficient conduct of the enterprise can be affected. Moreover, merely by increasing the number of partners in an estate, the transactions costs of major investment projects will be increased, and investment may be stopped short of the point to which it would be carried if there were only one landowner involved. We shall meet with examples of both of these adverse effects later and will argue that they were important in limiting the efficiency of Irish agriculture.

But, in fact we shall not find small Ulster tenants putting their land out at auction.* Only the aged, emigrants, or bankrupt farmers commonly did so. In other words, the tenant in the partnership did not act as the landlord would. The small tenant is not really to be thought of just as a manager of land; he is in fact primarily seeking to sell his labor. For

---

* Outside of Ulster, where landlord underrenting occurred, the tenant did not even possess the right to compensate. He had no tenant right at all; he had to consume the fruits of underrenting and could not dispose of them to another tenant. There was no way to price land at marginal product if the landlord-tenant market was imperfect.

him the going wage rate elsewhere in the Irish economy was very low—at times surely zero—and realistically the relevant figure may often have been the ruling wage rate in Australia or New England, with all the attendant discounting for risk, fear, uncertainty, and nonmonetary factors like family feelings that this would involve. A small, poor tenant who is underrented by his landlord will not necessarily be able to get a return for his labor elsewhere, and he will neither seek nor accept a bid for his land from someone who can make more profit from it.

The impairment of the landlords' right to evict and imperfections in the land market, in which tenant rights are not being auctioned off or do not exist, thus combine to keep land priced below its marginal product. In the first instance there is a redistribution of income from landlord to tenant. But there are other effects, too. This is clearly a case of misallocation of resources. The more efficient farmer is prevented from acquiring more land; the less efficient farmer is protected in his holding. If the small farmer is less efficient than the medium or large holder, a second consequence would be that the tendency toward consolidation of holdings is thwarted. A third consequence of underpricing land would be that we should expect factors to be combined in a way that uses more land and less of other factors than would be optimal. It is sometimes said that the high farming of the Lothians in nineteenth-century Scotland was partly the result of high rents; this tendency is inhibited when rents are kept below competitive levels. Thus we should expect that the tenure customs of Ireland protected inefficiency, discouraged consolidation, and encouraged backward technological methods.

We have argued that the historical fact that landlords do not evict rent-paying tenants and that large sums are paid for pure tenant right mean that land is priced below market equilibrium. This might sound like a curious result because it concludes that landlords were underexploiting rather than exploiting their tenants. But there is no necessary connection betwen exploitation and poverty; agricultural societies without any landlords at all can be desperately poor. If the working of the economic system in Ireland placed an intolerably low value on the services of the small tenant, then something should have been done about it, but there is no reason to conclude that it was the landlord's fault. Terms like "good landlord" and "bad landlord" have no place in a discussion with any analytical pretensions. If we say that land is rented at a price below market price, we do not attribute a necessarily generous nature to the owner of the land; the consequent resource misallocation may be very harmful. Moreover, we should be unwilling to assert that a man who accepts a market price for his land is by definition a "bad landlord."

No doubt England had wronged Ireland, wronged her grievously over many centuries. No doubt the landlords of Ireland were the visible embodiment of those historic wrongs. But it does not follow that landlord predominance in economic relationships—relationships expressed in terms of acres, prices, and rents—was the reason for Ireland's slow economic progress.

We have said that Irish landlords did not freely evict and clear or (what amounts to the same thing) charge a competitive rent, because it would have resulted in the disintegration of the social fabric. The course that was taken had, we have argued, unfavorable implications for economic development, nor was it an altogether satisfactory solution in other respects. The notion of a "fair" rent as distinct from a competitive rent is not completely unambiguous, and there are no economic forces tending to establish it. To keep rent below the competitive level, tenants must refrain from making, and landlords must refrain from accepting, bids for land at rents they would be willing to pay. Both sides must play the game. Also, the level of rent that will be acceptable will depend on some social consensus about fairness, and ultimately on the level at which people would revolt against the landlords. The result will not be a clear-cut determinate level of rent. What the Irish tenant faced was not impersonal market forces but a bewildering array of prices and practices, varying from landlord to landlord. This was true for Ulster, too, because free auction of tenant right was not the universal rule, and every landlord who did not allow free auctioning had his own office rules to restrict the bidding. Such a situation contains the seeds of endless resentments and frictions. In one sense there is no more secure tenant than the man who pays the competitive equilibrium rent: he knows the landlord has no incentive to remove him or raise his rent because no one will be offering more for his holding. The charging of "fair" rents instead of competitive equilibrium rents may avoid social unrest on the grand scale, but it does not necessarily promote amity and content.

When competitive rents are not charged, the potentiality of charging them never completely disappears: it always hangs over the tenant's head. Ordinarily, it would seem plausible that, if the custom were for landlords not to evict and not to charge competitive rents, this would communicate itself to the tenantry. There will always be instances of rack-renting landlords, the argument might run, but if they are really a rare occurrence, the tenants will be aware of this and act accordingly. But if there is discontent in the countryside—for historical or religious reasons—this kind of situation is evidently inflammable. It will be easy to stir up feeling with the example of one or two "bad landlords."

We have here an agrarian structure in which neither

party has complete freedom of maneuver. The landlord is restricted: he cannot freely evict and clear; if he wants to invest, he cannot easily arrange units of optimum size and he cannot be sure of getting a return on his investment because he is limited by custom in his rent-raising powers. He lacks the power to enforce his authority over techniques and farming practices, and he cannot replace a bad tenant with a good one. Tenants' customary rights are capable of blocking him in all these directions. The tenant is limited by the legal code, by the letter of the law if not by actual practice. The tenant has perhaps more possibility for investing than the landlord on the basis of the tenure situation, but if he wanted to improve he might feel, rightly or wrongly, the potential legal rights of the landlord hanging over him.

What Mr. Gladstone proposed to do was to strengthen the tenants' customary rights and to remove from them this supposed sword of Damocles—this landlord right to their improvements—that was thought to be the deterrent to investment and hence to progress in Irish economic development.

PROVISIONS OF THE LAND ACT OF 1870

The Landlord and Tenant (Ireland) Act of 1870 aimed to curb evictions and to secure to the tenants the value of their improvements. The fulfillment of these aims was felt to be, in the first instance, a matter of social justice and, in the second instance, an incentive to increased productivity and investment, and hence to economic progress. The act went on the assumption that the best means to this end was the firm establishment of Ulster custom where it existed and the introduction of its elements where it did not extend. Accordingly, the first section of the act established the legality of Ulster custom; the second section recognized the legality of any essentially similar custom that might prevail in the other provinces. Any tenant not holding under Ulster custom (and indeed any tenant who was entitled to claim the benefit of the custom but elected not to) was entitled under section 3 of the act to claim compensation for the loss of his holding whenever he was disturbed by action of the landlord. Ejection for nonpayment of rent was not an instance of disturbance, unless, for holdings valued at £15 or less, the court certified that the nonpayment was due to exorbitant rents. The landlord was to pay the compensation the court thought just, subject to the following maxima:

For holdings valued:	A sum not more than:
£10 and under	7 years rent
£10–30	5 years rent
£30–40	4 years rent
£40–50	3 years rent
£50–100	2 years rent
Above £100	1 year rent

A maximum award of £250 was set. Landlords were entitled to deduct from the compensation payments any sums due in back rent, or for deterioration arising from nonobservance of express or implied contract, or for taxes payable by the tenant. Tenants who subdivided without the written consent of the landlord, after passing of the act, were not entitled to compensation. Tenants holding by leases made after the passing of the act for not less than twenty-one years were debarred from claiming compensation for disturbance. Any contract by which a tenant agreed to surrender his claim to compensation for disturbance was declared void. These provisions for compensation for disturbance, then, were the weapons with which the Land Act of 1870 proposed to fight eviction.

Section 4 of the Land Act of 1870 provided that any tenant not claiming under Ulster custom should be entitled upon quitting his holding to claim from the landlord compensation in respect of all improvements made by him or his predecessor in title. Claims made for improvements dated twenty or more years before the passage of the act were limited to permanent buildings and reclamation of wasteland. Compensation for improvement was not to be granted where prohibited in writing by the landlord as being calculated to diminish the value of the estate (the court agreeing) and made within two years after the passing of the act or during the unexpired portion of a lease signed prior to the act. Also excluded were any improvements made in pursuance of a contract entered into for a valuable consideration; any improvements made in contravention of a written contract; any improvements the landlord had undertaken to perform (unless he failed to perform them within a reasonable time).

In general, compensation was not allowed if lease or contract made before the passing of the act expressly excluded it. Again, the landlord could deduct from the claim any back rents due him not exceeding three years, any sums for deterioration arising from nonobservance of express or implied covenants, and any taxes payable by the tenant. A provision was also made against contracting out of the benefits of this section for holdings below a certain value. The presumption was legally established (with suitable qualifications) that all improvements were deemed to have been made by the tenant, unless proved to the contrary.

Parts 2 and 3 of the act contained provisions for the purchase of holdings by tenants, empowering the Commissioners of Public Works to grant up to two-thirds of the purchase price repayable in thirty-five years at 5 percent.

These provisions were included in deference to John Bright, an unwavering supporter of land purchase for Ireland. They are important for the long shadow they cast ahead, but had little impact in the form they took in the Act of 1870.

The compensation for disturbance provisions of the act, designed to limit evictions, amounts to a combined tax and subsidy. Landlords are in effect taxed on every eviction, and the proceeds of the tax go to subsidize the evicted tenant, payments being inversely in proportion to the value of the holding. The objection was commonly made that these provisions would not curb evictions, since the landlord could recover the amount he paid from an incoming tenant. This argument is clearly weak, because, if the landlord could acquire any additional sum for his land from a new tenant, he had the incentive to acquire it before the act as well as after; moreover, the act lessened the amount he could retain of any enhanced rental. Thus a tax on eviction will certainly have a deterrent effect, and any landlord just on the margin of evicting will find it no longer profitable to do so. Like many economic policies, this mechanism works at the margin: not all evictions will be rendered unprofitable but some will. More than this, on land of given value it will be more unprofitable to evict numbers of small tenants than a few large ones. If a landlord has two estates of equal value and wishes to take one into his own hands, he will (other things equal) acquire the one with the fewer holdings on it. The small tenant is more protected than the large, and more assisted if he does get evicted.

If one aims at curbing eviction, and at assisting those evicted, especially small tenants, then the provisions for compensation for disturbance in the Land Act of 1870 will undoubtedly work toward those ends. The importance of the provisions and their influence on economic progress in Ireland will depend squarely on the prevalence of eviction. The act thus may be aimed at halting a major problem or mitigating only a minor evil. But there is a further point. To the extent that the act works, it may act as a barrier to realizing economies of scale. If economic progress is being impeded by the prevalence of holdings of substandard size and consolidation of holdings is urgently needed, then the better the act works in this respect the more it retards economic growth, and the laudable aim of subsidizing the small tenant associates the subsidy with the very perpetuation of small holdings that may be keeping tenants poor in the first place.

The effects of the provisions for compensation for improvements are less straightforward. Awarding a departing tenant the value of any unexhausted improvements is a clear gain in equity and in providing investment incentives. No doubt, such valuation would present many problems, but even imperfect awards are of some utility. The tenant who does not quit his holding must have his property in improvements secured to him, too. Under the Land Act of 1870, this comes about in the following way: if a landlord tries to increase rent on account of tenant improvements, the tenant can refuse to pay the rent and ask the court to award him the value of his unexhausted improvements. Ideally, this ought to work to prevent the landlord from ever making the attempt in the first place: he should realize that he will be frustrated in this endeavor. If he persists, then the tenant ought theoretically to be no worse off than before, since he will have the value of his improvements instead of the improvements themselves—theoretically, he should be equally well off either way. The court cannot force a landlord to set a certain rent, but the court can insure that no rent is charged on tenant improvements. (On the other hand, if the landlord offers a rent that the court considers fair, no claim for compensation is allowed.)

There are no logical pitfalls in these provisions. In legal terms, these provisions have the effect of extending to agriculture the right of removal of fixtures, thus granting the exception to the doctrine of waste that had long since been granted in the case of trade. The inherent difficulties in making good estimates of compensation awards should not be minimized; in addition there is a problem of bias in the court decisions in the historical circumstances. A more serious problem arises because of the awkwardness of the legal code: the tenant who refuses to pay a rent he considers unjust must relinquish his holding before the court awards are made. Without substantial confidence in the court, he will be unwilling to gamble. Nevertheless, one could legitimately expect, after a period of adjustment and clarification, that the courts would not fail to carry out the object of the act. There must have been ample experience in procedures in the business and trade cases. An act need not work perfect justice in all cases in order to improve a situation.

We conclude then that, if Ireland's economic difficulties were traceable to defects in tenure arrangements, the Land Act of 1870 was soundly conceived and well drafted. It was well designed to cure the evils it assumed. It would work to deter eviction and deter landlords from raising rents on tenant improvements. But if its assumptions were wrong, it could not hope to play a major role in improving the economic condition of Ireland. Its success rested squarely on the historical facts about the frequency of evictions, the course of rents, and the nature of investment incentives.

3.
The Assumptions of the Land Act: Evictions, Rents, and Improvements

In the evening I was in a whirl;
my mind jumped from a snatch of song
to a remembered page of economic history.

Ernie O Malley
Easter Week, 1916

If it should turn out that evictions in Ireland were rare and tenure was in fact secure, that rents were low and fairly stable, and that low investment was not the result of tenure arrangements, it would not be surprising if the Land Act of 1870 failed to have important effects.

EVICTIONS

We all have in our mind's eye (sometimes it appears on the dust jacket of best-selling books) a picture of a beautiful Irish girl, a shawl around her shoulders, standing sadly beside the smouldering ruins of a small cabin. Although such scenes unquestionably occurred, with all their heart-rending implications, after the Famine they were few and far between, and in the history of Irish agriculture in the mid-nineteenth century eviction would have a small chapter.

In round numbers there were about 600,000 tenants in Ireland after the large emigrations of the immediate post-Famine years. Of these, only a small proportion held land by lease; the overwhelming number (perhaps about 500,-

000) held as tenants from year to year. A year-to-year tenancy, we recall, was a letting for an indefinite period, but determinable on a six-months' notice to quit (after August 15, 1876, twelve months). We have seen that, while nothing sounds more precarious than this, tenancies from year to year existed for generations and descended from father to son. Tenants regarded them almost as a perpetual interest, and on this ground small tenants preferred them to leases.*

Although landlords undoubtedly had legal power to determine a year-to-year tenancy for any reason, testimony by individuals and from statistical sources is unanimous than an Irish landlord rarely evicted a tenant except for

* The reluctance of small Irish tenants to accept leases is a powerful argument for their confidence in their security as year-to-year tenants. (Large tenants and tenants of grass farms tended to hold by lease.) The following quotations from the Bessborough Commission are typical.

Watson 7495. "The tenants as a rule do not care about leases, they would rather be yearly tenants. The only time a man asks for a lease is when he wants to borrow money—they cannot borrow money except they have leases."

Quinn 6548. "I believe I have never been asked for a lease before or since the Land Act more than once or twice."

Sinclair 11434. "As to the objection to take leases, does that arise from fear of losing the tenant right at the end of them?—No, I think they had always the idea that they were pretty safe, but that when a lease falls in the landlord would be looking into the rent, otherwise the property went on and a man might be forty or fifty years without an alteration in rent."

Scott 15897. "They don't want leases—in fact, the leases we give are to Scotchmen, and large tenants, or people of that sort."

Scott 15899. "The smaller tenantcy don't value a lease?—They would not take it."

Mahon 21172. "You say the small tenants are not inclined to take leases?—They won't take them at all."

Mahon 21227. "Do you evict no notice to quit?—Never; you may say never, practically."

Mahon 21228. "Then the tenants on those estates without any law have fixity of tenure practically?—I think they have. That is the reason they would not have leases I suppose."

nonpayment of rent.* "Capricious eviction," by which is usually meant eviction for any reason other than nonpayment of rent, is infrequently alleged and rarely encountered in the entire inquiry of the Bessborough Commission, which covers the experience of all of Ireland for a decade or more before 1880. When one considers such valid reasons for eviction as dilapidation, bad farming practices, and prevention of subdivision, not even to mention consolidation, the small number of evictions is perhaps not a subject for congratulations.

In order to interpret any statements about eviction, it is necessary to remind ourselves again about the legal procedure for enforcing payment of rent. A landlord had three remedies for enforcing the payment of rent: (1) by a personal action against the tenant for breaking an express or implied contract, (2) by a proceeding for distress, which permitted the landlord to seize the tenant's goods

---

* Here are a few examples of typical testimony before the Bessborough Commission.

Wrench 5516. "We never bring an eviction except for nonpayment of rent."

Young 5868. "I never knew a case [of eviction except for nonpayment of rent] in my life."

O'Sullivan 25022. "Are there evictions in your district except for nonpayment of rent?—Well, sir, in the district that I speak of I am not aware."

O'Sullivan 25023. "Nonpayment of rent is the cause generally?—Nonpayment of rent is the whole mischief."

Robertson 1425. "I think virtually the tenants over Ireland have fixity of tenure now. [But not by law.]"

A numerical example that makes the same point is the following. For the 6 years ending in 1869, in Kerry there were 387 ejectment decrees, of which 92 were on notice to quit, 18 for expired leases, 277 for nonpayment of rent, the average term for which rent was overdue being 2 years, 2 months (*Reports from Poor Law Inspectors in Ireland as to the Existing Relations between Landlord and Tenant in Respect of Improvement on Farms, P.P.* 1870 [c. 31] XIV, p. 22).

on the premises, and (3) by an action of ejectment by which the landlord obtained possession of the land. The third procedure was already the commonest at the time of the Devon Commission (1844) and, for all practical purposes, is the only one of importance. Upon nonpayment of a year's rent, the landlord could bring an action for ejectment in the Civil Bills Court.[1] The action would then either be granted, dismissed, or otherwise disposed of. If the tenant paid the arrears of rent within a reasonable time, he could file a bill in chancery to redeem his interest and be put back into possession as tenant again; alternatively, he could be reinstated not as tenant but as caretaker and given a chance to redeem.

An ejectment decree was thus the landlord's first step in recovering overdue rent; it was designed for this purpose and not for the purpose of clearing away tenants. Any series of ejectment decrees entered, or even granted, will not give a picture of evictions. Also, any series of evictions granted, unless accompanied by series on readmissions as caretakers and readmissions as tenants, will not give an accurate picture of the numbers of tenants actually removed from their holdings.

Table 1 gives some idea of the magnitude of evictions in Ireland from 1849 to 1880. After 1870 the figures substantially overestimate actual evictions, since the readmissions column only includes those readmitted as tenants, not those readmitted as caretakers. Fortunately, we have for 1880 and for the first half of 1881 figures on readmissions as caretakers. These are presented in Table 2 and are given by province, so that the relative magnitudes of the readmission as caretakers and readmission as tenants may be seen in detail. Table 2 shows that, where we do have information available, 40 percent, 45 percent, and over 50 percent of those evicted were readmitted as caretakers.

Table 1. Eviction Cases with Readmissions, 1849–1880

Year	Evictions (Families)	Readmitted[a] (Families)
1849	16,686	3,302
1850	19,949	5,403
1851	13,197	4,382
1852	8,591	2,041
1853	4,833	1,213
1854	2,156	331
1855	1,849	525
1856	1,108	230
1857	1,161	242
1858	957	237
1859	837	346
1860	636	65
1861	1,092	274
1862	1,136	243
1863	1,734	183
1864	1,924	276
1865	942	183
1866	795	185
1867	549	90
1868	637	122
1869	374	63
1870	548	104
1871	482	114
1872	526	118
1873	671	152
1874	726	200
1875	667	71
1876	553	85
1877	463	57
1878	980	146
1879	1,238	140
1880	2,110	217
Totals	90,107	21,340

SOURCE: *Return, by Provinces and Counties, of Cases of Evictions Which Have Come to the Knowledge of the Constabulary in Each Year, 1849 to 1880.* P.P. 1881 (C. 185) LXXVII.

[a] The figures from 1870 to 1880 include those readmitted as tenants only.

It is apparent from Table 1 that after the immediate post-Famine years evictions are not numerous. Assuming that the aftermath of the Famine was over by 1854,[2] the gross evictions of 1855 to 1880 totaled 24,675. If we de-

Table 2.   Eviction Cases with Readmissions, 1880 and 1881, Quarters I and II, by Province (families)

		Readmitted as:	
	Evicted	Tenants	Caretakers
1880 Ulster	497	52	275
Leinster	484	65	189
Connaught	387	22	164
Munster	742	78	319
Total	2,110	217	947
1881-I Ulster	179	19	78
Leinster	60	2	17
Connaught	47	3	25
Munster	64	8	19
Total	350	32	139
1881-II Ulster	440	24	276
Leinster	171	12	62
Connaught	268	3	115
Munster	186	11	89
Total	1,065	50	542

SOURCE: *Returns of Cases of Evictions in Ireland in Each Quarter in Each Year, Showing the Number of Families and Persons Evicted in Each County, and the Number Readmitted as Tenants and as Caretakers, for 1880, P.P.* 1881 (2) LXXVII; *for 1881,* 1881 (285) LXXVII and 1881 (320) LXXVII.

duct those known to have been readmitted, there remain 20,007 final evictions. We are then still missing the number of readmissions as caretakers for 1870–1880, but for 1880 alone we know the figure to be 947. If we assume a third of those evicted in the 1870's were readmitted as caretakers, we are left with 17,775 final evictions for the entire period. Even if there were no turnover at all among the 600,000 tenants of 1855, this would amount to an eviction rate of under 3 percent; whatever turnover figure we assume will reduce the percentage.[3] When one considers that the eviction figures must include, for example, evictions due to family quarrels, evictions of felons and undesirables, and evictions for the sake of squaring farms (in which case, the evicted tenant is ordinarily resettled), it is hardly necessary to labor the point that the significance of evictions in Ireland in this period was extremely small.

It is interesting to go from overall figures to the level of individual cases. In Sligo, Mr. Cochran Davys, the Solicitor to the Grand Jury, presented evidence to the Bessborough Commission on his experience in the 1870's (1872 to the third quarter of 1880). In this period 1,012 ejectment decrees were granted, of which 725 were for nonpayment of rent and 287 for overholding and on title (22 of these 287 were for permissive occupancy). Of the 725 for nonpayment, 269 went to the sheriff; the rest were settled at once; of the 269 that went to the sheriff, 232 were reinstated at once and the rest later on. The majority of the 265 cases for overholding and on title arose between the tenants themselves; of these cases 124 went to the sheriff, as did 5 of the permissive occupancy cases.

"Everybody knows there is hardly ever a really final eviction for non-payment . . . the landlord is not at all anxious to get rid of a tenant," testified Mr. Cochran Davys. "I don't think that, taking one year with another, there are over three tenants in a year eventually lost their holdings." [4]

RENTS

If the Irish tenant did not live in constant fear of eviction, did he ward it off only by paying frequent rent increases? Was he faced with a confiscatory rent increase every time he made an improvement on his holding?

There are no rent series in existence that describe the course of rents in Ireland in the nineteenth century. Data on Irish rents do not become available until 1881, and then they are only partial. The assessments for lands under Schedule A of the British income tax returns, which are given separately for England, Scotland, and Ireland in the annual Reports of the Commissioners of Inland Revenue, are supposed to reflect agricultural rents;[5] for England and Scotland they do in fact reflect rents.[6] For Ireland, however, the annual series of Schedule A-Lands reflects only a single unrevised valuation, begun in the aftermath of the Famine and never substantially altered. Fortunately or unfortunately, so much controversy surrounded this single series that there exists a large literature on the subject, especially in parliamentary inquiries. The relation of the Schedule A assessments to rents is not the sole subject of any of these inquiries—they may be addressed to questions of local taxation or to whether Ireland is paying an equitable share of imperial taxes or even to why the valuation cost so much and whether there was discrimination against Roman Catholics in the Valuation Office—but in the course of pursuing them much light is thrown on the level of rents. The conclusion of Sir Josiah Stamp is, however, only too true: "Irish statistics [Schedule A] . . . should not be used . . . unless a careful study is first made of the most voluminous literature of this very difficult subject, and unless the principles of valuation have been fully understood." [7]

The first government valuation of Ireland was undertaken in 1830 under an Act of 1826 (and subsequent amending acts) to provide for the assessment of local taxes. The unit of valuation was the townland, a geographical area of which there were 61,000 in Ireland, averaging 350 acres each. The underlying principle was to evaluate the agricultural products of each townland according to a fixed schedule of commodity prices. Meanwhile, in 1838 the Poor Law had been passed for Ireland, and the poor rates required a valuation not for a geographical unit like the townland, but for each individual holding in Ireland. A Poor Law valuation was accordingly begun, the unit to be the individual tenement and the principle of valuation to be according to the actual rent paid. This followed English practice. The two valuations proceeded simultaneously until, in 1846, after a Select Committee had meanwhile considered their respective principles, a new valuation law was enacted by Parliament providing for a new tenement valuation on the principle of actual rent paid. The six counties not completed under the old Poor Law valuation were accordingly done under the new act. These figures were never published, because Parliament finally decided to change the basis of the tenement valuation to the older principle of applying a fixed scale of prices to the output of each holding. Under this last act, which was passed in 1852, the so-called Griffith's valuation was carried out for all of Ireland. It was used for county rates, for poor rates, other local rates, and, when the income tax was introduced in Ireland in 1853, for income tax purposes as well. The 1852 Act remained the basis of valuation into the twentieth century.[8]

It was a remarkable undertaking. Sir Richard Griffith carefully trained his men to investigate each holding, taking samples of topsoil and subsoil, and considering closely fertility, climate, and proximity to markets. They would first estimate the yield of the various crops and livestock that could be produced on each holding. Eight products were considered: wheat, oats, barley, flax, butter, beef, mutton, and pork. The physical yields were then multiplied by a fixed scale of prices to get the gross annual value of the holding. From this was deducted the cost of production, including labor, depreciation on equipment, 5 percent on an allowance for tenant's capital, and repairs and insurance. Rates and taxes were also deducted. These would comprise the county rates (grand jury cess), which went for roads, bridges, courthouses, infirmaries, and insane asylums; the poor rate; and other local taxes. The Dublin police tax and Belfast water tax were later included in this list. The result, after these deductions, would be the net annual value of the holding.[9] This figure would show what the tenant would be willing to offer a landlord for rent, and the valuators were instructed that their final figure should not exceed the fair letting value to a solvent tenant.

Sir Richard Griffith's men worked their way from south to north and valued every holding in Ireland, finishing the last county in 1865.[10] The prices for the eight chosen products were calculated from averages collected in forty market towns all over Ireland for the years 1849, 1850, and 1851. The poor rates were taken as the average of the five years preceding the date of valuation. It was intended in the Act of 1852 that a new valuation should be made at not less than fourteen-year intervals, but funds were never provided for any revision. Thus the series in the annual reports of H. M. Commissioners of Internal Revenue that bears the title "Gross Annual Value of Property and Profits Assessed as Lands for Income Tax Purposes" is for Ireland virtually stationary. It records the original valuations made by Sir Richard Griffith's men from 1853 to 1865, with a few minor additions. Although the Valuation Commission in Ireland each year recorded every transfer of acreage from one man to another, to correct for variations in the size of the individual holdings, the value of each acre by law remained the same. Nor were house assessments brought up to date. Annual additions were made for new structures and renovations, "toned down" to make them relative to the original values, but under the original act new farm buildings were not to be valued for the first seven years. Anyone in the towns could have his house revalued if he wished, by notifying the Valuation office; however, since values were increasing, it is hardly likely that people would rush to make voluntary applications to have their income taxes increased, so that very few changes were made.

Columns 1, 2, and 3 of Table 3 show for England, Scotland, and Ireland the annual value of lands assessed for income tax purposes. It is clear that, until such time as all the counties in Ireland were entered on the Griffith valuation instead of the previous Poor Law valuation, the series reflected the shifting of the individual counties from the latter basis to the former. By 1865 all of Ireland was on the Griffith valuation, and this effect was eliminated. The crucial question can then be put: in 1865, what relation does the valuation bear to the real value of agricultural land in Ireland, where value means rental?

In the first place, it would be difficult to find three years in which Irish prices were lower than in 1849, 1850, and 1851, the years averaged for the price scale in the Griffith valuation. Ireland then lay prostrate after the Famine; even the impetus given to prices by the scarcity of famine conditions was spent. Of the eight prices used in the valuation, only those of animal products exceeded the levels of 1836. Table 4 compares the prices of the Griffith valuation with corresponding prices in 1836, 1865, 1871, and 1881, and gives the prices also as percentages of those used by the Griffith valuation. We can see that, by 1865, the appropriate prices for crops would have been about 50–60 percent, and for animal products about 80 percent, above those ac-

Table 3. Rental of Land in England, Scotland, and Ireland, 1865–1881

	England (1)	Scotland (2)	Ireland Unadjusted (3)	Ireland Amended (4)	Ireland Alternative Amended (5)
1865–66	46,482	6,850	9,887	11,370	11,864
1866–67	46,556	6,965	9,992	11,661	12,110
1867–68	47,767	7,186	9,961	11,794	12,192
1868–69	47,799	7,217	9,952	11,942	12,301
1869–70	47,857	7,195	9,879	11,983	12,349
1870–71	49,011	7,301	9,886	12,110	12,437
1871–72	49,027	7,326	9,884	12,157	12,518
1872–73	49,035	7,363	9,885	12,208	12,593
1873–74	49,956	7,497	9,924	12,306	12,713
1874–75	50,272	7,493	9,923	12,354	12,791
1875–76	50,408	7,505	9,921	12,401	12,897
1876–77	52,016	7,690	9,938	12,482	12,989
1877–78	51,934	7,666	9,937	12,540	13,057
1878–79	51,870	7,668	9,940	12,604	13,131
1879–80	52,041	7,769	9,981	12,716	13,255
1880–81	51,847	7,712	9,981	12,776	13,305
Percent Change	11.5	12.5	—	12	12

NOTE: The source for columns 1, 2, and 3 is Josiah Stamp, *British Incomes and Property*, p. 49. Stamp's figures incorporate small adjustments, corrections, errors, and omissions from the official figures. For England and Scotland they vary very little from the official figures (as given, e.g., in the *Report of the Commissioners of H. M. Inland Revenue, P.P.* 1884–1885 [c. 4474], XXII), but I have used them because they are clearly an improvement. The main difference between Stamp's Irish figures (column 3) and the official figures is that the latter show a large jump after 1875 when farmhouses are included in Lands, as they are in the English and Scottish series. Prior to 1876 they were listed elsewhere in the Irish data. Stamp has restored them to the proper place and made other minor adjustments. For my own interest, I have made the crude adjustment of the official series by reclassifying houses (in 1876 and also, to a smaller extent, in 1874), and this crudely adjusted series is very similar to Stamp. Again, I have used his figures because they represent the best series obtainable.

The Irish series should ideally be augmented by an estimate of annual interest on Ulster tenant-right payments. This is unlikely to be very large, and in any case it would probably have little influence on *movements* in the series since 1865, which is our principal interest.

tually reflected. (Flax was abnormally high in 1865 because of the cotton shortage resulting from the American Civil War.)

The second abnormal aspect of the years of the Griffith valuation is the high poor rates. It is estimated that the total

Table 4. Comparison of Agricultural Prices with Prices Used in Act of 1852 (Griffith's Valuation)

Prices in the Valuation Act of

	1836 per cwt s.d.	% above or below 1852 act prices	1852 per cwt s.d.	1865[a]		1871[a]		1881[a]	
				per cwt s.d.	% of 52	per cwt s.d.	% of 52	per cwt s.d.	% of 52
Wheat	10–0	+33	7–6	12–4	+64	12–6	+66	10–2	+35
Oats	6–0	+24	4–10	7–6	+55	8–0	+65	8–0	+65
Barley	7–0	+27	5–6	7–9	+41	8–10	+60	7–9	+41
Butter	69–0	+5	65–4	119–0	+82	116–0	+77	96–6	+47
Beef	33–0	−7	35–6	65–3	+83	75–0	+111	63–9	+80
Mutton	34–6	−16	41–0	75–0	+83	79–4	+93	74–6	+81
Pork	25–6	−21	32–0	56–6	+76	41–0	+28	55–0	+71
Flax	—	—	49–0	106–0	+116	88–0	+79	54–0	+10

SOURCE: *Royal Commission on the Financial Relations between Great Britain and Ireland, P.P.* 1895 (c. 7720-I), XXXVI, Appendix VI.

[a] Averages from *Purdom's Almanac* (Dublin, yearly). Prices for 1836 and 1852 are contained in the respective Valuation Acts. By 1881 prices were officially collected and published.

poor rate expenditure for all Ireland was £1,113,472 in 1852; in 1865 it had decreased by 35 percent to £731,-852. Lord Lansdowne's agent, J. Townshend Trench, testified before the Cowper Commission that the average poor rate on Lord Lansdowne's Kerry estate in 1852, 1853, and 1854 had been 5s. 6d. in the pound. In 1886 it was 1s. 6d.[11]

On the other hand, county cess rates had begun to climb by 1865; expenditures in that year were already 21 percent above the 1852 level. The overall level of local taxation almost certainly fell after 1852, but the important point is that the southern counties first valued by Griffith's men were considerably undervalued compared to the northern counties, which were surveyed in a much more prosperous era.

The southern counties were relatively undervalued for another reason. There is much testimony that in the North yield was valued higher just because "times were better." Strictly speaking, if the valuation were made according to the letter of the instructions, it would make no difference whether "times were better," but clearly the valuation officials all thought it did.[12] One presumes that the valuers, traveling in the South in the early 1850's, seeing "ground untilled, some of it, thistles, docks, dilapidated cottages, ragged men," "like a drunk country fallen down to sleep amid the mud," were unable to visualize what the land could produce under normal conditions.[13] The 1850's were a decade of improvement in agricultural methods and in transportation. It is more than plausible that a valuer in the early post-Famine years would be biased downward in his estimates of the capabilities of the land.

For all of these reasons, the completed valuation in 1865 fell short of the actual letting value of Irish agricultural land, and the counties valued first were undervalued relatively to those covered later.[14] This much is generally agreed. If we can now form an estimate of how far the valuation fell short of the rental in 1865 and in subsequent years, we shall have an estimate of the course of agricultural rents in Ireland over that period.

Evidence on 1864 and 1865 is fragmentary. Stamp cites a draft report of the Select Committee on the Taxation of Ireland in 1864 in which one witness put the valuation at 10 percent below the rental. In the 1880 Royal Commission on Agriculture, Mr. Ball Greene was asked directly, "Do you not think that valuation represented the letting value of the land at that time?" His answer—"If the prices contained in the Act were the prices at that time it ought to represent the net value at that time"—is another way of saying "No." [15] When Sir J. G. Barton appeared before the Royal Commission on Local Taxation in 1897, he testified that the original Griffith Valuation was 15–20 percent below the rents of the day.[16]

The first important body of testimony dealing with this subject came from witnesses before the Select Committee on General Valuation (Ireland) in 1869. Ball Greene testified then that the valuation was a fourth under the letting value.[17] He outlined the reasons why Ulster was valued below the southern counties, but added further that Ulster was below the letting value by two shillings in the pound. A table prepared by the Valuation Office was put in evidence in the appendix of the report, showing the increase in the valuation of each county that would be necessary to bring it up to the level of Ulster. According to this table, an increase of 20 percent would be appropriate for the provinces outside Ulster.

When Sir Richard Griffith himself came to testify, he was both puzzled and puzzling. He contended that his original valuation for Ulster was "a fair valuation for rating this minute;" [18] yet it was patently obvious, as the questioners persistently pointed out, that prices had risen greatly between 1851 and 1865 and that the price of flax, which was a principal Ulster crop, had risen most spectacularly. "Yes; but I know that our valuation in the North is a fair valuation," insisted Sir Richard.[19] "The proof is that gentlemen have not raised their rents." [20] The explanation of this anomaly is that tenant-right prices, not landlord rents, had risen in Ulster. A correct definition of rent for the Ulster farmer would clearly have to add to the rent he paid the landowner the interest on the price he paid the previous occupant for the farm. Something would have to be added to the Ulster valuation to make it current, but it is no surprise that Sir Richard Griffith could not estimate that something from the rents.

This was made clear by other testimony before the Committee, from Mr. Henry Hutchings, an employee of thirty years' standing in the Valuation Office. Using current yields and prices, Mr. Hutchings calculated the net product per acre for a sample of thirty-seven Poor Law Unions in North and South, and compared the results with the original valuation. In this comparison it was Ulster, not the South, that was more undervalued. Using these calculations as a basis, Sir Josiah Stamp concluded that the Ulster valuation would have to be increased 20 percent to make it reflect current rent values, where rent includes (properly) interest on tenant right.[21] Stamp's estimate for all Ireland for 1868–69 thus gives the valuation at about 20 percent below the true letting value, an estimate which he found repeated for 1870 in the Annual Report of the Board of Inland Revenue.[22]

One final estimate relating to this period came to light in 1880 in Ball Greene's evidence before the Royal Commission on Agriculture. Here he testified that Sir Richard Griffith in 1871 "when prices were fully as high as they are now, wrote to the Treasury stating that if 30 percent were added to the existing valuation, it might be taken as a basis for rents, or the fair telling [sic] value."

Turning from the early 1870's to the later years of the period, we find that Ball Greene told the Bessborough Commission in 1881 that he had calculated in 1876 that Griffith's valuation was 33 percent below the letting value (Q744), and he told the Royal Commission on Agriculture in 1880 that "if Ireland were revalued tomorrow" a moderate valuation would be 33 percent above Griffith's (Q22,2).

After the Land Act of 1881, which set up a Land Commission empowered to fix rents, we begin to get direct data on rents. Up to March 31, 1893, 280,054 cases had been dealt with by the Land Commission, covering 8,666,-151 acres (roughly half of Ireland). The actual rental of these holdings had totaled £4,661,702, the valuation £3,975,697. Thus, for the first case for which direct data are available, rents were found to be 28.18 percent above the valuation. Sir J. G. Barton expressly affirmed to the Royal Commission on Financial Relations that he assumed "that the rents of Ireland which have not been dealt with in the Land Courts, bear precisely the same relation to the valuations of these lands that rent and valuation do to those which have been dealt with." [23]

On the basis of all these observations and a close reading of all the parliamentary papers mentioned, I should conclude that the actual facts are something like this: the Griffith valuation was a fairly accurate reflection of real rental values in 1848–1852, but already by the mid-1860's it was perhaps as much as 15 percent below real values and by the late 1860's 20 percent below. Around 1870 it was perhaps between 20 and 25 percent below value, and from 1875–1880 somewhere between 25 and 30 percent.

Columns 1 and 2 of Table 5 summarize my conclusions and compare them with Stamp's. Since mine were arrived at by using much of the same material and the same methods, it is not surprising that they are, aside from the earliest years, extremely close. It seems to me that a figure of 20 percent for 1868 is the firmest of the lot, resting for the most part upon calculations performed at the Valuation Office at the time, and I would argue that this figure should be adopted. My choice of the higher figure puts my series

closer to the views of Barton for 1865 and of Ball Greene
for 1868, although I am in agreement with Stamp in thinking that 25 percent and 28 percent are high enough for
1875 and 1880. The 28 percent figure for 1881 is also
firmly based, since it corresponds to the collection of actual
rental data.

Table 5.   Valuation below Real Value (by percent)

Date	Best Estimate (1)	Stamp[a] (2)	Alternative Estimate (3)
1852	0	0	0
1864	—	10	—
1865	15	—	20
1868	20	—	—
1869	—	—	25
1870	22.5	20	—
1875	25	25	30
1880	28	28	33

[a] *British Incomes and Property*, p. 158.

In column 3 I have constructed an alternative series of
estimates, based more closely on Ball Greene's opinions,
which have a claim to serious consideration. I have taken
his express figures for 1881 (33 percent) and 1869 (25
percent), and have adopted the upper limit of Sir J. G.
Barton's estimate on the original deviation of the valuation
(20 percent) for 1865. I have ascribed 30 percent to 1875
to complete this alternative estimate.[24]

If we now multiply the figures of Schedule A-Lands, given
in column 3 of Table 3, by the percentages given in columns 1 and 3 of Table 5 (interpolating the percentages
linearly for the missing years), we have two estimates of
the real value of the rental of agricultural land in Ireland

from 1865 to 1880. This is shown in columns 4 and 5 of Table 3; the figures are shown graphically in Figure 1.

An inspection of Figure 1 shows that the two series are nearly parallel, and if we are interested in movements in

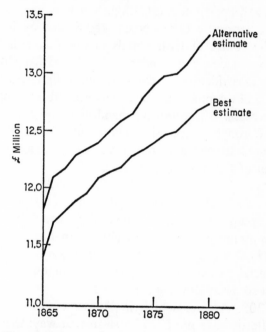

Fig. 1. Two estimates of agricultural rent in Ireland, 1865–1880 (£ million).

Source: Table 3.

the series rather than the absolute level, it will be a matter of indifference which we use. The rise in estimated rentals from 1865 to 1880 amounts to 12 percent, whichever series we use.

The period from the mid-1860's to the end of the 1870's was one of rising agricultural prices, and, for livestock, steeply rising prices. It was a period of great prosperity, and the value of Irish agricultural land, especially grazing land, could be expected to rise sharply. When we examine in Chapter 4 the evidence for the great increase in agricultural income in Ireland over this period, a 12 percent rise in rents will appear modest. English rentals increased over the same period by 11½ percent and Scotch by 12½ percent. The course of Irish rentals in this period is thus in line with experience elsewhere in the United Kingdom, and provides no evidence for the view that differences in Irish economic development are due to exorbitant or extortionate rent increases. The following handful of quotations from the Bessborough Commission, chosen at random from various parts of Ireland and from tenants as well as landlords, is typical of testimony about rents.

6903. We have been told that in some cases the rent has been increased from time to time, and that the effect is to do away with tenant right—is that so in your district?—No. There has been no increase of rent to any material extent within my memory in our district, at least so far as Down is concerned.

6208. Are rents high in Down?—I would say the landlords have not been harsh in that way; there are a few small men who do charge exorbitant rents.

150. And is there very little raising of rents?—Certainly [not] . . . [from Kilkenny.]

155. But on small estates with new men the feeling is very different?—I think so.

2027. Is land dearer [in Ulster] than in Limerick?—It is. I think Limerick, take it for all in all, is perhaps the cheapest let county in Ireland.

2029. Tipperary is moderately let, is it not?—Those

portions which are in the hands of the old proprietors are moderately let; but the parts of it which are in the hands of [Landed Estates purchasers] are let beyond their value.

5926. [From Antrim.] One can only judge from what one sees. I have never seen anything to make me think the tenants are influenced by a fear of the rent being raised. There are, perhaps, instances of small estates where the confidence would not be as great as among the larger men, but if you take the large estates, take the county generally, there is no rising of rent.

8300. [From a tenant farmer in Monaghan.] I think the landlords in our part of the county charge fair rents on the whole. I think the tenants have their holdings at a fair average.

Testimony (from tenants as well as agents) is practically unanimous that, on large and well-managed estates, rents are low and not often raised. The practice on large estates was to leave rents unchanged and to have occasional re-valuations of the entire estate, commonly at twenty-year intervals. Some estates followed the practice of making changes in rent upon a change of tenancy. Both kinds of practice tended to keep rent increases lagging behind the price rises in agricultural products from the 1860's on. The picture that emerges is that Irish rentals rose only slowly and "stickily" from the low levels of the Famine years.

Table 6 illustrates the truth of this conclusion from another source. This source is Irish Land Committee, consisting in 1880 of 1,826 large landowners whose holdings totaled nearly 7 million acres and were valued at £3.6 million; on these holdings were about 200,000 tenants. Since the total area of Ireland is 20 million acres, the total valuation £11.7 million, and the total number of holdings around 500,000, it is clear that the Land Committee represented a significant part of the experience of the country, probably over a third. From the respondents to the questionnaire (and there is testimony that members of the Land Committee that were nonrespondents cannot be identified as rent raisers), it can be seen that about 70 per cent of the area involved had rents set in the 1850's and before and not raised in the subsequent twenty years.

Table 6.   Dates at Which Current Rents Were Fixed and Area in Statute Acres of Estates Covered by Land Committee Questionnaire

Province	No. of Estates	Prior to 1830	1830– 1840	1840– 1850	1850– 1860	1860– 1870	1870– 1880	Total Acreage
Leinster	472	15,713	102,844	286,203	308,423	154,273	88,078	1,097,534
Munster	258	55,222	95,843	204,333	280,546	242,417	82,748	961,109
Ulster	357	121,671	340,036	243,205	447,211	361,406	171,863	1,685,392
Connaught	200	64,822	109,391	176,350	479,085	110,391	19,498	959,537
Totals	1,287	257,428	648,114	910,091	1,515,265	868,487	362,187	4,703,572

SOURCE: Bessborough Commission, 40138. Excludes grass farms.

The data in Table 6 explicitly exclude grass farms, on which rents were increasing during the period. There was general agreement about this. "The places where rents enormously exceed Griffith's Valuation," testified Charles Uniacke Townshend, were "the pasture lands of Meath, Limerick, Clare, and parts of Cork." [25] Tenants of grass farms did not complain, however; the rent increases were well justified by the increased value of their products. Rentals on grazing land of two, three, and even five times the Griffith valuation were not considered rack rents. [26]

It is much easier to prove that it was practically universally *believed* that small landowners who purchased in the

Landed Estates courts raised rents than to estimate the extent to which they actually did so. Many Landed Estates
purchasers were old landowners, perhaps adding to family
holdings or recovering some previously sold land; some
were men who came from England and farmed actively,
invested, and improved, and could hardly be blamed for increasing rents; some were men who merely raised rents
from levels of the 1840's in accord with price advances;
some were certainly purely speculators of the classic type.
It is possible to locate some of these "land sharks," but they
are most elusive; reference is made to them but they are
only rarely identified. We know from our overall data that
their impact on rents in Ireland must have been small.
Thomas Baldwin, superintendent of the agricultural department of National Education in Ireland for many years and
a man who knew every county in Ireland, put it this way:

> It is marvellous how the unjust treatment of one
> landlord creates a ferment in an entire county or prov-
> ince . . . whenever I went west of the Shannon, if a
> tenant grumbled or growled, his remark was, "Oh, he is
> as bad a landlord as so-and-so—a man named ****. I
> have heard that man's name mentioned two or three
> hundred times."
> And at great distances?—Actually 100 miles from
> where he has his property.
> In what county is that?—He lives near Tuam; the
> property is in Connemara. As I approached Donegal I
> heard the name of †††† in the same way, miles and
> miles from his property. The result was, I began to ask
> at last who was **** and ††††? I did not know either
> of them personally, and I did unearth at last this ****
> . . . I found the action of one unwise or bad landlord

brings disfavor in the whole class in the county or province, and actually drives terror into the minds of the people for miles and miles.

Reading the testimony of tenants and agents confirms Baldwin. Although these land speculators must have been few in number and small in their impact on rent levels, they played the role of the scapegoat. There is no need to deny the importance of social myths in economic history—economic historians can do much to account for some of them —but it is important to realize that this particular social myth had little influence on the course of rents.

When the spokesmen for the Irish tenants mounted their attacks on rents in 1880, their case was not buttressed by any demonstration of the course or level of rents but was based on the assertion that a "fair rent" was the Griffith valuation. Hundreds of cases were paraded before the Bessborough Commission in which tenants testified their rents were far above the Griffith valuation. It was as obvious then as now that this old valuation, based on abnormally low prices and totally different agricultural conditions, was an irrelevant standard for rents. (Parnell and Davitt were too intelligent not to have known this.) But its adoption was a brilliant political tactic. By that standard the majority of tenants in Ireland were paying "excessive" rents. The standard was simply understood, universally applicable, guaranteed to return the politically desired answer, and had a (spurious) semblance of impartial justice and governmental sanction. Even at that, the Land Committee's questionnaire showed that on 70 percent of the area covered, excluding grass farms again, rents were less than 20 percent above the Griffith valuation; only 14 percent of the area returned rents more than 30 percent and above the Griffith valuation (Table 7).

Tenants will understandably grumble about rents, whatever their level and however slowly they rise. Many allegations of rent-raising arose from misunderstanding. Cases in which rents were increased from the levels of 1857 [27] or

Table 7. Percentage above or below Poor Law Valuation at Which Lands Covered by the Land Committee Questionnaire Were Let, throughout Ireland, 1880 (thousand acres)

Amount of Rent	Acres
More than 10 percent below Poor Law Valuation	476.3
0–10 percent below Poor Law Valuation	580.6
At	424.0
0–10 percent above	1,718.6
10–20 percent above	1,288.6
20–30 percent above	989.3
30–40 percent above	476.8
40–50 percent above	229.9
More than 50 percent above	207.1
	6,391.2

SOURCE: Bessborough Commission, 40138. Excludes grass farms.

1866 [28] were cited as grievances in 1880. These are by no means isolated instances. The extreme case is perhaps that of William Gibson of Doomadonald, County Down, who complained in 1880 that his rent had been raised in 1860 from its level of 1782.[29] A tenant holding land within ten miles of Belfast complained when his rent was raised after twenty-five years, and a man with land within twelve miles of Belfast felt rents were being raised "on the improvements." [30] Ancient and irrelevant complaints were aired.

The very rarity of rent increases in Ulster made almost any increase seem a grievance. It would be too much to expect the Ulster farmer to understand that "the price of corn determines the rent of land and not vice versa." He felt that, since he customarily made the improvements on the land, *any* rise in value was somehow due to him and should be appropriated by him. It was certainly true that any increase in rent lowered the value of tenant right; although the Ulster farmer always maintained that the landlord was entitled to "legitimate" rent increases, he resented any infringement on the value of his tenant right. But the two were logically inconsistent. Since landlords were reluctant to adjust rent during the term of a tenancy, they (naturally) did so at the termination of a tenancy. This immediately reduced the value of the tenant right at the point of realization, which was felt to be a grievance. It may be imagined what an outcry would have arisen had landlords tried to renegotiate rent during the period of the tenancy.

There is no reason to discount all the testimony about rent increases on the grounds of misunderstanding. Convincing cases of rent-raising on tenants' improvements certainly occur. In Ulster many appear, in Londonderry and Tyrone, as well as Donegal, though throughout Ulster generally rents were slow to rise and were felt to be low or reasonable by many tenants. Even in Connemara rents in 1880 were very commonly a quarter or a third above the Griffith's valuation. But in the Southwest rents were certainly raised frequently and steeply, right through the 1870's. Kerry stands apart from the rest of Ireland in this respect, and conditions prevailed in Kerry in the 1870's that had not been known for decades elsewhere.

The overall picture, then, is that Irish agricultural rents rose about 12½ percent between 1865 and 1880, much in line with the course of rent elsewhere in the United Kingdom and in accordance with rises in agricultural income during the period. Rents rose most on lands suitable for grazing, but graziers did not complain, because price increases amply justified higher rents. Testimony agreed that small landowners were raising rents exorbitantly, but if one subtracts from the overall figure of 12½ percent something for the well-justified increased rental of the rapidly expanding grazing sector, not much force remains to be exerted by these rapacious small landlords.

IMPROVEMENTS

It is hardly necessary to document the prevalence of the common belief that in England and Scotland all permanent improvements were made by the landlord, while in Ireland they were made by the tenant. From the Devon Commission on, this assertion will be found everywhere.[31] As a generalization it is partly untrue, in varying degrees, for England, for Scotland, and for Ireland.

Compensation for unexhausted improvement, including some permanent improvements, was a lively issue among English agriculturalists from the 1870's on. Various local customs providing tenants compensation for permanent improvements existed all over England.[32] In Scotland, it was the improvements of tenants on nineteen- or twenty-one-year leases that made the Lothians the model of nineteenth-century high farming. In Ireland the question of who made the improvements can only be answered in one way: "It varies." Any conclusions drawn from the premise that Irish landlords do not invest, while in England and Scotland only landlords invest, are going to be incorrect.

In every county it is probably safe to say that there were districts in which the tenants made all the improvements and districts in which the landlord contributed; there are isolated instances, not numerous but significant, of landlords who made all the improvements. If we examine the improvements by type, we do find a general pattern throughout Ireland. Building was done by the tenant; the landlord typically provided timber and slate. The tenant would generally make the interior fences, the landlord the exterior. The landlord frequently gave an allowance for lime or an allowance of so much a foot for drainage; major arterial drainage was undertaken by landlords.

If we look at the pattern by size of farm, we find that on large and moderate-sized holdings the improvements were joint. This was even true in Ulster. Drainage was the principal permanent improvement, and major drainage works were usually undertaken by landlords with funds borrowed from the Board of Works. The Land Committee found in its questionnaire that landlords had invested £3.5 million in this way, their own funds and those borrowed from the Board of Works, over the period 1840–1881.[33] Writing in 1870, Samuel Horseley, Poor Law inspector in Cork, Kerry, and Limerick, put it this way: "All the real and substantial improvements under the heads of farm houses and offices, fences and thorough drainage have been the joint creation of landlords and of tenants." Dr. Brodie, another Poor Law inspector, writing in the same report, tells us that in his district, on large estates, improvements were joint; his district was composed of parts of Cavan, Clare, Galway, King's, Leitrim, Mayo, Sligo, Roscommon, and Tipperary.[34]

The tenants who made all the improvements themselves were most likely to be found among the small occupiers. They built, drained, and fenced frequently with no aid from the landlord beyond slates and timber or a small allowance for drainage. Aside from parts of Ulster, where substantial tenants sometimes made all the improvements, improvements of this kind can often be called so only by a stretch of the imagination. In the first place very little was done on these holdings. The improvements might be open sod drains that cattle could destroy in a season, a small pig sty, or the reclamation of a bit of cutaway bog. Moreover, anything that was done frequently tended to *decrease* the value of the land.[35] If land is held in quantities beneath the minimum necessary to support a family, every fence or cottage represents a negative return; they would have to be torn down and leveled in order to raise the productivity of the land. To establish compensation for an "improvement" of this kind would merely be to encourage further noneconomic investment in substandard holdings.

Much the same may be said of another "improvement," one that is more important in Ireland than in England and Scotland. This is the reclamation of bog or mountain land. This was invariably undertaken by small tenants, primarily because it was an investment that did not pay the landowner. The common arrangement was that a landlord would allow a tenant who had reclaimed a piece of land undisturbed occupation (rent-free or without a rent increase) for a sufficiently long period to compensate the tenant for his capital and labor. This customary arrangement is met with in all parts of Ireland.

We can see by concrete examples that the assumptions of the Land Act of 1870, that the tenants do the investing and are prevented from investing more by a defect in the land laws, are not borne out by the facts. While on *some* estates low rent and secure tenure may have encouraged tenant investment, on many others no such result followed. William Heron, a valuer and surveyor, described one of the latter cases to the Bessborough Commission as follows:

> 14051. There is the townland of Drumartin, the people hold it forever at a rent of 7s. 6d. an acre, and I defy you to say there are more comfortable homes there, or any better farming, than anywhere else.
>
> 14051. Chairman—These are perpetuities at a moderate rent?—Yes.
>
> 14053. And you see no difference between their state

and the state of the tenants who pay the higher rate?—I venture to say that, if you take a townland on Colonel Ffolliott's property close by, you will say they are a thousand degrees better off than the perpetuity men. You may account for it as you please, but it is a fact. Of course, it is absurd to say that a man is better off with a high rent to pay; but just as a horse with a light load may get skittish, so a tenant, who has not something to make him industrious, may become lazy.

This testimony is echoed many times. There is no need to attribute laziness to the tenants of Drumartin; the point is that tenant investment was determined by many factors beside tenure conditions.

The problem was less that land laws prevented tenants from investing than that the actual tenure customs we have observed deterred the landlords from investing. After all, no English landlord would have provided houses and offices for his tenants if he had had to build a few dozen houses on 200 or 300 acres. But Irish landlords were severely limited in exercising power over their own estates. "In order to get the estate into order," testified one landowner, describing a badly subdivided section in Mayo, "no man's life would be worth sixpence purchase if he attempted to do what would be necessary." [36]

Making consolidated farms from land in rundale (common holdings) had always been difficult for landlords, but "the difficulties are so great now [since the Land Act] that we would rather let them be as they are, sooner than attempt to make any change." [37]

Drainage schemes involved similar difficulties: When a main drain runs through several farms "some of the tenants will want to get the land drained, and others will oppose the draining of the land, and it is often very hard to arrange amongst the tenants about the running of the drain." [38] Even if this obstacle were overcome, landlords had persistent difficulties with tenants about keeping drains clear: "In my part of the county [County Limerick], at all events, draining is a thing that will pay very well, as a rule, if other processes are carried out afterwards. In some cases it is necessary only to till the land, so as to level it, and eradicate the grasses and rushes, which grow in wet land; in other cases it is necessary to lime it and till it, and so on. Well, if the landlord could do all these things the improvement would probably pay him very well if he had the lands in his own hands, but he cannot practically do it, because he cannot get up the land from the tenant to do it, and if he happens to have an idle or ignorant tenant, the money which he lays out on his drainage may be to a certain extent unfruitful." [39]

A consolidating landlord was thought to be "the devil himself," testified a Kells landowner, who however did not evict anyone. "Some people might say if I turned out these men and let it for grazing . . . I would have got more money, meanwhile I might not be here to give evidence," he explained.[40]

"It is a very curious thing," said Professor Baldwin, "that what the people call a good landlord is a man who lets them alone. My idea of a good landlord is a man who will try and use his position in such a way as to obtain the largest gross produce out of the land, and leave to his tenants a good margin to live on." [41]

Going back to the time of the Enclosure Acts to make the relevant comparison, one would hazard that English landlords had more, not less, power than the Irish landlord of the second half of the nineteenth century.

Thus, not only is it wrong to assume that tenants do all

the investing, but any action based on the assumption, for example, strengthening tenants' rights and claims, runs the risk of diminishing landlord investment by more than it increases tenant investment.

It is clear from a study of examples that improving Irish landlords needed patience, persistence, determination, and a robust indifference to public popularity if they were to succeed. Investment in Irish agriculture came about in the face of enormous difficulties. It was one thing to buy an estate and quite another to acquire control over it. William Bence Jones took over a neglected property in 1838: "When I got it the estate was cut up in all sorts of ways. There was a field here and a field there, and I found my farms subdivided in all kinds of ways. It was only by sacrificing any increase of rent for more than twenty years that I got them together. When one man went away I had to take seven or ten acres that were part of his farm, and give them to another man, on condition that he give up five or six acres that adjoined another farm distant from his. In that way I readjusted the whole estate, and got the fields of all the farms conveniently together, so that every man had his land near his house. I could not have done that if there were any payments for tenant right to be made. As it was, it cost me a lot of money to do it." [42]

In the early years the tenants grew potatoes, followed by wheat, then "oats, oats, oats," until the land was exhausted. They then let the land rest (i.e., grow weeds) until some organic matter was restored, then pared and burned the land for a renewed cycle, beginning with potatoes again.

Bence Jones introduced turnips and clover, distributed Scotch plows as prizes, brought in a Scotchman to instruct ("I could not farm well without my Scotchman"); drained, constructed buildings, built roads. The fodder enabled stock to thrive and in turn the manure improved crop yields. "It is impossible for the course I have taken to be popular," he wrote in his memoirs, "and indeed the rules I act on are not often liked." [43]

When some tenants fled after the Famine, Bence Jones found land on his hands, which he slowly began to improve. Although it was the worst land on the estate, eventually he estimated it yielded in gross produce four times the land of the small tenant occupiers. "I believe myself that if I laid out all my land in grass . . . I could make more money by it than I do," he told the Bessborough Commission. [44]

William Talbot Crosbie of Ardfert in Kerry was an improving landlord whose story is similar. He succeeded to an estate in 1838 on which "no one knew, from year to year, what farm he had to till, they used to divide every field, and divide the crops every year, and nothing could be worse than the condition of things." [45] Fortunately, there was a portion of the estate that was underpopulated, and Talbot Crosbie was able to resettle the tenants on farms of adequate size and arrangement. Without such resettlement he could not have gone on with his subsequent improvements in construction, drainage, fencing, and housing. [46]

When landlords were faced with large numbers of small holders and no untenanted land, it was virtually impossible for them to arrange farms of a size sufficient for profitable investment. Neither Bence Jones nor Talbot Crosbie was in this position, and both made a point of saying that they had not cleared away tenants but had provided for them all. On the Pollok estate in Galway, an improving landlord found it impossible to take the land into his hands for rearranging without paying considerable sums to the outgoing tenants; for this he became "at one time the best abused man in Ireland," and of course the profitability of his investment was severely curtailed.* Landlords who invested on their estates without having the power to prevent continual subdivision of holdings—examples are Murray Stewart, the Earl of Leitrim, Wybrandts Olphert—soon found pockets of poverty building up with which they were utterly unable to deal and which nullified the hope of any return on their investment.

Thus there is ample evidence that the flow of capital into Irish agriculture was impeded by the inability of landlords to establish farms of optimal size and to introduce improved farming techniques. It was the prevailing tenure customs— of not evicting and not charging market prices for rent— that blocked the way. Edward O'Brien, a gentleman farmer from County Limerick, summed up the influence of tenure customs on investment this way: "The landlords, on the one hand, have not the power to improve their land to the extent that would be required to bring the country into the condition which it ought to be. To do so they would be obliged, in many instances, to make considerable changes in tenancies, which, as a general rule it is out of their power to do. The tenants, on the other hand, have not sufficient security to

* See Chap. 4 below for details of the Pollok estate. The following exchange before the Bessborough Commission describes the situation well (the witness is Richard John Mahony, an improving Kerry landlord):

"25041. About twenty years ago a tenant who had a farm in an unreclaimed condition (but it happened to be in a good situation) broke down. I saw that it was a suitable subject, and I set to work improving and thorough draining it. The only portions which had been tilled before had been absolutely exhausted by taking tillage crops off it. I took it up, sub-soiled it, drained it, fenced it, built a villa on it, and soon got a tenant for it. It was in a very nice situation. I have since given that tenant a lease for ninety-nine years, and he has laid out £10,000 upon it. If I had left that farm in that man's lands, or that he had the power of sale [sic], he would have sold it to somebody else of the same type, and it would be in the same condition still.

"25042. You might have bought it yourself and it would not be in the same condition?—Why should I buy my own property?"

warrant the very large outlay that would be needed on their part if the improvement of the country were to be carried out chiefly by them. They have always the fear of a rise of rent impending over them." [47]

In this situation, the simple assumptions that underlay the Land Act of 1870 were wrong in fact, wrong as an explanation of past investment patterns, and wrong as a basis for future legislation.

EVALUATION OF THE 1870 ACT

The Land Act of 1870 could hardly make much contribution to Irish economic development because it was based on an incorrect diagnosis of Irish economic problems. Instead of a class of rack-renting, freely evicting, oppressive landlords, we find the old landlord class dedicated to a "live and let live" policy. Evictions were rare, rents were moderate and sticky, many improvements were made jointly with the tenants. The statistical tables we have looked at for all Ireland reflect heavily the habits of this class. The small landlords who purchased under the Encumbered Estates Act were invariably identified as the rent-raising or rack-renting landlords. Not all Encumbered Estates buyers were of this type, but their existence is confirmed by the testimony of dozens of expert witnesses, and hundreds of nonexpert witnesses, before the Bessborough Commission. Their actions do not show up in the statistical tables, first, because their numbers were few compared with their renown and, also, because the rent increases that tenants considered such a grievance (and to the small tenants they were indeed a terrible hardship) were frequently increases over a twenty-five-year-old rent level or increases of a few pounds.

Compensation for disturbance had an infinitesimal effect in a situation in which evictions of all kinds were rare and evictions for reasons other than nonpayment of rent rarer still. Since almost the only tenants who were evicted were hopelessly in arrears, virtually nothing would be left for an evicted tenant after the landlord was paid.

The provisions for compensation for improvements filled a real gap in the land laws, and many examples occur in which these clauses prevented injustice when a man was relinquishing his holding. But since most of the people who relinquished their holdings were not improving tenants but broken-down small holders, the contribution of these compensations to the well-being of Ireland was not notable. No doubt many tenants said, and sincerely believed, that they had not invested in their land because they had lacked assurance of compensation for the investment. But when we find that they rejected leases, and when we further find many examples of land held in perpetuity at low rents among the worst farmed in Ireland, we may doubt that these tenants fully understood their motivations. No great flurry of tenant improvements followed the Land Act of 1870.

The provision of compensation for improvements had two important unforeseen consequences. First, it put an abrupt stop to landlord improvements.[48] It was a rare landlord who continued to invest in lands in the hands of tenants after 1870, unless he could induce the tenant to sign a lease contracting him out of compensation for improvements. While many legitimate awards for compensation were granted by the courts, many inflated claims were made, too. Landlords were naturally reluctant to incur a future liability of uncertain amount in a political atmosphere in which they had little hope of getting a return on the investment by raising the rent. This is a direct and important consequence of the 1870 Act. It can hardly be stressed too much that landlord investment in Ireland virtually ceased in the very years when it could have been preparing the Irish economy to meet the foreign competition that lay ahead.

Second, the compensation clauses in the Land Act of 1870 made it easier for tenants to get credit. The increase in rural credit cannot be wholly ascribed to the Land Act, but it is frequently mentioned as a contributing factor. An increase in bank credit for investment on good security would, of course, have been a real contribution, but what commonly occurred was a further sinking into debt by the small tenants to merchants and moneylenders not only for fertilizer and supplies, but also for Indian meal and other provisions for consumption. As in other poor agrarian countries, the Irish tenant carried a heavy burden of debt borrowed at very high rates and used often to finance consumption, so that no ray of hope of escaping from the burden ever appeared. During the bad seasons of the late 1870's this credit network collapsed, and the Irish tenant was under enormous pressure from his creditors, under more pressure in many cases than from his landlord.*

The Land Act of 1870 was the remedy for a disease that was not seriously afflcting Ireland in 1870. It is hardly re-markable that it did not "solve the Irish land problem." It had little immediate effect in all: some effects for good, like the compensation for improvements to outgoing tenants; some effects for bad, like the diminution of landlord im-provements. Had it worked, as Gladstone hoped, to discour-age eviction and to encourage investment in very small hold-ings, it would have been a sad victory. A small tenant who was encouraged to stay in Mayo or Kerry in 1870 was going to be facing starvation by 1879.

* In County Sligo, for example, there were 8,392 civil bill processes in-stituted for recovery of small debts in 1879, nearly double the number for 1867 (Bessborough Commission, 14008). A sheriff's officer in Donegal testified in 1880: "I can tell you that I suppose I have for execution at present in the district nearly 150 decrees for shop debts outside rent. It is seldom we get a decree for rent" (Bessborough Commission, 14958).

The deepest failure of the Land Act of 1870 was due to the way in which it posed the problem: this exacerbated landlord-tenant relationships and, second, blocked any alternative approaches to the solution of Ireland's economic problems by more fruitful policies. In a book written in 1868 that probably had some influence on Mr. Gladstone, George Campbell wrote that the Irish land problem was the problem of two claimants to the right of occupying land. To set up the problem this way, as an adversary procedure, merely heightened tension in a country in which the social and religious division between landlord and tenant was enormous to begin with. In places where feelings ran high, as in Kerry, the Act was a signal to both sides to "look to their rights" and gird for further battle. But the real problem in Ireland was not the division of a given pie, but the provision of a larger one: to raise Ireland from a poor to a prosperous country, to make the economy grow and progress, to improve yields and practices and methods, by a variety of policies that were not unknown at the time, which could have been pursued by landlord and tenant together to the joint benefit of both. The real failure of the Land Act of 1870 was the path not taken.

4.
Real Factors in the Development of the
Irish Agricultural Economy to 1876

Lord Lucan has cleared his ground.
"Cruel monster!" cry all people.

Carlyle

In running my eye over the account which
I wrote of English agriculture in 1850, I
find descriptions of good farming in nearly
every part of the country . . . Lord
Lucan, . . . in Ireland . . .

James Caird

Sometime in the 1850's a Scottish landowner and farmer named Pollok bought in the Encumbered Estates Court 30,-000 acres of farmland in County Galway near Eyrecourt. Eyrecourt lies about equidistant from Ballinasloe and Portumna, and is close to Banagher, where a Postal Inspector named Anthony Trollope had had his headquarters from 1841 to 1844. (If Trollope ever revisited Banagher before leaving Ireland in 1859, and if Pollok was a hunting man, they may well have met.)

Relying no doubt on his Scottish experience, Pollok thought he could come to Galway and begin to farm his land. He found instead that the land was peopled by small tenants whom it would be both expensive and difficult to displace, if indeed it were even possible. Instead of pursuing a vain attempt to get possession of his land by law, Pollok arranged to buy out certain of his tenants, paying them for their crops and their stock such an amount as would induce them to leave. For this Pollok became for a time "the best abused man in Ireland." The lands that thus fell into his hands he drained, improved, and divided into large farms, on which he built houses and other farm buildings. These farms, suitable for both tillage and grazing, he then let to tenants on nineteen- or twenty-one-year leases at rents of from £200 to £2,000 a year.

But on one section of his land Pollok left in undisturbed possession two hundred small yearly tenants. Their aggregate rent, which remained unchanged, amounted to £1,800; it was reduced in the 1870's. The land was wet and needed draining. These tenants had built their own homes and had never made substantial improvements of any kind, although Pollok stood willing to assist them if they wanted to improve; in fact, he did help them in small ways. These holdings were so small that tenants could not always pay the rent from them, and the men had to migrate seasonally to England and Scotland to earn money by helping with the harvest there. Sometimes the men got home too late to harvest their own crops. Pollok's large tenants provided the small tenants with some employment but could not possibly hire them all. Tillage farms required laborers but grazing farms practically none. The small holdings grew still smaller through constant subdivision which it was impossible for Mr. Gairdner, the agent, to prevent. If a tenant left for America, his farm might be thrown in with the adjoining holding, but since there were twenty applicants clamoring for every such vacancy, consolidation did not make much progress.

Pollok made a profit on his investment in County Galway —he was a skilled and energetic farmer—but the costs of getting the land into his own hands were so great that his Irish venture was a disappointment. The story of the Pollok estate, which was told by the agent to the Bessborough Commission, contains the main elements of the (agricultural) economic history of Ireland from the 1850's to the end of the 1870's.

ECONOMIC SIGNIFICANCE OF THE FAMINE

The years of Ireland's great population rise (1780–1845) define a unique episode in her economic development. From medieval times to the present day, the business of Irish agriculture has traditionally been animals and animal products, but in the half-century preceding the Famine the predominance of the livestock economy was challenged by a tillage economy as never before or since.

Without industrialization, a population increase as large as Ireland then experienced can only be borne by recourse to more and more intensive forms of agriculture. The growing of potatoes is one of the most labor-intensive forms of agriculture known to man, and potatoes made the population increase possible, as the population increase made potato-growing necessary. These years saw, moreover, the considerable development of corn crops in Ireland, encouraged by protectionist measures which the Irish Parliament passed in 1784 (Foster's Act) and by the price rises of the Napoleonic era later on. Ireland became an exporter of wheat, barley, oats, and flour. Even within the livestock sector, these years saw a relative shift to dairying, a much more labor-intensive occupation than sheep-raising or cattle-grazing. Ulster contrived to support her dense population by a tillage economy in which flax was the principal market crop, again a labor-intensive crop and one that provided a great deal of ancillary employment.

On the eve of the Famine, then, owing to the enormous pressure of her population and in some measure to price trends, Ireland was allocating her resources to tillage, to corn, potatoes, and flax, in greater measure than ever before; the number of cattle in Ireland was perhaps lower than at any time since the early eighteenth century, and sheep-raising was at an ebb so low that it never recovered until the end of the nineteenth century.

But the population problem was beyond the capabilities even of the potato, and when that mainstay of the economy collapsed in the late 1840's the agricultural structure that replaced it was to develop along different lines. The Famine resulted, as every schoolboy knows, in the most drastic population losses (by starvation, by disease, and by emigration) known to modern Western society.

It is impossible to compare pre-Famine with post-Famine Ireland accurately because of the deficiencies in the agricultural statistics in the census of 1841 that have been brought to light by Bourke.[1] Using Bourke's amended data, however, we see that there was a decrease in the number of agricultural holdings above one acre of about 25 percent between the immediate pre-Famine situation (1845) and the 1851 census. The great change in the number of holdings was virtually completed in this decade, however. Between 1851 and 1861 the decrease was negligible: between 1861 and 1871 only about −4 percent; between 1871 and 1881 about −3 percent. Moreover, decennial figures are deceiving. Holdings dropped sharply every year until 1853, when they stood at 550,000. From 1853 to 1861 they increased every year, and did not fall below 550,000 again until 1866. (After 1866 holdings declined gradually until they stood at 529,-000 in 1876.) The continuing emigration after the Famine reflects the failure of the Irish economy to absorb population; it does not reflect until much later any substantial decline in the number of agricultural enterprises.

The population decrease after the Famine naturally caused a profound change in the average size of farm and altered the size distribution of holdings. Although Bourke's work shows that the much-quoted figures from the 1841 census, showing that farms between one and five acres accounted for 45 percent of total holdings, cannot be taken seriously, still a very substantial shift in the size distribution occurred.

Table 8 shows that, although the trend to fewer small farms and more large farms continued throughout the century, the important change had already been effected by 1851.

Table 8.   Changes in the Size Distribution of Farm Holdings above One Acre, 1845–1881 (percent)

	1–5 Acres	5–15 Acres	15–30 Acres	Greater than 30 Acres
1845	24	40	36	
1851	15	34	25	26
1861	15	32	25	28
1871	14	31	26	29
1881	13	31	26	30

SOURCE: Figures for 1845 are derived from P. M. Austin Bourke, "The Agricultural Statistics of the 1841 Census of Ireland," *Economic History Review*, 2nd series, 18 (August, 1965), table 4. Other figures are derived from census data. Census data on holdings are reproduced in the annual *Agricultural Statistics*, which also give annual holdings data, though with a slightly different breakdown.

Thus, as population declined, land became relatively less scarce and was held in larger amounts. It was labor's turn to be relatively scarcer, and one significant aspect of the post-Famine years was the decrease in the availability of agricultural laborers. These men came from the cottier class and from the small tenantry, precisely the classes hardest hit by the Famine. After the initial impact of the Famine, when population continued to decline but numbers of holdings did not, it is not implausible to assume that the landless men were being drained away. It was often said that the price of labor doubled between the Famine and 1880.

Both the high price of labor and the reduced pressure on the land would tend to shift the economy away from labor-intensive forms of agriculture, but we have seen that a great part of this adjustment was already made by 1851. There can be little doubt that over the long run it was from the demand side that the greatest impetus came. Writing in 1880, James Caird, the historian of English agriculture, put it succinctly: "Thirty years ago, probably not more than one-third of the people of this country consumed animal food more than once a week. Now, nearly all of them eat it, in meat, or cheese, or butter, once a day. This has more than doubled the average consumption per head; and when the increase of population is considered, has probably trebled the total consumption of animal food in this country. The increased supply has come partly from our own fields, but chiefly from abroad. The leap which the consumption of meat took in consequence of the general rise of wages in all branches of trade and employment, could not have been met without foreign supplies, and these could not have been secured except by such a rise of price as fully paid the risk and cost of transport." [2] The enormous increase in the demand for animal products was translated to the Irish farmer in terms of the prices he faced. Thomas Barrington's work on Irish agricultural prices enables us to see precisely what occurred.

BEHAVIOR OF PRICES
In a paper read to the Statistical and Social Inquiry Society of Ireland in 1926, Barrington presented price series

for the principal Irish agricultural products back to 1845.[3] Official Irish price series begin in 1881, but the Department of Agriculture had published an unofficial series going back to 1840, based on the average of highest and lowest prices appearing each year in *Purdom's Almanac* and the *Farmer's Gazette*. From these two series, which he felt did not offer serious problems of incomparability, Barrington constructed indexes for fourteen products on a basis of 1840 = 100, which he presented in conjunction with the Statist-Sauerbeck index of wholesale prices for Ireland.

These price indexes fall naturally into two classes: tillage products and animal products. The six tillage products are wheat, oats, barley, hay, potatoes, and flax. Hay, perhaps, should not be dignified to the status of a crop. Almost all the hay produced on the farms was used by livestock or used as seed, so that hay is not really a product but an input of animal products. Much the same may be said of potatoes, with the important exception that a significant proportion was consumed by farm families. The only estimates known to me show that 68.3 percent of the potato crop (by value) was used as livestock feed or for seed, while 13.2 percent went for human consumption on the farm, and 18.5 percent was marketed.[4]

At the other end of the scale, all of the flax crop was marketed either for home consumption or export; while for wheat, oats, and barley in 1908 48.0 percent, 24.3 percent, and 70.8 percent, respectively, of the total value of the crop came to market. Since flax is a highly localized crop and responds to a different set of world market conditions, it ought to be considered separately. Wheat, oats, and barley, then, are the principal crops with which we shall deal as tillage products. Of these, oats is by far the most important.

There are eight price series for animal products: butter,

pork, wool, eggs, beef, mutton, store cattle one to two years old, and store cattle two to three years old. Of these I shall not consider egg production, at that period an enterprise organized principally to utilize the surplus labor of farmers' wives. The livestock industry comprises the dairy industry, based on milch cows, and the meat industry, based on dry cattle. Final fattening for the London market was not done in Ireland, and the animals were kept until the late stages as store cattle and shipped live to Great Britain.

I have converted the Barrington price indexes to five-year moving averages and (aside from flax, potatoes, eggs, wool, and hay) the results are presented in Figure 2 for the period 1845–1876. The price experience revealed by the chart is not hard to summarize. Until the early 1850's general prices fell, agricultural prices fell but by less than the general (wholesale) price level, and tillage prices maintained their position relative to animal prices. From the early 1850's to the end of our period, all prices rose except wheat and, for whatever the Sauerbeck index is worth, agricultural prices rose more than the general price level. But the divergent experience of animal and tillage prices is beautifully illustrated. Tillage prices are grouped at the bottom of the graph; meat prices and the one dairy price are grouped together next, showing a significantly greater rise; and the store cattle prices at the top of the graph show a steep increase.

Aside from the minor matter of production of hides, we should expect the price of beef to govern the price of store cattle, but they may diverge for many reasons. The early years of the period we have chosen saw the development of railroads in Ireland and steam transport between Ireland and England, and brought the Irish farmer within range of the English market for live cattle. Pasture in Ireland that had been worthless because it was remote now produced candidates for the London dinner table. Even if (London) beef prices were constant, this cheapening of transportation would tend to raise the price of cattle to the Irish farmer; in fact beef prices were themselves advancing. There are other conceivable reasons for the rise in store cattle prices, including an improvement in the beef-producing qualities of cattle and the cheapening of foodstuffs fed in the final stages of fattening (both of which Barrington suggests); but without detailed study it would be impossible to assess their importance compared with the transportation factor.

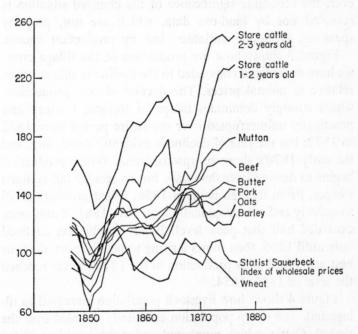

Fig. 2. Prices of principal agricultural products (five-year moving average of prices expressed in index form). Annual data on basis of 1840 = 100; for store cattle, 1845 = 100.

Source: Thomas Barrington, "A Review of Irish Agricultural Prices," *Journal of the Statistical and Social Inquiry Society of Ireland,* 15 (1927).

OVERALL ADJUSTMENT OF THE ECONOMY TO 1876

In response to these changed population and price conditions, the face of Ireland changed markedly in the post-Famine years. The area under crops decreased and the area in grass or pasture increased. Within the area under crops, meadow took steadily a larger share. If we consider that a better contrast between tillage and animal products is between ploughed area, on the one hand, and pasture plus meadow, on the other, the shift is even more marked. However, the economic significance of the changed situation is revealed not by land-use data, which are not, properly speaking, economic variables, but by production figures.

Figure 3 shows how the production of the tillage crops we have considered responded to the decline in tillage prices relative to animal prices. The decline of oats production, which strongly dominates tillage in Ireland, is steep and practically uninterrupted over the entire period from 1852 to 1872; but the rate of decline is evidently decreasing, and the early 1870's show an upward trend. Wheat production begins to decline later than oats, but its secular fall is much steeper. From its high point in 1858, wheat production fell so quickly and catastrophically that, after 1861, it only once exceeded half that peak level. Barley production declined only until 1866, then shows a rising trend. Even so, the four best years for barley production in the 1870's never reached the level of 1851–1854.

Figure 4 shows how livestock population increased as tillage fell. The sheep population essentially doubled over the period. Cattle, which numbered under three million at the beginning of the period, were running over four million at the end. The increased pig production is not nearly so marked but can fairly be described as showing a gently rising trend.

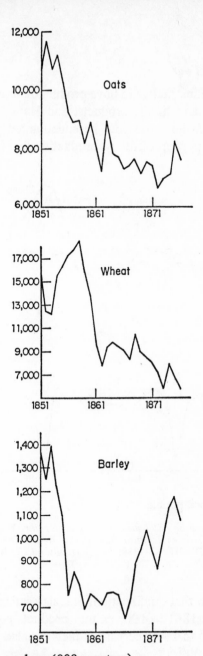

Fig. 3. Total produce (000 quarters).

Source: Agricultural Statistics of Ireland for the Year 1864, P. P. 1867 (LXXI) 3766; *Agricultural Statistics of Ireland for the Year 1874, P. P.* 1876 (LXXVIII) C.-1380; and *Agricultural Statistics of Ireland for the Year 1876, P. P.* 1877 (LXXXV) C.-1749.

It would be instructive to have production indexes for animal products and tillage products, and Hans Staehle once attempted such an index; but he encountered problems in isolating that portion of tillage production that is not a final

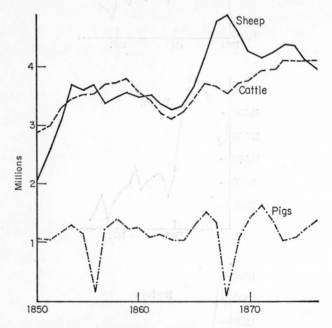

Fig. 4. Livestock population (millions).

Source: Agricultural Statistics of Ireland for the Year 1864, P. P. 1867 (LXXI) 3766; Agricultural Statistics of Ireland for the year 1874, P. P. 1876 (LXXVIII) C.-1380; and Agricultural Statistics of Ireland for the Year 1876, P. P. 1877 (LXXXV) C.-1749.

product. With that qualification, Staehle's index shows that, on a base of 1861 = 100, animal products equaled 39 in 1847 and 245 in 1909; cereal products equaled 135 in 1847 and 132 in 1909.[5]

It is hardly possible to doubt that the readjustment of the

Irish economy over this period resulted in a considerable increase in per capita income. Staehle's index of total physical output of agricultural production in the twenty-six counties, again on a basis of 1861 = 100, rises from 66 in 1847 to 213 in 1909. Agricultural production in the six excluded counties also rose, and the rise in industrial production there must have been spectacular. Set against a steadily declining population series, it scarcely needs arguing that per capita income increased dramatically in the quarter of a century after the Famine. My guess is that the readjustment I have outlined results in continuous improvement until 1876, although some salient elements of the readjustment are already spent before then and others continue after that date. Such dating is necessarily arbitrary in the nature of the case, but there is fragmentary evidence that gives some confidence to the choice of 1876. The population of Ireland, which had been declining at a decreasing rate between censuses since 1841, actually rose slightly from 1876 to 1877. The marriage rate was above the average and the death rate low; and emigration in 1876, 1877, and 1878 the lowest since the Famine. Railway receipts for those years were the highest on record (not equaled until 1883); the count of spindles was high; beer and whiskey consumption also was high. All these indications of income or well-being turn downward by 1879 or 1880. Population begins to decrease again, the emigrations are larger in number than for any of the thirteen preceding years; the death rate in 1880 was the highest on record since the Famine and the marriage rate the lowest; railway traffic was low in 1879, 1880, and 1881; whiskey consumption was low in 1880.[6]

THE IRISH AGRICULTURAL ECONOMY IN 1876

We have stated that the Irish agricultural economy in the quarter-century after the Famine experienced great gains in per capita income, owing primarily to decreased population density and to a marked shift to livestock production, as a response to the changed relative prices of tillage and livestock products, the changed price relation being due to very great price increases in livestock and livestock products. We now propose to subject the economy of 1876 to a closer examination. Once this is done, we shall be able to say something about the pattern of adjustment, how it was distributed in 1876, not only by geographical area, but also by size of farm; something about the historical pattern of the readjustment, which regions changed most and which least; and finally something about the nature of the regional economies in 1876, what the prosperity of each depended upon and where their weaknesses lay. With such a detailed breakdown we shall be able to get a good picture of the evolution of the post-Famine readjustment and its distribution at its culmination, and we shall have a clear idea of the economic structure on which the blows of the future were to descend.

Northern Ireland in 1876 remained a region of dense population and small farms. Industrial areas aside, the population density in the rural Poor Law Unions of Ulster east of the mountains rarely stood below 200 persons per square mile of improved area. As one moved west across Ulster, the population thinned out, only to increase again sharply in the Donegal unions on the Atlantic coast. Inishowen and Dunfanaghy unions had in 1876 more than 300 persons per square mile of improved area; they were more densely populated than any rural unions in the east, more even than some industrialized parts. The farmer in Eastern Ulster (i.e., east of the mountains) devoted a far higher proportion of his land to tillage than farmers in any other part of Ireland. A typical Poor Law union tilled between 30 and 40 percent of its land. Corn crops were extensively grown, primarily oats but still wheat in some areas; almost every union still grew some flax. Even so, between 40 and 50 percent of the land in Ulster unions was already being devoted to pasture and meadow (this allows roughly for 10 percent in waste). Sheep were not numerous, but many cattle were raised. In the west, however, in what was sometimes grandly called ultra-montane Donegal, very little land was devoted to tillage, rather more to pasture and meadow, and vast areas of waste were common. For example, Glenties union, in Donegal, devoted but 7 percent of its land to crops (54 percent of this area was in potatoes); 43 percent of Glenties was grass and meadow; and the remaining 50 percent was waste.

The population densities in Leinster were much lower than in Ulster, fewer than 150 persons per square mile of improved area and quite commonly fewer than 125. Farm size was correspondingly larger than in Ulster, but the median farm was still very modest in 1876. Leinster was emphatically not a tillage area—in one (extreme) Meath union more than 90 percent of the land was in pasture and meadow. This is the great midland grazing area of Ireland. Here the dry cattle two years old and over were heavily concentrated, and vast herds of sheep were raised for meat. Whatever tillage land there was in these areas was primarily devoted to corn crops, but turnips were a crop of some importance, too; potatoes here, as in Eastern Ulster, rarely occupied as much as a quarter of the tilled area.

One can discern in the rest of Leinster, in the southeast corner of Ireland fanning out from County Wexford, a second tillage region, though tillage shares remain well below Eastern Ulster. Nevertheless, much of the barley that Ireland produced was grown here, and oats were an important crop; here again potatoes played a modest role in the tillage economy.

The density of population in Munster was generally greater than in Leinster, though less than in Ulster. If Ulster densities may be characterized as over 200 and Leinster under 150, Munster may be said to range between 150 and 200. The unions with the densest populations in Munster were found in west Clare, Kerry, and along the coast of Cork west of Kinsale. The median farms in Munster were by far the largest in Ireland in 1876.[7] Munster was very definitely not a tillage region. No union in Clare or Kerry tilled so much as 10 percent of its land. Most of the land, accordingly, was in pasture and meadow; but where waste was extensive, as in Clare and Kerry and parts of Cork, the share of grass and meadow was severely curtailed. Munster was the home of the dairy herds in Ireland. In Limerick and Kerry and the adjoining parts of Cork and Tipperary, dense concentrations of milch cows were to be found. If we inquire what crops were grown on the (small) tillage areas in Munster in 1876, we find for the first time (apart from Donegal) the potato playing a major role in the tillage economy. In the western two-thirds of Munster, whatever land was tilled was devoted in large measure to potatoes: up to 70 percent in the case of two extreme unions and nearly a half or more in almost all the rest. A handful of Clare unions, for example, each with 9 percent of the area in tillage, had 50, 51, and 57 percent of that in potatoes. For Kerry, with pitifully small amounts of arable land, the dependence on the potato was as great.

The Poor Law unions of Connaught were as densely populated as Eastern Ulster, some unions in Mayo (Belmullet, Swineford) matched the Donegal unions with population densities above 300 per square mile of improved area. Median farms were tiny. Some Mayo unions had median holdings as small as eight and nine acres; five had thirteen acres as the median holding. Tillage occupied under 15 percent of the land in almost all the Connaught unions, under 10 percent in very many, with large tracts of waste sharing the remainder with pasture and meadow. Belmullet is an extreme case. With a very high population density, this bleak peninsula, jutting out of northwestern Mayo into the gray Atlantic, was able to raise crops on 5 percent of its area and to pasture livestock on 13 percent. The rest was waste.

Potatoes played the same important role in the tilled fields of Connaught as in Clare and Kerry and west Cork. For example, Clifden and Oughterard in Western Galway both devoted over 52 percent of their crop area to potatoes. Eastern Galway was the only part of Connaught with a potato share of tillage as low as 35 percent; even 35 percent is well above Eastern Ulster and all of Leinster and the eastern third of Munster.

DISTRIBUTION OF THE POST-FAMINE READJUSTMENT

Without an equally detailed study for some early year, we cannot say with precision how the post-Famine adjustment was distributed geographically, and it is only possible to form some rough idea. Some calculations made by John Hooper, in his introductory essay to *Agricultural Statistics 1847 to 1926,* are particularly useful.[8] The principal potato-growing counties in 1926 were much the same as they had been in 1859. Milch cows were densest in the same counties in 1859 as they were in 1926 (and in 1876). But in 1851 "the best tilled counties were in the eastern half of the country and included what are now the great grazing counties. Meath in 1851 had the tenth highest percentage ploughed." [9] In 1847 Meath and Limerick were included in the group of counties densest in *wheat.* For the excluded Ulster counties we know that it was after the Famine and during the 1860's and 1870's that the economy shifted to the livestock-producing orientation that Northern Irish farms now show.[10] None of this can be taken as conclusive evidence, but it certainly does suggest that the shift from tillage to livestock occurred more decisively in Eastern Ulster and in the East in general, and that the shift in the midland plains must have been especially marked. If Eastern Ulster and the Southeast remained in 1876 the preeminent tillage regions, this is not incompatible with the suspicion that in 1847 or 1851 they had been far more predominantly, perhaps almost exclusively, tillage regions. The West and the Southwest seem to have changed least. Thus, the evidence is that the readjustment of the economy after the Famine occurred most markedly in Ulster, the Midlands, and the Southeast; while Donegal, Connaught, and the Southwest shared to a lesser degree. Since the shift to livestock production was associated with the increased income over the period, we must conclude that the West and Southwest lagged behind the rest of the country.

It was suggested at the outset that the increased farm sizes after the Famine contributed an impetus to the growth of livestock and decline of tillage. The size factor is unlikely to have played as large a role as relative price movements did: we saw that by far the greatest change in farm size had been effected by 1851; yet 1851 was the year of maximum tillage for Ireland. Nevertheless, it is legitimate to wonder to what extent the shift from tillage to livestock occurred on large farms and on small farms.

A modern estimate of labor requirements for different agricultural products in Northern Ireland will give at least some idea of the relative orders of magnitude of labor-intensiveness in tillage and livestock husbandry. Naturally, it is unwarranted to use these figures for the earlier period, but changes in techniques in the intervening years are unlikely to have been large enough to obliterate the main features that are evident. Table 9 shows the standard mandays of labor per acre per year required by various agricultural enterprises as calculated for the Small Farmers scheme in Northern Ireland in 1958.

A farmer with a given amount of land and labor will choose from all the possible combinations of enterprises that fully employ his land and labor that combination

Table 9. Labor Requirements for Different Agricultural Enterprises, Northern Ireland, 1958

Crop	Standard Man-days per Acre per Year Required
Potatoes	21
Flax	15
Oats	4½
Wheat, barley, rye	3½
Dairy cows	15
Bulls	7
All other cattle	3
Sows	5
Sheep, excluding lambs	⅔
Grass for hay	2
Grass for grazing	¼

SOURCE: Leslie Symons, ed., *Land Use in Northern Ireland*, p. 57.

which yields him the greatest profit. Aside from dairying, tillage is by far more labor-intensive than livestock raising; and potatoes and flax stand out conspicuously. The small farmer, with a higher endowment of labor than land, will tend to select enterprises with large labor requirements to take advanatge of his situation. The large farmer, finding labor less abundant than land, will have a tendency to specialize in those enterprises in which labor requirements per acre are low.

It is not surprising to find then that the share of land in crops decreases as the size of the farm increases, and that

the share of land in grass steadily increases as the size of
the farm increases (until we get to very large farms, where
high proportions of waste obscure the relationship; see Table 10). Since, within the crop acreage, the share of

Table 10.   Percentage of Land in Crops, Grass, and Waste by Size
of Farm, 1871

Size of Farm	Prop. in Class	Crops	Grass	Bog and Waste
Less than 1	8.2	85.1	5.5	8.4
1–5	12.6	63.5	27.5	7.9
5–15	28.9	47.4	42.9	9.0
15–30	23.4	40.6	48.1	10.7
30–50	12.3	35.3	51.1	12.8
50–100	9.3	28.9	54.8	15.1
100–200	3.6	21.3	57.2	19.4
200–500	1.4	12.7	52.5	31.4
Over 500	0.3	3.2	33.2	60.3
All Ireland		27.7	49.6	21.0

SOURCE: *Agricultural Statistics of Ireland, 1871, P.P.* (1873) LXIX, c. 762.
NOTE: Percentages do not add to 100 because of minor omissions, e.g.,
timber plantations.

meadow increases markedly with size, the association between smallness and tillage is even stronger if meadow is
not considered with the tillage crops.[11] Small farms thus
tend to specialize relatively in tillage and in milch cows,
young cattle, pigs, and poultry, while large farms specialize
in grass with dry cattle and sheep.[12]

The nature of the *dependence* of different size farms on
different types of husbandry is clear; but whether the overall *change* in the economy was due merely to a change in
farm sizes is not self-evident. Hooper investigated this question and found that between 1854 and 1912 "the smaller

the holding the larger the increases in the densities [per thousand acres of crops and pasture] of all live stock, except dry cattle two years and over, and the larger the decrease in density of ploughed land." [13] It is quite natural, as Hooper observed, for largest densities to experience largest absolute changes, but even the proportionate changes were greater on smaller holdings (again except for cattle two years old and over). Thus the (relatively small) transference of land from small holdings to larger holdings played practically no role in reducing tillage or increasing livestock, comparing 1854 to 1912. The years of the great transference of land from small to large holdings came about by 1851, and this was unaccompanied by a shift from tillage to livestock. The shift must have come about because of relative price changes and labor cost changes. These simple conclusions do not hold up, however, when the period is broken at 1874: from 1854 to 1874 tillage decreased more on larger farms; then from 1874 to 1912 tillage decreased so much more on small farms that the latter period determined the net result for 1854–1912. Hooper also concluded that the rate of increase of dry cattle two years old and over was greater on small than on large holdings from 1854 to 1874, but less from 1874 to 1912. An examination of his figures in Table 11 suggests perhaps that no single tendency is evident from the figures on dry cattle.

Where the population density was moderate and farms were of moderate size, the chances of a favorable economic adjustment were greatest. Regions of dense population had less flexibility; here intensive farming was a necessity, and intensive farming meant tillage, whether of corn crops or potatoes. We recall that in Eastern Ulster population remained dense and farms were small. This dense population was supported by an economy in which tillage played a large part; the tillage crops, moreover, included the profitable flax crop that was ideally suited to small farms by virtue of its large labor requirements per acre.[14] Corn crops still played a considerable role in Eastern Ulster. A livestock-based sector was already well established in Eastern

Table 11. Percentage Changes in Area Ploughed and Number of Dry Cattle Two Years Old or Over per 1,000 Acres of Crops and Pasture in Ireland

| | | | Size of Holding | | | | | |
	1–5	5–15	15–30	30–50	50–100	100–200	200–500	Over 500
Area ploughed								
1854–1874	−16	−18	−21	−23	−24	−31	−34	−43
1874–1912	−41	−33	−31	−25	−18	−7	−8	+27
1854–1912	−50	−45	−45	−43	−39	−36	−39	−28
Dry cattle 2 yrs. or over								
1854–1874	19	35	29	27	23	25	26	0
1874–1912	0	3	0	0	7	10	25	66
1854–1912	19	40	30	30	33	37	58	66

SOURCE: John Hooper, Introductory Essay to Saorstát Eireenn *Agricultural Statistics 1847 to 1926*, p. xiv. Hooper's conclusion about dry cattle is not, I think, warranted by the figures.

Ulster by 1876, too. Where tillage is possible, a farm of a given size can support a greater livestock density the higher the proportion of land it tills, by providing foodstuffs for the animals, so a small Ulster farm could support more cattle than a Kerry farm of the same size.

In Leinster where the population was much less dense, there was less need to turn to labor-intensive agricultural enterprises, and it was in the midlands in Leinster that full advantage could be taken of the great price rises in dry cattle and sheep. Here tillage was severely diminished, for

some places it would not be an exaggeration to say abandoned. Still, whatever small holdings remained dependent
on tillage were able to grow corn crops. In the southeast,
and in Eastern Cork (in Munster), where population densities remained relatively low, more tillage was apparent, including barley, a crop whose yield was rising impressively
from the 1860's on. In the population trends that underlay
the low density figures of this part of Ireland lay the germs
of a future system of larger farms. Already, in 1876, though
median farms were still small, impressive numbers of large
farms could be counted in Leinster. In a cursory comparison with Eastern Ulster, the distribution of farms around
the median showed no such phenomenon: the size distribution of Ulster farms closely clustered near the median.

The fatal combination of dense population, small farms,
and no possibility of a profitable tillage crop imprisoned
Connaught and the Northwest in virtually a pre-Famine
mold. The statistics have demonstrated the pitifully small
amount of tillage that was being carried on in these regions,
and only by tillage could such a dense population be supported. Synge's account of the making of a field on the
Aran Islands provides a more vivid understanding of these
low tillage figures than any statistical tables could:

> The other day the men of this house made a new field.
> There was a slight bank of earth under the wall of the
> yard, and another in the corner of the cabbage garden.
> The old man and his eldest son dug out the clay, with
> the care of men working in a gold-mine, and Michael
> packed it in panniers—there are no wheeled vehicles on
> this island—for transport to a flat rock in a sheltered
> corner of their holding, where it was mixed with sand
> and seaweed and spread out in a layer upon the stone.
> Most of the potato-growing of the island is carried

on in fields of this sort—for which the people pay a considerable rent—and if the season is at all dry, their hope of a fair crop is nearly always disappointed.[15]

This description of the difficulties of tillage on the Aran Islands can be matched by equally vivid accounts of the men of North Kerry, for example, going for miles to the shore for their seaweed, to mix with a bit of earth to spread on flat rock. And on these wretched fields, often nothing could be grown except potatoes. The rye yield on Inishmaan (the middle Aran island) was so low, wrote Synge, that "a field hardly produces more grain than is needed for seed the following year, so the rye-growing is carried on merely for the straw which is used for thatching." [16]

The potato remained as vulnerable in 1876 as it had been in 1846. It was not until 1885 that the first use was made of Bordeaux mixture, which continued until a few years ago to be the standard spray for potato blight and is still in use today in some places, in conjunction with other sprays. The potato crop had been disastrously bad in 1860 and 1872, and this is reflected in very low yield figures for calendar years 1860 and 1861 (also 1862), and for calendar years 1871 and 1872 (see Figure 5). (Yields are calculated for the calendar, not the crop, year, so that the effects of a crop failure in one year will be spread over two calendar years.) In addition to the year-to-year precariousness of the potato, it was also believed that yields never recovered their pre-Famine levels. "I have been informed," wrote Dr. Hancock in his *Report on the Supposed Progressive Decline of Irish Prosperity* in 1863, "by persons of great experience that the produce of potatoes per acre has never since the Famine at all equalled what it was before 1846, being on an average about one-half." [17] Figure 5 suggests that yields fell after the mid-1850's, and, except for particularly good crop years like 1874–1876, remained substantially below the earlier recorded levels. For the twenty-six counties, Hooper's data show that the yields of the early 1850's were never attained again until after

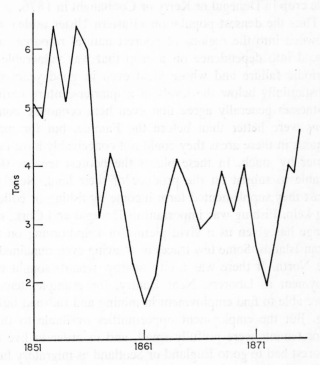

Fig. 5. Potato yield per acre (tons).

Source: Agricultural Statistics of Ireland for the Year 1864, P. P. 1867 (LXXI) 3766; Agricultural Statistics of Ireland for the Year 1874, P. P. 1876 (LXXVIII) C.-1380; and Agricultural Statistics of Ireland for the Year 1876, P. P. 1877 (LXXXV) C.-1749.

1910.[18] For pre-Famine years we shall have to rely on Hancock's "persons of great experience," for there are no comparable statistics available. When one considers mod-

ern practices in potato culture—keeping the plants con-
stantly under the new manganese- and zinc-based sprays
from May until harvest, and not planting the same ground
to potatoes in too many successive years—it is easy to believe that the potato was neither a dependable nor a profitable crop in Donegal or Kerry or Connaught in 1876.

Thus the densest population (Eastern Ulster aside) was
crowded into the regions of poorest natural resources and
forced into dependence on a crop that was vulnerable to
periodic failure and whose yield even in good years was
substantially below the levels of a quarter-century earlier.
Witnesses generally agree that even here economic conditions were better than before the Famine, but for many
tenants in these areas they could not conceivably have been
better by much. In these places the poorest tenants were
unable to subsist on the produce of their land. Near the
coast they supplemented farm income by fishing or collect-
ing kelp. Fishing was important in Donegal and Cork, and
Synge has given us a vivid picture of kelp-burning on the
Aran Islands. Some few traces of weaving even remained in
the North. If there was a city nearby, tenants sought employment as laborers. Near Bantry, for example, tenants
were able to find employment in mining and railroad building. But the employment opportunities available to these
poor tenants were pitifully small, and in order to live the
poorest had to go to England or Scotland as migratory farm
laborers. (Some Armagh men also found work in the English iron mills.)

The number of migratory laborers has probably been exaggerated—some estimates exist of 100,000 to 300,000.
The first census of migratory laborers was taken in 1881,
and only 16,836 were enumerated.[19] However, by 1881
the English and Scottish demand for agricultural labor had
diminished sharply, and with English and Scottish labor un-

employed it is hardly likely that there would be work for Irish labor.[20] Even so, in Mayo, the only county in Ireland in which migratory labor was a principal factor in the economy, 14.3 percent of the males twenty years of age and upward were still seasonal migrants to England and Scotland in 1881. For some localities, moreover, the proportion approached a hundred percent. An Irish priest from Castlebar testified before the Bessborough Commission:

> In Achill, I was there one time, and I was greatly amused, I saw whole families going off in the spring, and locking their doors and sending their cattle off to the mountains and going over wholesale, every one of five or six villages, and then coming back about the 1st of August . . . about Louisburgh [on the mainland] any man able at all goes to England, and the female portion of the family stay at home. He leaves the potatoes sown, and the oats and the heavy portion of the work done, and leaves the rest of it to be done by the female portion of the family and the children.[21]

Roscommon, Donegal, Galway, Leitrim, and Sligo—and Armagh—were the counties ranking next in migratory workers, all far behind Mayo. They sent between 1.4 and 4.4 percent of their adult males to England and Scotland in 1881, possibly several times that in earlier years, when demand for agricultural labor was higher.

The continuance of pre-Famine conditions in these areas is due in the first instance to the perverse population developments of the period we are considering, perverse because population increased most in the areas of poorest natural resources. The fundamental work on population developments has been done by S. H. Cousens in a series of articles.[22] His studies establish the demographic forces behind the regional differences in density figures we observed in 1876. From the 1850's to 1881, the areas of increasing rural population (or those experiencing the least decrease) were concentrated almost entirely in the west of Ireland, the areas losing most of their population were concentrated almost entirely in the East. The geographical distribution of emigration, Cousens found, was fairly even, so that population changes are explained by differential rates of natural increase. To give Cousen's conclusions in his own words:

> Natural increase was much greater in the west than in the east, a pattern inherited from the pre-Famine period. The differences in natural increase, considerable in the sixties, were still marked in the seventies but had declined very much by the eighties. The regional differences in natural increase were largely the result of remarkable variations in the degree of celibacy and the age at marriage.
>
> The whole period from 1851 to 1881 was a distinct phase in the demographic history of Ireland, bridging the gap between the period of great increase in the west and a lesser increase in the east of the early nineteenth century, and the emphatic decline of most of the west and lesser decline of the east which has marked the trend of events since 1881. Although this period was characterized by a gradual extension westwards of family limitation through celibacy and late marriage, as a whole it was one in which the pressure of population on resources was considerably eased in the east and north, whilst if anything it grew worse in the poorer parts of the west, where population increase was a persistent phenomenon in the poorer, more remote areas.[23]

Thus, the change in Irish family patterns from the pre-Famine pattern of early and nearly universal marriage with large families to high celibacy rates, late marriage, and smaller families occurred with a distinct geographical lag; not until after the 1881 census does the West emerge from the pre-Famine demographic pattern.[24] And the West offered the least opportunity for the intensive farming that dense populations need.

The case of Eastern Ulster shows that dense population and small farm sizes are not sufficient conditions for poverty; the case of the Southwest shows that they are not necessary conditions. Only two unions in Cork, and none at all in Kerry, showed population densities above 200, while densities above 200 were commonplace in Connaught and Donegal. And the size of the median Munster farms was the largest in Ireland. This part of Ireland, we recall, was (and is) primarily grassland. Now where tillage was profitable, a farmer could live on a holding of, say, 15 acres, keeping an acre or so in oats, and an acre or two in potatoes, and devoting the rest to meadow and pasture for livestock. To keep 25 cows on good grassland a farmer might need 40 or 50 acres; 15 cows was described as a bare minimum and this might occupy 30 acres. Where the grassland was of good quality, as in Limerick and parts of Clare, the median holding could support the population nicely. Where the grassland was poorer, a family could not manage even on 25 or 30 acres. Land was commonly rented by "the cow's grass" in this part of Ireland, and the area so denoted varied greatly according to soil and other conditions.

Consider the union of Dingle in Kerry. There were about 2,000 holdings in Dingle union in 1876, a quarter (514) were below 15 acres, another quarter (492) between 15 and 30 acres. In all of the union there were fewer than 10,000 milch cows (11,500 other cattle, 25,000 sheep, 5,000 pigs). Only 10 percent of Dingle union was in crops and a third of the crop area was in meadow. Thus a person with a holding below 30 acres might very well be unable to graze enough cows to make a living for his family—and family size was large in Kerry—and the possibilities of profitable tillage crops were simply not open to him. And precisely half of Dingle holdings were below 32 acres (the median holding).

Where grassland was poor, then, even fairly large farms might fail to support a family, and the plight of the small holder in a nontillage region was desperate indeed. As a region the Southwest never showed the dense network of tiny potato patches characteristic of Donegal and Connaught, but in isolated areas these conditions do appear. In the Southwest they are probably not due to the same historical forces, but are rather the result of the economic adjustments that had occurred since the Famine: where small holders appear they frequently turn out to be the descendants of agricultural laborers displaced when tillage lands were laid down to grass. For 1841 Cousens found the proportion of laborers highest "where holdings of over 30 acres were most common, notably in Cork, and especially in the unions of Dunmanway, Kanturk and Macroom. West Limerick and parts of Tipperary and Waterford in the South and West, and parts of Meath and Louth in the East also recorded a high proportion of population without land . . . In the poor law union of Killarney less than a tenth of the population were without land, and in Listowel less than a fifth. To the east, over 60 percent were without land in Newcastle, over 50 percent in Macroom, and over 70 percent in Dunmanway." [25] These high proportions of laborers were associated with what we identified earlier as tillage regions in the 1840's. The contrast between Kerry (Killarney, Listowel) and Cork (Macroom, Dunmanway) is especially suggestive. Where tillage receded and rates of natural increase did not adjust (e.g., in Cork), there remained pockets of squatters and small holders.

Like Mr. Pollok's Galway estate, Ireland in 1876 had regions in which farms of reasonable size supported a modest population by tillage or, increasingly, by taking advantage of favorable price trends to move into livestock breeding and grazing. But in the same way as on Pollok's estate, the population pressed most insistently outside of these regions. It was not possible for the population to move to the more prosperous livestock industries because very little labor was required there. If, as in Ulster, a labor-intensive tillage economy was able to absorb population—to say nothing of a rapidly growing industrial sector—all would be well. If population pressed on impoverished lands in the West, farms remained, as before the Famine, too small to support the population. In Connaught and Donegal, where the tradition of tiny holdings was long established, subdivision remained a problem. In Kerry, where such a pattern was not the rule, the population pressure raised rents. Rents could (and did) double or triple on good grazing land without causing distress, but rents on small holdings in Kerry or Mayo could have fallen to zero without enabling a tenant to make a living from them.

The year 1876 was a prosperous one in Ireland. So had been the previous two years. The average yield of wheat in 1876 exceeded that of any of the previous nine years. In fact, so high a yield had never been attained since returns were first collected in 1847. More important, the yield of oats also exceeded any of the previous nine years, except

1874, and (with that exception) the oat yield had been unrivaled since 1854. Barley, though below the 1874 and 1875 yields, was still at high levels, and bere and rye yields also exceeded any of the previous nine years. Potatoes were doing exceptionally well; the 1876 yield was higher than any seen in the previous decade, and 1875 had been better still. The hay crop, exceptional in 1875, remained above average in 1876 as well. Not only the tillage farmers but also those dependent on potatoes and meadow crops had a banner year in 1876; for many it was the third banner year in succession. Under these conditions, even the small Western tenants were surviving. The readjustment of the Irish agricultural economy after the Famine must have seemed in 1876 very nearly a success story. The continuance of this success story would depend for Ulster mainly upon the tillage economy, for the Midlands upon the livestock economy, for the Southwest upon the dairy economy, for the West (and Southwest) upon potato yields and on auxiliary employment in England—as well as upon the continued acquiescence of these poor tenants in their pattern of life.

5.
The Downturn in Irish
Agriculture 1877–1879

*The Land League was not begotten by
oratory, but by economics.*

T. M. Healy

During the month of March 1877, when Irish farmers
were preparing to till their soil and plant their crops, it
rained for twenty days.[1] Then it rained for twenty-four days
in April. In August when the crops should have been ap-
proaching maturity for the harvest, it rained for twenty-
seven days. With the exception of one crop (hay), the
harvest was disastrous. The yield of every other crop fell,
and potatoes suffered particularly, declining from an average yield per acre of 4.7 tons in 1876 to 2.0 tons in 1877.
The following year the weather was more nearly normal.
The wheat crop recovered; oats and flax and rye yields
were as high as any since 1869, aside from the records set
in 1875 and 1876; the hay yield maintained its previous
year's level. Thus there was a general recovery, though not
to 1876 levels. But, for potatoes, the average yield in 1878
stood at 3.0 tons an acre, a ton above the previous terrible
year, but scarcely a good yield. And although 1878 was a
better year for potatoes in Ireland as a whole, it was a
worse year in Munster, where the average yield fell again,
from 2.1 tons in 1877 to 1.9 in 1878. In Kerry the figure
for 1878 was 2.0 tons, in Limerick 1.6 tons, in Cork 1.5
tons. From Bandon, Bantry, and Castletown in Cork came

reports of very bad potato crops. From Clonakilty: "The potatoes in this locality have not been so bad since 1848, small and wet, but not much of the disease in them." But there was blight in South Cork, blight in Dunmanway, blight in Mallow. From Kanturk: "With the exception of the potato . . . the produce of the crops this year has been nearly an average. Potatoes very bad." In Macroom the potato crop was spoken of as a failure. In Kerry there was blight in Listowel; Kenmare reported the worst potato crop in years.

It is almost impossible for the imagination to devise a worse combination of weather conditions than befell the Irish in 1879. Not only was the mean temperature of every month from January to September, inclusive, considerably below the average of the preceding ten years, but it was in July and August that the cold was most unusual. There simply was no summer heat. The mean amount of cloud cover exceeded the average of the previous ten years, and the worst excess came in June and July. Not only did the rainfall far exceed the average, but the four months of greatest excess included June, July, and August. For June and July the rainfall was more than 100 percent above the average of the past ten years. Crop yields plummeted. The potato yield fell to 1.3 tons for all Ireland, half a ton below the last recorded *famine* year (1872).[2]

"That loss which has been brought upon us by natural causes we may trust to nature with time to repair," wrote Caird of the European weather of the late 1870's. "But the agriculture of America has been stimulated in an extraordinary degree by the rising demand occasioned by this long-continued diminution in our own crops, and in those of Western Europe generally . . . The increase in the last three years has been unprecedented."[3] The measure in which the presence of American agricultural products on the European scene can be ascribed to the crop failures of these years or to lower ocean freights may be a matter of doubt, but there can be no doubt of the sharp increase in American grain exports in the late 1870's. The European farmer was denied the usual compensation for crop failure in the form of higher prices, as imports from America moved in to fill the deficiency. Ireland was perhaps relatively favored, having already substantially moved out of wheat production into oats and barley, where American advantages were less. The lack of sun in Ireland underlay her choice of corn crops, and the one thing the American Midwest could not compete with was the amount of cool cloudy weather that Ireland could provide the oats and barley. But, despite differences in timing and severity, Ireland felt the blow, too.

The late 1870's initiated a period of falling agricultural prices in Ireland of longer duration and steepness than at any time since just after the Crimean War. The Barrington price indexes show not only declines for the main tillage crops, but also for store cattle; wool and butter prices had started to fall even earlier.

Table 12 illustrates the decline of principal tillage prices on the Dublin Corn Exchange over the course of the 1870's. The prices of 1876–1877, 1877–1878, and 1878–1879 are below the averages for the first seven years of the decade. The decline in oats and barley prices would be even more drastic had the average been struck for five years instead of seven. The years of worst crop failure thus coincided with the years of relatively low prices, and income declines for tillage farmers were drastic indeed.

Livestock prices also fell from the levels of 1876, but their story is more complicated. The average cattle prices estimated by *Thom's Almanac* declined in 1878 and 1879, but neither sheep nor pig prices did so; they remained steady at 1876 levels until 1880, when sheep prices rose and pig prices began to fall. However, average cattle prices do not tell the whole story, since age and quality vary. The fall in cattle prices from 1877 to 1879 recorded at the

Table 12. Average Prices on the Dublin Corn Exchange, from 1869–70 through 1878–79

	Wheat	Oats	Barley
(Nov. 1–Oct. 31)	Bbl. 20 stone	Bbl. 14 stone	Bbl. 16 stone
1869–70	25s.– 9½d.	13s.–11½d.	16s.–3 d.
1870–71	31 – 3	14 – 3½	17 –9½
1871–72	31 –11¼	13 – 8	18 –3¼
1872–73	29 –11	14 – 8½	18 –4½
1873–74	32 – 1	16 – 8¾	20 –5½
1874–75	24 – 6	16 –10	18 –2
1875–76	24 – 9	14 – 3	17 –4
Average of the above 7 years	*28 – 7*	*14 – 9¼*	*18 –1*
1876–77	28 – 5	14 – 2½	18 –0
1877–78	26 – 7	14 – 8	18 –0
1878–79	22 – 0	11 – 2	17 –0

Source: *Thom's Almanac and Official Directory of The United Kingdom and Ireland.*

Ballinasloe fair and reported in *Thom's Almanac* resulted from a sharp decline in the price of first-class cattle, a mild decline in the price of second-class cattle, but increases in the prices of third- and fourth-class cattle. After 1879 all classes moved together, and a general upward price trend was evident during 1880–1883. Thus third- and fourth-class cattle prices at the principal Irish market rose every year (except one—1881) from 1876 to 1883; second-class prices declined somewhat in 1878 and 1879 but otherwise showed the same upward trend until 1884; for all of these groups the prices of 1883 were well above those of 1876. The initial declines in the prices of first-class cattle were so great that the recovery in the early 1880's never returned prices to the peaks of 1876 and 1877.

For one important livestock product, butter, the bottom fell out of the market. Table 13 shows high and low butter

Table 13.   Butter Prices Quoted in *Farmer's Gazette* (shillings per cwt 112 lbs)

Year	Low	High	Average
1868	120	130	125
1869	108	113	110½
1870	110	130	120
1871	114	118	116
1872	100	126	113
1873	110	140	125
1874	110	150	130
1875	115	140	127½
1876	110	154	132
1877	89	126	107½
1878	90	115	102½
1879	61	131	96

SOURCE: Compiled from Bessborough Commission, 1627.
NOTE: Prices taken from reports from butter markets in Cork, Dublin, and other leading markets in Munster.

prices at the principal markets from 1868 to 1879, and a simple arithmetic average between them. This series clearly shows a drastic decline after 1876. Since more sales are made at the low than at the high prices, a properly weighted average would reveal a still more disastrous price decline. At Cork first-quality butter was quoted as low as 76s. and 77s. in July and August 1879.

By the blows of these years all Ireland was affected. The succession of bad seasons inflicted damage on the tillage crop directly in terms of yields and quality. With the co-incidence of the price declines, the tillage farmer was pros-trate. The estimated values for all crops in Ireland, which stood at £36.5 million in 1876, fell to £32.7 million in 1878 and to £22.7 million in 1879.[4]

There was damage in the livestock economy as well. Wet seasons left pasture infested with weeds and rushes, fewer animals could be maintained, and fewer animals meant less manure—the damage cumulated. There was a deterioration in quality, and disease broke out. Still, by the time the Bess-borough Commissioners arrived in 1880, prices were mov-ing upward again. The livestock farmer felt the crises of the late 1870's as a temporary setback, not as the end of an era.

"Butter," wrote one of the inspectors superintending the collection of agricultural statistics in County Limerick, "calculating upon quantity and quality, is at least one fourth less than it was in former years." The cheaper grain that did little to help the Irish dairy farmer was a consider-able boon to the Danes, who carried on winter dairying and indoor feeding with imported grain.

For the subsistence farmer in the West the story of the late 1870's had an all too familiar sound. A young English civil servant traveling in the West as Secretary to a Com-mission of Inquiry into Poor Law and Lunacy administra-tion brought the situation to the notice of the self-deluded, eternally sceptical administration in Dublin Castle. In his memoirs, Henry Robinson recalls:

> I was in Galway late in the year 1879 and was spend-ing a week-end at Recess, when I happened to take up a Dublin Newspaper in which there was an article de-scribing the famine and starvation in some mountain villages near by, and which declared that some infatu-

ation must be paralysing the Government. I met a young priest—Father John Connolly—and in course of conversation referred to these newspaper reports and premised that they were grossly exaggerated.

"Come with me tomorrow into the mountains," he said, "and I'll learn ye whether they are exaggerated or not; that is, if ye don't mind a six-mile walk over the wet bogs."

I was glad of the experience, so we started off early next day for a mountain village called Derryvoreda. I never got such a shock before or since. The people were living skeletons, their faces like parchment. They were scarcely able to crawl. Even the few pigs and fowls were hardly able to stand, and so far as I could see there was not a house with any food in it. It was appalling. I urged the priest to send a special message for a relieving officer, who would get them into the workhouse and give them temporary relief till they could be removed. He promised to do so, but believed they would die at home rather than enter the workhouse.[5]

There was starvation and destitution in Clare, in Kerry, in West Cork. The small farmers depended on the potato for their food, and for their cash expenditures on fishing or kelp, going to England or Scotland to help with the harvest, and perhaps the sale of a few livestock. With what is commonly called the luck of the Irish, everything failed them at once. The price of kelp fell from £7 to £2 a ton. Even the fish were alleged to have fled the Donegal shores. Livestock were for a time unsalable. The agricultural depression had not spared England—far from it—so the demand for agricultural labor dwindled away. The small western farmers had evolved an economy so delicately balanced on the edge of subsistence that the removal of any single prop would have been a serious matter; by 1879 no prop was standing. One tenant told the Bessborough Commission in 1880: "What we ate three years ago is not paid for yet." [6] Although for those who suffered through it the situation was as grave as the Famine, the resources for meeting it were far better developed. While the government was not conspicuously successful in its relief efforts,[7] private relief funds flowed in. Aid came from the Duchess of Marlborough's Fund, the Mansion House Fund, the Society of Friends, the Dominion of Canada, the New York Herald Fund: 1879 was not 1847. And the changed political climate in 1879 was if anything even more important than the meteorological.

The Irish Home Rule Party that Isaac Butt led in the House of Commons in the early 1870's was a loose association of gentlemen and landlords who were supposed to forward their leader's program of Home Rule and the three F's: fixity of tenure, fair rents, and free sale. As they respectfully pursued these aims in perhaps a desultory way, there lumbered into their midst the figure of Joseph Gillis Biggar, the Belfast provision merchant who had won a seat for Cavan in the 1874 elections. Biggar's contribution to the Irish question was the policy of obstructing the business of the House of Commons. Obstruction, of course, was hardly a program, but rather a technique of harassment and an expression of contempt for the British Parliament. Among the handful of Irish members who were attracted to this form of aggression was the young Charles Stewart Parnell, who was elected to Parliament for Meath in 1875.[8] Biggar was no isolated figure. Both he and another "obstructionist," John O'Connor Power, were members of the supreme council of the Irish Republican Brotherhood, the

Fenian organization.[9] Parnell was thus brought into contact with the Fenians, and, more importantly, through them with Michael Davitt. In December 1877 this (to me) most attractive figure in the Irish nationalist movement was released on ticket of leave (parole) from the prison sentence he had been serving since 1870 for his Fenian activities. According to Moody, Davitt first met Parnell when he went to thank him and O'Connor Power for their efforts on behalf of his release from prison.[10]

Davitt's vision for Ireland began to take shape in the months after his release from prison. It was a vision that ultimately went back to an earlier revolutionary of the 1840's, James Fintan Lalor, though Moody has evidence that Davitt had reached some of the same conclusions two or three years before he read Lalor. Lalor had seen the revolutionary Irish nationalists as a set of chiefs with no Indians, or, in his metaphor, a railroad engine without a string of carriages. The missing rank and file lay close at hand in the impoverished Irish tenantry. "Repeal is the question of the town population; and the tenure question is that of the country peasantry; both combined, taking each in its full extent and efficacy, form the question of Ireland—her question for the battle today." [11] The weapon Lalor devised was the rent strike: the tenants should refuse to pay rent to "the present usurping proprietors, until the people, the true proprietors . . . have in national congress . . . decided what rents they are to pay and to whom." [12]

The proposition that "the land of Ireland belongs to the people of Ireland" is a sentiment to which we may all subscribe. It is a nationalist political slogan. It is an entirely different proposition from maintaining that every small tenant in County Mayo should be encouraged as a matter of economic policy to remain on his substandard holding. It was the genius of Fintan Lalor to see that the two could usefully be confused for revolutionary ends, and the greater genius of Davitt not only to perceive but to implement the vision. In the spring of 1878 Davitt broached to Parnell his program of uniting both the moderate and extreme nationalists behind a vigorous attack on "landlordism." Parnell was sympathetic, though, with the great political wisdom that stayed with him almost to the end, he declined to join the IRB or to enter a formal alliance. Davitt's next move was to America, where he spent the summer and autumn of 1878, lecturing to Fenian audiences and hammering out with sympathetic Irish-Americans the details of his program. He was never able to gain the support of the orthodox Fenian revolutionaries, but he found a powerful associate in John Devoy. Having done his best with Parnell and with the physical-force nationalists, in both cases with only partial success, he now turned to the third branch of his policy: the tenantry. Mayo was Davitt's birthplace and to Mayo he now returned. The role of the agrarian collapse of the late 1870's became now of crucial importance. Davitt's first organized demonstration, at Irishtown near Claremorris, was a resounding success, for it gave the distressed Mayo tenants an outlet for their misery and a channel to direct action. Agitation in the West had begun, and Parnell was presented with the choice of leading it or dealing with it as an outsider. In the famous Westport meeting of June 1, 1879, he took his stand as head of the agitation, and when the Land League was formed some months later, Parnell became its president.

On May 17, 1880, T. P. O'Connor, the recently elected member for Galway, was walking to the Mansion House meeting in Dublin, where the Irish party was to choose its leader for the new parliamentary session. William Shaw was considered certain of reelection. O'Connor owed his election to Parnell and Davitt and the land agitation, and as he walked toward the Mansion House he suggested to his companions, John Barry and Timothy Healy, the possibility of nominating Parnell. "We met Parnell on the way to the City Hall," wrote O'Connor later. "He did not give us any encouragement, seemed rather taken aback by the proposal." [13] To the general surprise, Parnell was elected, 23 votes to 18.

Parnell accepted the weapon Davitt had forged for him: the organization of the tenantry along quasi-revolutionary lines. (Some might, with justice, quarrel with the "quasi.") It was a weapon neither Davitt nor Parnell could wholly control. The interests of the tenants were not identical with Parnell's: political independence by parliamentary methods. If the tenants could be appeased prematurely by satisfactory concessions to their land aims, they were in danger of being detached from Parnell's leadership. If unappeased, the violence of their agitation represented a potential danger to Parnell's parliamentary strategy. Having achieved power with the help of the Land League, Parnell's policy was to keep at one remove from it—maintaining the other bases of his support intact and, brilliantly, establishing himself as the sole alternative to anarchy in Ireland. The skill of Parnell, to which his aloofness, his bad health, and his frequent absences for personal reasons contributed much, transformed the parliamentary situation almost overnight.

When the English Parliament failed to grant the Irish any measure of Home Rule in the nineteenth century, it bestowed upon her instead an abundance of commissions and inquiries and statistics and debates so illuminating and so complete that the modern researcher may perhaps be excused for wondering if it were not really worthwhile missing Home Rule altogether. One of the richest of these sources is the Bessborough Commission, whose report and voluminous evidence were presented to Parliament in 1881. The Bessborough Commission, under the chairmanship of a noble Irish landowner, included William Shaw, the deposed chairman of the Irish parliamentary party; Richard Dowse, one of those numerous ornaments of the Irish bar of the nineteenth century whose reputation for wit has survived any authentic examples thereof; the O'Conor Don, an Irish Catholic landlord, whose title went back to before 1385; and Arthur MacMorrough Kavanagh, a remarkable person—born without arms or legs, he became a proficient horseman, yachtsman, and hunter and a leading landlord, and had perhaps the most incisive mind of any member of the Bessborough Commission.[14] There were no Parnellites on the commission. The commission held 65 sittings, from September 1, 1880, until January 5, 1881; visited Belfast, Londonderry, Sligo, Donegal, Castlebar, Roscommon, Galway, Limerick, Killarney, Cork, Skibbereen, and Clonmel; and heard 80 landowners, 70 land agents, 500 tenants, and a rich assortment of experts, officials, clergymen, M.P.s, barristers and solicitors, land surveyors and valuers. It is our luck that they never stuck to the point of the inquiry, but ranged over all possible questions connected with Irish agriculture over the past twenty-five or thirty years. From the pages of the Bessborough Commission evidence, we can derive an unrivaled picture of Ireland at the economic downturn of 1877–1879. We have already at hand a detailed picture of the structure of agrarian Ireland before the downturn, at the culmination of her post-Famine adjustment. We also have a catalog of the blows that fell after 1876—bad seasons, potato famine, price collapse, and depression in England—and a picture of the new political forces, the Land League and a more militant parliamentary party, that were emerging. The evidence of so many con-temporary witnesses enables us not only to assess the effect of these blows on the economy, but also to see how people interpreted what was happening, what they considered the cause of their difficulties, and what their demands for the future were going to be.

Ulster was hit hard in the downturn. The Ulster tenants traditionally had been better organized than the Southern Irish, and the representatives of their many local Tenant Farmers' Associations and Tenant Defense Associations poured in to testify before the Bessborough Commission. They rehearsed their old complaints about landlords' inva-sion of Ulster custom. Complaints about eviction were so rare that it is a fair assumption that eviction was practically unknown. Rent-raising was the principal grievance, some-times just the choice of the timing of a rent increase. Also, many complaints were made against landlords who tried to restrict the market for tenant right.[15] We have argued that eviction and excessive rent-raising were rare in Ireland and that tenure arrangements did not play a major role in the development of the economy. It is hard to see what they could have contributed to the plight of Ulster in 1880 and hard to see what help a strengthened Ulster custom could have provided in improving that situation. A few quota-tions will show how the Ulster tenant tried to reconcile in his mind what really had occurred (price collapse) with his traditional explanation (tenure arrangements) of all the ills of Ireland.

The controversies over limitations of the sale of tenant right received a wider hearing than their importance de-served. If anything was established, it was that the customs surrounding the sale of tenant right varied from estate to estate. Any attempt by landlords to limit the price was ha-

bitually thwarted by sub rosa payments from the incoming
to the outgoing tenants. The exercise of the landlord veto
no doubt could limit the market, but many tenants felt it
was well within the landlord's right to refuse a tenant who
was personally unacceptable. There is much evidence that
the sale of tenant right was primarily resorted to by poor,
broken-down tenants, and in such cases the first charge on
the proceeds of the sale always went to the landlord to pay
for arrears.

The real difficulties that drove the Ulster tenants to complain to the Bessborough Commission are not far to seek:

> 7795. Do you know how long before you got into oc-
> cupation was the rent raised—how many years has the
> rent been at the present rate?—I should say it has been
> at the present rate for twenty or thirty years, but prices
> were high previously and the people did not feel it. It
> is the competition we have met with and the deprecia-
> tion that has come over the staple trade of Ulster that
> has prevented us from paying the rent.
>
> 7796. Why do you say your landlord is an exacting
> landlord when he did not raise the rents for thirty
> years? [Co. Antrim]
>
> 10877. There is a great feeling of bitterness in con-
> sequence of those rises of rent—there is a great deal of
> talk about it. Those tenants are all respectable farmers,
> many of them friends of my own, and they had in most
> cases, greatly improved their farms before the increased
> rent was put on them. They say that with the occasional
> bad seasons and the fall in price, owing to American
> competition, they are not able to pay those rents, and
> I believe if there is not some check put upon this rising
> of rent, the greater part of the Ulster settlers will have

to leave the country. We are not going to shoot our landlords here, as they sometimes do in the South, but certainly we have great grievances to complain of.

10878. The O'Conor Don. When did that increase of rent on the farms you mention on Lord Abercorn's property take place?—In 1866. [Co. Tyrone]

3161. Has there been any general rise of rents upon [your landlord's] estate?—No.

3162. He is a very liberal landlord I believe?—He is a very charitable and good landlord, and has a first-class agent.

3167. Mr. Kavanagh—Do I understand your complaint to be that your rent is too high?—My complaint is that no matter what we do we cannot make ends meet. The produce is low, wages are high, labour in every way is dear, taxes are multiplied these last ten years . . . Everything is very much higher than it was ten years since, and the produce is very much less. [Co. Down]

2837. Baron Dowse. You say you have good landlords?—Yes.

2839. You don't complain of the landlords?—No. What we want is fixity of tenure, fair rents, and free sale. That is what we want and what we must get in the end. The county is on the verge of bankruptcy, and when the farmers of Louth are badly off the farmers elsewhere are worse off.

2844. It was not the Land Act that did that?—No, it was nothing but the bad times . . . The Americans will ruin us. [Co. Louth, in a tenant-right district]

These quotations speak for themselves. The Ulster farmer had been going along since the middle of the century with the particular tenure customs of his estate. Rents had risen mildly and gradually from the low levels of the post-Famine years, as prices rose and prosperity increased. When the bad years and American competition struck, the Ulster farmer was hit hard. He hit back. At his landlord.

> 5100. You think that if allowed to hold his land at a fair rent, and secured in the value of his improvements, that, notwithstanding the American competition, the tenant-farmer in Ireland could still "hold his own," as the saying is?—Yes; I think so. Give us good land laws, and I shall have no fear for the future agricultural condition of Ireland. [Testimony of Thomas Shillington, Jr., Chairman of the Armagh Tenant Farmers' Association]

In 1880 rents were not rising in Ulster; abatements were being granted. Improvements ceased because prices were low, not because tenants felt insecure. Landlords' office rules were not restricting the prices of tenant-right sales; tenant right was not selling because there were not buyers.[16] The sad truth of the matter was that the lowering of transport costs and the opening up of the American prairie had permanently diminished Ulster's comparative advantage in tillage: "As corn can now be carried from Baltimore to Derry for 13s. 9d. per ton, while it costs farmers in Donegal as much to send a ton of their oats to Derry, their best market, new and serious conditions affecting our agriculture have arrived."[17] All of European agriculture would have to adjust to these new and serious conditions. The Ulster farmer wanted to think the high cost of land in Ulster (relative to Kansas) was due to grasping landlords. But it was due to the balance between land and labor in Kansas (or Saskatchewan) compared with Ulster, and no change in land laws was capable of altering this relation.

Distress in the West had a different aspect. The small holders of Ulster depended on a tillage economy based on corn crops; the small holders of Donegal and Sligo and Mayo depended on a tillage economy based on the potato. "If you cannot insure the potato crop to grow, you cannot have a prosperous small tenantry," a Sligo valuer told the Bessborough Commission.[18] Moreover, population was pressing hard on the means of subsistence as it had in pre-Famine times. The Malthusian model was still at work.

Consider the following case. The Earl of Leitrim held 60,000 acres in Donegal.[19] The farms had been continually subdivided until they were too small to support a family by farming, and the subdivision was continuing, despite all efforts of the Earl's bailiffs. The farmers, if they can be called farmers, grew green crops after potatoes, and perhaps a little oats and hay on mountain tracts. They lived on potatoes and, with whatever other earnings they managed to scrape together from fishing or kelp-gathering, they purchased corn meal and paid the rent. When the potatoes failed, they faced destitution and starvation.[20] The Earl of Leitrim did not know where to turn, as he told the Bessborough Commission:

> 11222. Chairman—When a lease drops are these people [subdividers] taken on as direct tenants?— Leases have fallen in since I have been in possession of the estate, but I have not dealt with them so far. I have had so much distress to deal with that I had not time, but as a rule they are. One has power under the Act to deal with these cases of subdivision summarily, but the hardship is so great if you do deal with them summarily

that one doesn't exactly know what to do. If one cannot see these people out of the country in some sort of
way you have not the heart to turn them out.

Wybrants Olphert, another Donegal landowner, with an
estate of 20,000 acres, reported that he had 500 small tenants with holdings of four, five, or ten acres, renting for
£2, £6, and £8, respectively. Tenant-right prices fetched
thirty to forty years' purchase, and sixty to seventy years'
was not unknown. "That is the great difficulty a landlord
has to deal with, to prevent subdivision; it is a thing almost
impossible to prevent. The smaller the holding, the poorer
the people, the more inclined are they to subdivide." [21] Insecure tenure and landlords' raising rent on tenants' improvements sound very strangely as battle cries in Donegal.

The population pressure made the competition for land
intense. If a landlord failed to charge a high rent, the tenant took advantage of the demand situation by subletting
(as in the above cases) or by selling his tenant right for
whatever it would fetch. The Earl understood this well:
"The result of letting it reasonably is that that man will put
in another man at an unreasonable rent." [22] The road-mak-
ing, fencing, and draining had been done by the Earl's
grandfather, and he himself borrowed £17,000 from the
Board of Works during the awful winter of 1879–80 for
relief works. The tragic condition of his tenants was neither
due to his actions nor remediable by them; the most perfect
working of Ulster custom would have availed nothing on
his estate.[23]

"I am paying for twenty years £13 18d. 4 d., and I can't
stand it any longer." [24] This is the cry of a Mayo tenant.
The small tenants of Connaught, like those in Donegal, did
not date their suffering from the downturn of 1877–1879.
They were never far above the level of destitution, and

thousands had never been able to make a living from their holdings. It is tempting to quote case upon case, to build up a picture by the accumulation of authentic detail; to select one example is utterly inadequate to portray the situation. However, the islands off Mayo may serve as an instance. On the Achill Mission estate on Achill Island, 600 tenants held about 2,000 acres of wretched reclaimed land. Plots of four acres had to support a whole family. The weather was awful: rain and storms from the Atlantic. The islanders lacked adequate boats for fishing. There was insufficient seaweed to fertilize their plots. The agent for the Mission estimated "if you took two-thirds off the rest might live." [25] Reclamation, aid to the fishing industry, provision of alternative employment—all of these he felt would be inadequate to maintain the current population of Achill. Furthermore, "The tenants I speak of, their rents are very small indeed." [26] The islanders earned their living by going to England as laborers. The Achill Mission's tenants were at least better off than the tenants of the other principal island landlord, a man named Pike, who extorted the last possible cent he could squeeze from his tenants.

Population pressure in Connaught, as in Donegal, pressed against rents. "They bid against each other and then they complain of the high rent," observed one landlord. The general impression one receives is that rents in Connaught had risen only moderately from their levels of twenty or twenty-five years previous, and stood at around 25–30 percent above Griffith's valuation. Exceptions, of course, were numerous. The pressure of population vented itself in subdivision and, to a lesser extent, subletting. To give just one example, Patrick Noon, a tenant of Lord Claremorris in Galway, spoke to the Bessborough Commission on behalf of 40 tenants (probably 200 people) whose total holdings amounted to 18 acres. In other words, it mattered little that the landlords' rents remained fairly stable; tenants or heads of households would then be the rent raisers.

If the fall in tillage prices had been Ulster's main problem, and the continuance of pre-Famine conditions, with the periodic potato famines that these conditions entailed, had been Donegal's and Connaught's, the difficulties of tenants on the southwestern grassland regions were more varied. Although Limerick and Clare, Cork and Kerry, were primarily grassland, we have seen that the small holders there depended on tillage, on corn and potatoes. The decline in tillage prices thus hurt some Clare and Limerick tenants, and the cry went up that small tillage farms no longer pay. Since the pressure of demand for land was aimed at small holdings, rents were prevented from falling—in Kerry they were even rising through the 1870's.

Although the median farms were larger than in Connaught, there were pockets of small holders scattered here and there whose situation resembled the pre-Famine conditions of Donegal or Mayo: fishermen near Skibbereen, squatters on Ardfert Commons, the tenants on Dursey Island. To the problems of tillage price collapse and potato famine were added the collapse of butter prices. Finally, the larger farmers of Limerick and Clare came in to complain to the Bessborough Commission, too. They did not always complain of their economic condition, but they evidently felt that, if remedial legislation were going to be enacted, they wanted their share. They complained of being debarred from the benefits of the Land Act of 1870, and some were at pains to show that large farmers were unable to rent land as cheaply as small farmers. When feelings ran high, even well-to-do farmers would raise a clamor.

From the Southeast no deputations poured in to the commission, although tillage farmers must have been hard hit. Perhaps their greater resources enabled them to sustain losses for a time. The cattle graziers of the Midlands were also conspicuously absent, and we know from subsequent commissions that they were well able to make themselves heard if they chose. Not surprisingly, they appear to have weathered the storm of the late 1870's fairly well.

The cry of the Ulster farmers and their tenant associations had been for the three F's; in the West and the Southwest there was no such cry, there was direct action. Many Farmers' Clubs and Tenant Associations there had been converted to Land League sentiments, and the aim of the Land League was perfectly clear. Even Parnell had gone so far as to say, "it is the duty of the Irish tenant-farmers to combine among themselves, and ask for a reduction of rent, and if they get no reduction, then I say it is the duty of the tenant to pay no rent." [27] And so the cry of the day rang out in the popular song by T. D. Sullivan, the Nationalist politician:

> Farmers far and near,
> Long despoiled by plunder,
> Let your tyrants hear
> Your voices loud as thunder.
> Shout from shore to shore
> Your firm determination
> To pay in rents no more
> Than Griffith's valuation.

In the background cries of "No rent" and "Pay nothing" were ominously heard.

It might be interesting to hear in his own words the story of the most famous victim of the rent strike:

I was instructed by the Earl of Erne to collect his November rents of 1879, and to allow his tenants 10 per cent abatement. I cannot speak accurately to a pound, because I am only going on memory, but the gross rental is either £30 or £31 18s. 6d. over Griffith's valuation. His lordship was allowing 10 per cent on that, and asking for the November rent of 1879 in some cases, and in respect to yearly tenancies the May rent of 1879. The tenants all refused to pay—all but two—unless they got an abatement of 25 per cent. I referred the matter to his lordship, and he said he would give no more than 20 per cent. I first sent a letter to them to pay, and they declined, and I then took out ejectment processes . . .

The ejectment processes were served on the 22nd September. The process server only succeeded in serving three of the ejectment processes. He had a force of police with him to protect him, but they were beaten, and he only succeeded in serving three of the notices, and there has been no attempt since to serve the remainder . . . I am certain that they cannot be served without a very large force of police . . . but if they were evicted nobody would take their land, and they would be reinstated again as is done everywhere in Ireland now. They would be put in again by mob force and kept there . . .

On the 24th September, a mob came up to my house and ordered off every person in my employment. There was not a single person left but one that I had brought from Dublin, and since then he is the only person I have been able to get. I have, with the assistance of my nephew to drive in the cows, and drive them out, and draw out water to the cattle, take out the horse and cart and drive them, under an escort of police, and there is not a single sort of person allowed to help me. My herd has given up his holding, but he will not give up the house in order to prevent it being given to a stranger. Others have given work, but the people will not work

for me. I have the magistrate's orders for ejectment, but
I can get nobody like a special bailiff to serve. Even last
Tuesday the woman who washed clothes for the house
said that she dare not do so again.

I cannot get my potatoes dug nor my hay saved. I
cannot get my corn threshed, nor my mangolds cut . . .

The police have to bring me my letters now . . . I
am living with ten policemen in my house at present,
and I have to be escorted wherever I go by policemen.[28]

This was no isolated case. When the time came to collect
rents in 1880, the strike was in effect everywhere. The Land
Committee organized a deputation of landlords and agents
to testify to the brilliant success of the Land League tactics,
as reported to the Bessborough Commission:

40193. In my examination before in Sligo I was asked
a question as to rents coming in, and the prospects of
payment, and I stated that there was a movement in the
direction of payment of rent as far as my property went.
The evidence was given early in October, and certainly
within one week after giving it the movement took an
entirely opposite turn. Since the 17th October, I think
there is a complete change in that district, and in other
places where I hold property.

40194. Mr. Shaw—The organization has spread
through the country?—Completely. [Testimony of Col.
E. R. King-Harman]

40213. Up to the beginning of this month [November
1880] the rents were paid freely by the tenants, but since
that the combination has extended to all parts we have
to deal with, in Tipperary, Kilkenny, and Wexford.
[Testimony of Charles Uniacke Townshend]

32241. . . . you have the remarkable fact that even

on Sir Richard Wallace's estate [Co. Down], managed in such a princely way, there are tenants refusing to pay their rents. I found a man refusing to pay his rent to Sir Richard Wallace, and I was able to trace that he had £1700 on deposit in the neighboring bank. [Testimony of Prof. Thomas Baldwin]

The rent strike had spread from the destitute lands of Mayo and North Kerry to the prosperous districts of Meath and Kilkenny. Landlords were powerless. If some who deserved it were brought to ruin, so were many who had been helpful and reasonable. If unjust evictions were stopped, by the same token worthless old reprobates were upheld in their refusal to pay reasonable rents. It is naïve to say (as some did) that the tenants had been coerced by agitators and kept in line by terror and intimidation; equally naïve to suppose that the situation could have been achieved without leadership and organization and discipline—or that the tenant who chose to defy the Land League could expect much better treatment than a landlord.

Many memoirs exist that give excellent pictures of Ireland in these days. Two novels are especially valuable: Trollope's posthumous (unfinished) *The Landleaguers* (1883) and Liam O'Flaherty's *Land* (1946). Both authors, who normally maintain tight control over their characters, have been betrayed, perhaps by the wildly emotional climate of that time, into melodrama, with heroes larger than life. Trollope's hero is a police inspector, O'Flaherty's is an Irish revolutionary. Trollope leaves out the poverty of the tenants and the legitimate nationalist aspirations of the Irish; O'Flaherty leaves out the injustice and inhumanity that accompanied the Nationalist movement in those times. Once we rise above the heroes-and-villains view of history, perhaps what the Land League experience illustrates is that an alien ruling class, however it conducts itself, is likely to be the object of resentment and hatred never far below the surface. Many landlords who never received a penny's rent again after 1880 were disturbed far more by the ease with which their tenants turned their backs on them. But the measure of what they thought was their tenants' passive devotion turned out to be the measure of repressed hostility.

The success of the Land League began a period of seven years that is rightly called the Land War in Ireland. Economic variables can no longer be understood in simple economic terms: refusal to pay rent is not necessarily a sign of poverty; neither is the accumulation of arrears; refusal to grant abatements is not necessarily a sign of landlord inflexibility; evictions are a weapon in a political struggle. By the use of physical intimidation and the boycott but, more important, by virtue of the widespread moral support of the community, the Irish tenantry had laid its hand on the control of the rent-setting mechanism. Tenants wanted to control the mechanism to maintain their incomes by reducing their rent payments; Davitt wanted to control the mechanism to drive out landlords and eventually to nationalize the land; Parnell wanted to control the mechanism as a show of strength that would wrest Home Rule from Parliament, after which the land question could be dropped. Economic policy was going to be made in a setting in which the economic well-being of the Irish people would be a minor consideration, if indeed a consideration at all.

No one could foresee in 1880 where it would end, but a thoughtful man could catch a glimpse. "Is not the tenant of a farm . . . at the mercy of his landlord?" Baron Dowse asked a small landowner from Tuam named O'Flaherty before the Bessborough Commission.

19435. Upon my word I think the balance is very little in favour of the landlord. Supposing a crisis like this arises, which every man of ordinary sagacity might foresee, I think the landlord is in the worse position of the two, for how can he meet his payments, interest, annuities, jointures on his property, and his other outgoings—if the Land Leaguers induce the tenants to refuse to pay their rents.

19436. We are not always, I hope, to have the Land League?—I fear you may consider the Land League as a permanent institution.

19437. You think so?—I do—that is my opinion. Of course I speak with the utmost deference, but I believe whatever Bill you recommend, even if it be carried in the next Session of Parliament, will fail to satisfy the tenantry; and even if it should temporarily satisfy them, you will see the same agitation spring up again before the end of ten years. I think there is a fixed desire or passion on the part of the Irish peasant to get the fee of the land.

19438. Without paying for it?—Well, on cheap terms at all events.

19460. Would not the same difficulty arise if a peasant proprietary were established?—Do you mean between the Government and the tenant?

19461. Yes?—I think not; the Government is not like a landlord—one is an unsubstantial body which cannot be assailed or frightened, the other is an individual whom we can denounce or shoot.

19451. They could not get rid of them [the government] without rebellion or civil war?—Yes; and they regard that as chimerical.

6.
The Land Act
of 1881

*If you value rents you may as well for
every available purpose adopt perpetuity
of tenure at once. It is perpetuity of tenure
only in a certain disguise. It is the first
link in the chain, but it draws after it the
last.*

W. E. Gladstone

The structure of Irish agriculture that was built up in the
third quarter of the nineteenth century rested on the successful adjustment of the economy to rising agricultural
prices, especially for livestock and livestock products. But
this successful readjustment was unevenly distributed and,
owing to differing regional population trends, the West and
Southwest had a smaller share in it. The downturn of the
late 1870's threatened the whole fabric. Bad seasons resulted
in a direct and disastrous decline in incomes, and the appearance of American grain in Europe suggested that the
tillage sector might never recover. For livestock there was
for the moment less cause for pessimism. The tragic failure
of the potato crop so crucial to the West and Southwest was
no novel catastrophe, although it was exceptionally severe
in the late 1870's and coincided with other adverse developments for these people. What was new in the West was the
effective organization of the tenantry by Davitt and his associates in the Land League. Although descriptions of Ireland
in 1880 contained such grand phrases as "on the verge of

rebellion," "society in dissolution," and "social revolution," what was happening was the perfection of the techniques of the rent strike. Shooting at landlords, resisting sheriff's officers, boycotting, maiming cattle—all were primarily developed to ensure the efficacy of the widespread refusal to pay current rents. In any case, the Land League was in control in parts of Ireland, and "English" law and order could not be maintained any longer.

GENESIS OF THE LAND ACT OF 1881

When Gladstone returned to power in 1880, the "severity of the crisis," in his own words, "rushed upon us like a flood." Before the election, Mr. Gladstone, although nominally retired from the leadership of his party, had made a furious onslaught on Disraeli's foreign policy—on "Beaconsfieldism"—in the celebrated Midlothian campaign. His mind was on Constantinople, Kabul, and the Cape. It was Disraeli who tried to make Ireland a campaign issue and, with perhaps greater sensitivity to agricultural problems, gave evidence of understanding the dangers.[1] Caught unaware when it came to power after the election, the Gladstone government allowed the law conferring special powers on the Irish executive (Coercion Act of 1875) to lapse. One attempt at Irish legislation failed. The House of Lords threw out the government's bill to provide compensation to evicted tenants, and nothing was done during the session to cope with the continuing serious situation in Ireland. The story is familiar how, in the subsequent session, Parliament passed the Coercion Act of 1881 when the Speaker of the House put the question in spite of the obstructionist tactics of the Irish party. The stage was now set for a new attempt at land legislation.

The Land Act of 1881 was obviously not preceded by intensive study and long memoranda on the part of Mr. Gladstone. For the current state of thinking on the Irish land problem, the best source is probably the reports of two royal commissions that were issued in January 1881. The Disraeli government had appointed a Royal Commission on Agriculture[2] in the summer of 1879, and while the commission was not confined to Ireland it directed much of its attention there. Under the chairmanship of the Duke of Richmond, a great Tory landowner, the commission held hearings and heard expert testimony on Ireland through the summer of 1880. When Gladstone came in, he appointed a commission of his own, Bessborough, which was more specifically directed toward Irish land legislation. The Bessborough Commission sat for testimony in the autumn of 1880. Both commissions then published reports in January 1881.

Much of the testimony before the Richmond Commission stressed overpopulation and small holdings as the main source of Irish difficulties. The real trouble lay in the West, and in the West, farms were below a size capable of supporting a family. The commission also heard evidence on the deplorable level of agricultural practices in Ireland, and considerable testimony was devoted to the very important butter industry. Thomas Baldwin served as the Richmond Commission's agent in Ireland and testified at length after making special on-the-spot investigations. He was a man who knew his business of agricultural techniques well; his testimony is attractive because he confined it to matters of personal knowledge. In 1880 he may have been the only man in Ireland who had not made up his mind on what scheme of land reform was going to solve everything. Baldwin located the problem squarely in the West and Southwest. He estimated that 100,000 farms were "too small to give continuous employment to an able-bodied male." Nevertheless, he told the commission that the Irish farmer could double his income by "even moderately good farming." [3]

The policies he recommended were emigration and resettlement, better agricultural practices, credit for the small farmer, railroads, and drainage ("I know of nothing that would be more beneficial than a comprehensive system of arterial drainage").[4] He confessed to being puzzled about the role of rent.*

Baldwin found many dairy farms in "a deplorable condition . . . very much neglected," [5] and his testimony was corroborated by that of other witnesses. Once Irish butter had monopolized a large share of English imports, but it could no longer compete with Danish and French (Normandy) butter; by 1880 very little Irish butter was sold in London. The trend had started much earlier. By 1866 foreign butter imports into England were up by 100 percent over 1855 and Irish down to 25 percent of 1854.[6] The years from 1867 to 1876 were perhaps the most prosperous decade dairy farmers ever knew in England, but the Irish were unable to share in the prosperity. It was a problem of quality. The best Irish butter could indeed compete on equal terms with Danish or French butter. William Bence Jones told the Richmond Commission that he shipped his butter directly to London, where it fetched a much higher price than could be got in Cork. He labeled it, however, "from a

* "I never could find from my own experience any instance of bad treatment by the old landlords," he testified. "Then to some extent," he was asked, "this fear of bad landlords is a superstition, and not based on reality so far as the old landlord is concerned?" "But then," said the professor, "supposing one of these land jobbers is in a county, he may drive terror into the rest of the tenants" (Richmond Commission, 3403–05). Cf. p. 73 above. It is only fair to add that some time later Professor Baldwin told the Cairns Commission that he was surprised at the amount of rack-renting he encountered as subcommissioner under the Land Act of 1881. The Cairns Commission is the name we shall use for the following series of volumes: *First Report from the Select Committee of the House of Lords on Land Law (Ireland), P.P.* 1882 (249) XI; *Second Report, P.P.* 1883 (204) XIII; *Fourth Report, P.P.* 1883 (279) XIII.

private dairy," since as Irish butter it would not have sold.[7]

The Irish problem was partly due to lack of capital and organization, but behind that to ignorance and indifference. Irish butter was dirty. Many small farmers had no dairies at all, but kept milk in the sleeping room. "If they have dairies, they are of the poorest possible class, with earthen floors and dirty thatched roofs," testified an agent from the Southwest.[8] Butter was sold by the firkin, and by the time a small farmer could produce enough butter to fill the top of the firkin, the butter at the bottom was likely to be rancid. At the very best such butter was not of standard quality. Adulteration was not uncommon. Much criticism was directed against the Cork butter market, which financed and handled a large share of the trade, and closer examination of this institution would probably be well repaid.*

A good summary of some of the things the Richmond Commission heard may be found in the testimony of the Marquis of Lansdowne: his Kerry tenants kept old breeds of worn-out Kerry cattle, made bad butter, had no systematic system of cultivation but practiced continuous cropping, used old diseased seed, and could not be induced to grow more green crops. He attributed these things to ignorance, laziness, and low rents. The Lansdowne estates in Meath

---

* The rise of the Danish butter industry had started from the same point. The price of manor house butter (like Bence Jones's or Mahony's) was much greater than peasant butter at first, but as the Danes improved their production and marketing techniques through the cooperative movement, the price of peasant butter rose more and more until it came to equal that of manor house butter. The Danish cooperative movement was begun and developed entirely without government assistance. Of course, the Danes had advantages in education and literacy, as well as a tradition of self-government. Nevertheless, although the Irish are rightly annoyed at always having Denmark held up to them as a good example (Irish dairying was "outdoor" dairying because of cost considerations, not out of perverseness), there remains much in the history of Danish agriculture that stands as a reproach to Irish farming.

and King's, he told the commission, were nothing like the Kerry estate.[9]

Against this background, the majority of the Richmond Commission in a preliminary report dated January 14, 1881, recommended emigration and resettlement, and public work assistance in the form of drainage, railways, fisheries, and agricultural education. Any recommendation for the three F's was conspicuously absent. Thirteen (of nineteen) members signed the majority report. Proponents of the three F's (even of peasant proprietorship) were also heard by the Richmond Commission, and the minority report echoed these views. To the minority the problem remained a fear of capricious eviction and rent-raising; industry and investment were deterred by rent increases: the Land Act of 1870 had failed because it had not prevented undue and unreasonable rent increases. A tribunal should therefore be set up to settle rent; Ulster custom, though having "certain drawbacks" and providing "a security still imperfect," should be imitated by introducing free sale and fixity of tenure everywhere.

A cynic could not be blamed for supposing that the Bessborough Commission had been appointed in order to bring in a verdict for the three F's. The Tories in fact accused its recommendations of being "pre-ordained" and thought the dirty work had been done in unseemly haste.[10] But the cynic and the Tories were probably wrong; at least we have Morley's word that Mr. Gladstone was astonished when he learned of the recommendations of the commission.[11] "In a word," reads the *Report* of the Bessborough Commission, ". . . we advocate the reform of the Land Law of Ireland upon the basis known as 'The Three F's,' *i.e.* Fixity of Tenure, Fair Rents, and Free Sale." [12] The commission hoped rents would be set by arbitration and, failing complete success along those lines, envisaged an independent tribunal as the ultimate authority for rent-setting. The argument advanced for the adoption of the three F's was that they already substantially existed by tradition in Ireland; the discrepancy between the unwritten and written law ought to be reconciled in favor of the former. The commission was clear that Irish rents were below market value and that landlords were very nearly without power to evict.[13] The "great grievance" of Ireland, in this view, was the discrepancy between the law and the tradition. And what of the masses in the West and Southwest, "where it is said they are not able, if they had their land gratis, to live by cultivating it?" The Bessborough *Report* excused itself from worrying about them: "It is thought [by some] to be an almost insoluble problem." [14] The *Report* merely hoped that the three F's would somehow do something to improve their condition and "that the tranquility which will follow on a well-considered measure of Land Tenure Reform will be a blessing alike to all classes, and especially to the poorest." [15]

There are three classes of objections to the legislation recommended by the Bessborough Commission: one on a fairly abstract level concerning optimal forms of land tenure; another on a more concrete level concerning the potential contribution of the legislation to income and development; another concerning political effects. Cogent arguments under all these heads were presented in supplementary reports to the Richmond and Bessborough commissions. Bonamy Price wrote a memorandum for the Richmond Commission in which he summarized the economic arguments against the three F's in a form that could hardly be bettered today. The land law of Ireland had been defective, he wrote, insofar as it had permitted rent-raising on tenant improvements. The Land Act of 1870 had been framed to remedy this defect; if it had failed, it should be amended along the lines laid down. "But legislative inter-

ference with the value of rent is a wholly different matter."
To give tenants tenure is effectively to prevent landlords
from investing in agriculture and to rob them of the power
to introduce technical improvements. The right of tenure
for the Irish tenant perpetuates small holdings, subdivision,
and bad farming. As for free sale, he wrote, the tenant's
right to the value of his improvements should be firmly secured to him. Let a cheap and easy method be devised of
valuing these improvements and let the tenant be granted
this value. Beyond that, he saw, the tenant has nothing to
sell. If the value of his improvements is reserved to the tenant, then, a rational allocation of economic resources re-
quires that the rent be set by market forces. To set a lower
rent would be to protect inefficiency and to paralyze hopes
of readjustment. Price's conclusion is worth quoting at
length:

> What a particular tenant can pay is no rule for deter-
> mining the fair rent—the rent which, if he understood
> his business, he ought to and would be able to pay . . .
> This F.—this determination of fair rent other than by
> free contract—strikes at the root of all improvement in
> the agriculture of Ireland. It takes as its standard the ig-
> norance, the indolence, the apathy, the want of capital,
> of the unhappy tenant, who is protected in his want of
> industry by the adjustment of the rent to his state and
> habits.
>
> The 3F's, consequently, ought to be condemned as
> false on principle, both socially and economically, as
> calculated to perpetuate the particular evils from which
> Ireland is suffering, and to arrest that increase of pro-
> duction from which alone she can hope to advance to-
> wards prosperity.[16]

The O'Conor Don, who signed the majority report of the Bessborough Commission, wrote a supplementary report as well. In it he expressed, among many other points, the total irrelevance of tenure reform to the tenants in the West:

There are parts of Ireland in which the condition of things is such that no alteration in the tenure of land or the amount of rent could really accomplish any lasting effect. There are portions of Ireland in which the land is so bad, and is so thickly populated, that the question of tenure and rent are mere trifles. If the present occupiers had the land forever, and for nothing, they could not in the best of years live decently, and in bad years they must be in a state of starvation . . . The simple fact that the rents in many localities average £3 and £4 a year, and that the lowest annual amount which an average family would require to support themselves is £60 or £70 must be convincing proof that the doubling of rent or its abolition could not make the difference between even moderate prosperity and destitution. The loss of a small pig or of one rood of potatoes would be a greater loss to one of these tenants than even the doubling of his rent, whilst the production and good sale of one firkin of butter would be worth more to many of them than the forgiveness of a whole year's rent.[17]

But to show that the land tenure legislation recommended by the Bessborough Commission was widely realized to be on economic grounds either wrong or irrelevant is to miss the whole point. The legislation was recommended with a view to halting the agitation in Ireland; it was recommended less as an economic policy than as a political stroke. A dozen years later Mr. Gladstone confessed: "I must make one admission," he told Parliament, "and that is that without the Land League the Act of 1881 would not now be upon the Statute Book." [18] The Bessborough Commissioners felt that the vast majority of tenants would be satisfied by it and would thus be split off from the "extremists." They also felt that many Irish landlords had indicated a willingness to support such legislation. Such a measure would be aimed at the heart of the Lalor-Davitt approach and might well wreck Nationalist hopes.*

The progress of the Land Act of 1881 (44 & 45 Vict. Ch. 49) through Parliament must have been as agonizing for members to endure as it is for the historian to read. Par-

---

* They were possibly right. The Land Act of 1881 posed a very difficult situation for Parnell from which he was extricated when the Gladstone government clapped him into Kilmainham jail in October 1881. Tim Healy, who was Parnell's closest advisor at this time and in a good position to judge, thought the action was the "main blunder in England's relations with Ireland in the nineteenth century" (Timothy Healy, *Letters and Leaders of My Day,* 1:137). Parnell's arrest was followed by a winter of such violent agitation that Gladsone was forced to release him (the "Kilmainham Pact" of April 1882). There followed within four days the assassination of Lord Frederick Cavendish at Phoenix Park. The political situation was thus transformed beyond anything the Bessborough *Report* could have envisaged.

It was felt by some, however, even before the Land Act of 1881 was passed, that its effectiveness in pacifying Ireland might be short-lived and that moreover it contained the seeds of the eventual destruction of the landlord system. Cf. the O'Conor Don: "I fear that any Act based merely or mainly on proposals to modify the conditions under which the occupier is brought into relation with the owner, will be only like the Act of 1870, a mere temporary expedient, fit for a transition period, but containing within itself the seeds of failure as a permanent settlement. Another slice, and a very large slice of what is now recognized as the legal property of the owner, will be taken away without satisfying the occupiers, and above all without establishing any just principles on which this transference of property should take place" (Bessborough *Report,* p. 38).

The O'Conor Don thought any judicial setting of rents would be the signal for another round of "new and most formidable agitation" (ibid., p. 39).

liament has had ample revenge. Debates on the bill occupied 58 sittings; 14,886 speeches were delivered, 6,315 of them by Irish members; nearly 2,000 points of order had to be raised by the Speaker or committee chairman; the House of Lords made 93 separate amendments in the final bill, which the Commons had to consider. Morley tells us that few British members understood it and none mastered it. None cared about it.

Certainly the Land Act of 1881 lacks the elegant clarity and simplicity of the Land Act of 1870. That measure assumed that defects in land law restrained economic development, and then proceeded to frame a simple direct remedy for the defects. The fault lay in the assumption, not in the legislation. The Land Act of 1881 reflected no principle, no hypothesis, and thus there was no shaping of legislation to correct a situation or fill a need. There was no policy framed, only demands granted—and hastily.

Part I of the act sets out ordinary conditions of tenancy. Section 1 grants the tenant the right to sell his tenancy for the best price he can get. This is subject to certain conditions: the sale must be to one person only; the landlord must be notified; the landlord may purchase the holding either at an agreed or at a court-determined price; the landlord can refuse to accept the new tenant on reasonable grounds, reasonableness to be decided by the courts; the landlord is to receive from the purchase money any arrears or other debt due him; and there are various other qualifications concerning the circumstances of the sale. Naturally, a tenant who avails himself of free sale is not entitled at the same time to compensation for improvements or disturbance, nor is a tenant who has received such compensation entitled to avail himself of the right of free sale. These two compensations were introduced in the 1870 act as equivalents to the right of free sale. Yet the 1881 act does not supersede the 1870 act; in fact, it liberalizes the compensation benefits conferred. Thus a tenant who gives up his holding may claim under the (amended) 1870 act or exercise his right of sale under the 1881 act or, if he is from Ulster, may sell according to that usage or custom. None of this is difficult to understand, but it does not make for a tidy piece of legislation.

Section 2 of Part I prohibits subdividing and subletting; and Section 3 deals with the devolution of tenancies by will or in the event of intestacy.

In Section 4 the bill makes a circuitous approach to the question of rent. It outlines four courses of action open to a tenant who is faced with an increase in rent: if he accepts the increase, he acquires statutory tenure (defined later in the act); if he refuses, he can sell his tenancy, but he is entitled to receive from the landlord compensation for the amount by which the rent increase is deemed by the court to have diminished his selling price; or, if he chooses not to sell the tenancy, he can claim compensation under the (amended) 1870 act; but, finally, he need neither accept nor reject the rent increase but can apply to a court to have the rent fixed.

In Section 5 the incidents of tenancy under the statutory term are defined. A tenant so holding has his rent fixed for the term and cannot be evicted from his holding as long as he observes certain specified conditions: he must pay his rent on time; must not commit persistent waste by dilapidation of buildings or deterioration of the soil; must not subdivide or sublet without permission; shall not vest the tenancy in an assignee in bankruptcy. To the landlord are reserved certain rights: taking minerals; quarrying; taking timber and turf; making roads, drains, fences; passage to the seashore; viewing and examining; various hunting, shooting, fishing, and game rights. The landlord is granted the right to increase rent in consequence of any capital outlay on his part, but the capital outlay and the rent increase are both subject to agreement with the tenant.

Part II of the act outlines the role of court intervention. The tenant or the landlord or both together have the right to apply to the court to fix a fair rent for the holding. This rent would stand for fifteen years, during which time the tenant was fully protected in his holding as outlined in Section 5 of the act. The only glimmer of a definition of fair rent are two conditions that limit the court's discretion. The first is contained in a celebrated clause due to T. M. Healy: "No rent shall be allowed or made payable in any proceedings under this Act in respect of improvements made by the tenant or his predecessors in title, and for which, in the opinion of the court, the tenant or his predecessors in title shall not have been paid or otherwise compensated by the landlord or his predecessors in title." The second provides that the amount of money paid for the tenancy shall not be a ground for increasing (or decreasing) the rent.

Part III outlines two new kinds of tenancy to which the Act of 1881 does not apply: judicial leases for thirty-one years or more and a fixed tenancy paying a fee-farm rent. Existing leases are exempt from the working of the act, although the court is empowered to void any lease that contains terms unfair or unreasonable to the tenant which the landlord procured by threat of eviction or other undue influence.

Finally, the act contains clauses providing funds for land purchase by tenants; providing loans for reclamation, drainage, building laborers' cottages, or any other agricultural improvement; providing funds for the assistance of groups of emigrants.

The reader who persevered through all sixty-two clauses of the Land Act of 1881 would be justified in envisioning a country with a bewildering variety of tenures and customs and practices. Some tenants might be planning to purchase their holdings by applying for loans. Some tenants might be selling—to other tenants or to their landlords. Possibly, these persons would then apply for funds to assist them in emigrating. Or they might be seeking compensation for improvement and disturbance. Others might remain as they were before the act, perhaps seeking loans for agricultural improvements, or working out agreements for landlords to make the improvements. Leaseholders would be unaffected by the act, except those who sought to have old leases revoked on the ground of unfair landlord pressure. Some tenants might be facing demands for increased rent, to which a variety of responses might be made. Some might try to convert to the newly established judicial or fixed tenures. Some might join the landlord in submitting the rent to arbitration. Some might ask the court to fix a fair rent for the statutory term of fifteen years (or register with the court a rent fixed by agreement with the landlord).

Any and all of these actions were possible under the Land Act of 1881. But only the last mattered. It would not be much of an exaggeration to say that all the provisions except the rent-setting provisions were a dead letter: to the extent that it was operative, the Land Act of 1881 was simply a rent control act.* This was the strategy for meeting

* This is abundantly clear from the first annual reports of the Irish Land Commission, and subsequent reports only reinforce it. Cf. also the testimony of John Edward Vernon, one of the commissioners, before the Cairns Commission in April 1882 (Lord Tyrone is questioner):

"4280. [The arrangement] as to purchase, you say that is not working? —That is not working.

"4281. Is the provision with regard to emigration working?—No.

"4282. As to reclamation of waste land, is there anything being done under that?—No.

"4283. We have had, of course, evidence as to the arrears showing that that clause does not work?—The amount advanced altogether is small."

the altered economic situation that Ireland faced after the downturn. The courts were to apportion the diminished agricultural income between landlord and tenant in some completely unspecified way, governed by no principles or criteria. How this would contribute to the readjustment of the economy in the new situation and how it would strengthen Ireland's competitive position—to these questions there is not the hint of an answer. It is of this bill that Morley writes, "Many will be disposed to give it the highest place among Mr. Gladstone's achievements as lawmaker." [19]

The Land Act of 1881 was passed on August 22. By October 1 the forms to transact business were ready, and on October 20 the first sitting of the court commenced. Tenant applications were dated as of August 22, so that all rent reductions would be retroactive. The termination of the first sitting of the court was announced for November 12. Applications from tenants poured in at the rate of several thousand a day; on November 12 they amounted to 12,000. "I believe we are only at the beginning of it," a witness told the Cairns Commission in 1882. "I believe that more than three-fourths of the yearly tenants in Ireland will serve notice to have their rents fixed, or, indeed, a great deal more than three-fourths; it costs them little or nothing to risk it. They have only to pay a guinea for the solicitor; they have not to pay a valuator, and it is worth their while, for the sake of getting a reduction for 15 years, to chance their guinea, and I believe they will all go into court." [20]

Why indeed would a tenant not go into court? He had to make no case, meet no criterion, prepare no bill of particu-

---

Statistics on voiding leases and construction of laborers' cottages are given in the annual reports of the Irish Land Commission; very little was done.

lars, make no list of his improvements. He had merely to ask a neighbor, perhaps the schoolmaster, to testify that his rent ought to be lower, and it was lowered. Old rents, low rents, rack rents; improved farms, unimproved farms; Ulster, Connaught, Leinster, and Munster—rents were everywhere lowered. Nothing could be better established than the Land Commission's complete lack of rationale for the wholesale lowering of rents. The three Land Commissioners testified in turn before the First Cairns Commission to this effect.

Lord Salisbury asked Justice O'Hagan, the chairman of the Land Commission of the First Cairns Commission:

4007. When the Sub-Commissioners [i.e., the rent-setting tribunals] were appointed, was there any kind of communication from you to them as to the principles on which you would wish to administer the power delegated to them?—Not the least.

4008. None whatever?—None whatever. We thought it would be very wrong to say anything of this kind to them considering that we were the judges of appeal.

4026. You have to cut the cake into two morsels, but there is no principle whatever upon which to decide what those morsels shall be?—Except this, that the valuer who has been accustomed to value land knows, just as a person who values any other commodity knows, that the land would be dear at one price and cheap at another.

4027. That introduces the fatal element of competition? —To a certain extent there must be the element of competition, but it is not an extreme competition.

By extreme competition Justice O'Hagan meant what we would call competition. Not only was there "not the least" of principles to guide the subcommissioners in setting rent, but tenants were not even required to furnish a list of claimed improvements. Here is Lord Tyrone of the Cairns Commission questioning Edward F. Litton, Q.C., another of the land commissioners:

3209. Is any course taken, or do you think any course would be desirable without pleadings, to inform the landlord, as he is in the position of defendant in all these cases, what the case of the tenant will be with regard to his claim as to improvements?—No; my colleagues and I considered that question very carefully, and having regard to the aspects of it on both sides, we came to the conclusion that the course we adopted was the wiser course of the two.

3210. What was the course you adopted?—The course of not requiring particulars to be stated.

3211. What led you to adopt that course?—That I do not think I can answer; at least I must respectfully decline to answer, because to do so would be to enter into the reasons which influenced the exercise of the discretion vested in us by Act of Parliament.

But his Lordship drove the point home.

3251. We understood that, in the first instance, in the instructions and forms which you sent down to the Sub-Commissioners, you require them to state, as part of their findings, the value they put upon the tenants' improvements and interests?—Yes, that is so.

3252. That is no longer part of the information they are required to give, is it?—There was a change made, and from that time to the present that information has not been insisted upon. It is proposed to get that information, as far as possible, in future returns again. There are great difficulties in the way, but we intend to try to do it so far as we can in the future.

3253. I suppose I may infer from that, that you think there would be very considerable advantage, if it can be done, in obtaining that information?—I am doubtful about that. We do it rather to show that we are anxious to meet the views of persons who place a value upon it. We think that it will not lead to any very practical results of a satisfactory character, or, at all events, that it may not. First of all, we do not think that we can get accurate information in all cases; in the second place we think it is extremely hard to put a money value upon them and then to fix a reasonable relation between the money value and the rent.

3254. But without at all disputing what you suggest now, namely that it would be very difficult to do it, is it not one of the difficulties that the tribunal has really to cope with and to meet?—Yes; and it would be a matter of absolute propriety if the difficulties of the tribunal in fixing a fair rent were defined and could be reduced to a mathematical or arithmetical calculation.

3255. But, is it not a matter which the tribunal ought to have in their own mind before they come to a decision? —Yes, they ought.

The third member of the Land Commission, John Vernon, testified to the same effect: it was impossible to enunciate principles of rent settlement, and it was undesirable to describe and define improvements.[21]

It was a miserable performance altogether. The subcommissioners were sent forth to set fair rents for Ireland; fair rent was undefined, except that the competitive level was not to be an element in the definition, and no rent was to be paid on account of tenant improvements, which were expressly not required to be listed. The commissioners refused to be drawn on why improvements need not be listed. The most the Cairns Commission could extract was the admission from Justice O'Hagan that "great discontent and quarreling" might arise.[22]

It is hard to avoid the conclusion that it was the mission of the courts to lower rents in order to prevent tenant income from falling "too much": "too much" to be defined as that amount which would induce the tenants to continue agitation. The courts were to do this with no explanations offered, and landlords were to be presented with a fait accompli.

There was not much landlords could do. Costs weighed heavily on them. Solicitors' and valuers' fees had to be paid during long court delays. In some places valuers were afraid to appear on the landlord side.[23] It might cost the landlord more to contest or appeal than the property was worth, and small landlords were under especially great financial pressure to settle out of court.

Thus the Land Act of 1881 granted the Irish tenant the three F's: a fair rent, for which there was no definition; a fixed tenure, which involved no great change; and free sale, by which, although landlords' income was fixed by court, tenants' property could be valued on the open market, so that for any property so sold the new tenant would be paying a competition rent. By this act a drastic decline in tenant income was to be avoided—tenants' incomes were increased by the amount of the rent reduction. What of the secondary effects? Incentives to readjust the economy in the face of new international conditions were to some extent paralyzed.

There is no need to take too seriously landlord contentions that everybody rushed to court and neglected his farming, but if tenants could increase income more by litigation than by changing agricultural techniques, they would certainly do so. If valuers were swayed by appearances, a premium was even put upon worse farming, and consequent dilapidation. "They calculate on getting the reduction, and put an exaggerated value on what it is going to do for them," a land agent told the Cairns Commission. "They think if they get a reduction, that reduction is going to make gentlemen of them, but in comparison with what the increased produce would be if they minded their farms properly, it is a mere nothing . . . the Irish tenants think the rent is everything. They do not consider that an extra barrel of corn to the acre would be worth more than any double reduction of rent that they can get, and it rests with themselves if they properly cultivated their land . . ." "They look to some political machinery or result to give them that which should come from their own industry?" asked Lord Tyrone. "Yes" was the reply.[24]

Not alone from their own industry, but from intelligent economic policy, too. But with the tenants of Ireland crowding into court, no one was thinking about agricultural education, credit and marketing programs, improved cropping, selective breeding, and, in general, ways of assisting tenants to adjust to changed economic conditions. No one was thinking what could be done to help the tenants in the West who could barely live on their land if they held it rent-free.

However, the Land Act of 1881 did not come about by mistake. "The immediate necessity for Mr. Gladstone's land bill was a condition of things in Ireland which bordered on social anarchy. This was largely, if not entirely, the deliberately planned work of the Land League . . . [The Land

Act was] a concession to the tenants so as to detach them from the League." The trap was laid and sprung: Parliament passed in the Land Act of 1881 "a legislative sentence of death by slow processes against Irish landlordism." [25]

7.
Rent and Income in the 1880's

*All my life I have been for the underdog.
Why, I was even for the English in the
Boer War.*

John A. Kaposey

When agricultural incomes are falling, the way the burden is shared between landlords and tenants will depend on the elasticities of supply and demand for land. These will vary according to available alternative uses of land and labor. It is not implausible to consider the supply of agricultural land very inelastic; its alternative uses are either as demesne land or as industrial land, and these do not seem pressing alternatives for the large amounts of agricultural land available. The demand elasticity for rental land will depend on employment opportunities elsewhere in the economy. The elasticity of demand for land was likely to have been much greater for England than for Ireland in the 1880's.

These simple expectations are borne out by the course of English agriculture in the 1880's. As agricultural prices (mainly in tillage) fell, farmers' incomes fell. Unable to pay rents at the old level, farmers left the land in large numbers for towns and cities. Faced with the prospect of untenanted lands, owners lowered their rents drastically and suffered severe losses.

In Ireland one would expect landlords to bear less of the

burden of the agricultural price fall, because the elasticity of demand for land was probably much less than in England. But the Irish tenants, faced with a potential fall in incomes that were already extremely low, simply refused to accept the market solution. As in England, the market situation began to lower their incomes and made them unable to pay the old level of rents. They had no place to go; hence they could exert no pressure on landlords to lower rents. So they went on strike. They attempted to maintain their previous income level by expropriation of landlords. They simply refused to pay rents at the old level. The landlord was practically powerless to evict them, and even if he did, he would be unable to relet the lands. The magnificent organization that Davitt had wrought in the Land League paralyzed market forces and left landlord and tenant confronting one another as sort of bilateral monopolists. Economic considerations alone would certainly not determine where rent would settle in a situation like this. This was Ireland's predicament when the Land Commission came on the scene and began to reduce rents in 1881.

It is obvious that rent strikes can be organized whether incomes are falling or not. Some people felt that the no-rent agitation was unjustified by income declines. Lord Salisbury, for example, viewed the movement as "a wholesale system of fraudulent bankruptcy,"[1] whose primary objective was to banish the landlords without compensation. (This view reinforces Lord Salisbury's claim to be, simultaneously, the most acute and the most wrong-headed English statesman of the nineteenth century.) The origin of the rent strike is clearly in the period of great economic distress of the late 1870's, and its renewal in 1886 coincided with another drastic income decline, rent strikes apparently being easier to organize among people who have not got any money. Of course, industrial workers will not strike in depression: they will be unable to achieve their demands and would merely drive employers to bankruptcy. But this bankruptcy was precisely what the Land League wanted to effect: the rent agitation was to be a means ultimately to political independence.

The economic consequences of the rent reductions in Ireland in the 1880's clearly must be seen in the context of declining incomes. In this chapter we shall present estimates of Irish agricultural income for 1876, 1881, and 1886, and set against them the estimates of rental of agricultural land for the same dates. We shall be able to calculate the ratio of rent to income before and after rent control and say something about the course of tenant and landlord income in the 1880's.

The general course of the Irish agrarian economy in the 1880's is clear from literary sources. The peak of the mid-1870's was followed by the disastrous seasons of 1877, 1878, and 1879. Then there occurred a leveling off in 1880 or 1881, and a partial recovery for 1882, 1883, and 1884. But in 1885 and 1886 depression struck again. To grasp the quantitative impact of these developments, it is necessary to have a measure of income in Irish agriculture for the peak year (1876), for the year just after the downturn (1881), and for the year of renewed decline (1886).

The first measure of the value of Irish agricultural output was made for 1908 by the Department of Agriculture and Technical Instruction.[2] The department supplemented the data available from the annual agricultural statistics with special inquiries and reports on particular points from its county instructors and other experts on its staff. Without these supplementary studies it would be impossible to form a reliable estimate of the value of Irish agricultural output, but using the information contained in them it is possible to make the desired estimates. Strictly speaking, the estimates measure, for 1876, 1881, and 1886, gross value added in Irish agriculture, in current pounds. To get from gross value added to income, deductions would have to be made for certain taxes and depreciation and for imported seeds and fertilizers. A detailed description of the derivation of the estimates is given in Appendix B.

Table 14 shows the gross value added in Irish agriculture

Table 14.   Gross Value Added in Irish Agriculture in Current Prices, 1876, 1881, 1886 (£000)

Sector	1876	1881	1886
Crop			
Wheat	929	958	287
Oats	2,249	1,746	1,261
Barley	1,222	923	561
Flax	1,737	1,564	1,234
Potatoes	5,090	3,605	2,241
Hay	685	598	505
Other	627	495	320
Subtotal	12,539	9,889	6,409
Livestock			
Cattle	9,747	9,675	6,999
Butter	7,963	5,841	4,631
Milk	3,513	3,450	3,293
Pigs	8,523	6,286	5,972
Sheep	2,424	1,385	1,254
Wool	927	552	493
Eggs	2,068	1,772	1,594
Other	1,851	1,524	1,276
Subtotal	37,016	30,485	25,512
Total	49,555	40,374	31,921

NOTE: For a detailed description of the derivation of the table, see Appendix B.

for the years measured. (It will be less awkward to say "value of output" or "income" instead of "gross value added," always bearing in mind that their value differs slightly from what has in fact been estimated.) At the peak of its nineteenth-century development, then, the value of the agricultural output of Ireland stood at £49.5 million. The livestock sector contributed £37 million and the crop sector only £12.5 million. This shows, incidentally, how far the economy had gone in the shift from tillage to livestock, which was earlier identified as the main trend of the post-Famine period. By 1881, a date that excludes some of the temporary effects of the downturn of the late 1870's, the value of agricultural output had fallen to £40.4 million, or by 19 percent. Crops had fallen by 21 percent, the livestock sector by 18 percent. But a finer breakdown is necessary to see what had happened. The potato crop fell by 29 percent in value; crops other than potatoes only by 16 percent. Dry cattle, the single most important livestock product, did not really decline at all, by less than 1 percent. It was in butter and pig production that the decline occurred.

In 1886 the value of output fell again, to £31.9 million, or 21 percent below its 1881 level (and down to 64 percent of the 1876 level). Crops were down to 65 percent of their 1881 value; the other crops fell by about the same as potatoes this time. Livestock values were 84 percent of their 1881 level, but dry cattle fell by much more than other livestock products, the value of dry cattle output falling by 28 percent. Butter fell sharply again in value, but other livestock products registered only mild declines, pig production, for example, decreased only 5 percent.

Over the decade 1876–1886, the value of Irish agricultural output declined by 36 percent. The value of crops fell by half, the value of livestock products by a little less than a third. Potato, butter, and pig production fell most in value in the early stage; potatoes, other crops, cattle, and butter fell most in the second stage; thus potatoes and butter, along with other tillage crops, were the most spectacular victims of the debacle.

There are important implications in these figures for the history of Irish agriculture, which we cannot pursue here. The crisis of the 1880's for English and continental agriculture was a crisis in tillage crops. It was for Ireland, too, but only for that small part of the economy that had not yet moved out of tillage. The collapse of potato production, in price and quantity, provides another important chapter in the history of that plant in Ireland. For the rest, Ireland apparently was experiencing declines in just those branches of agriculture that were the best solution for European agriculture: the "breakfast table foods"—butter, bacon, and eggs. The readjustment of agriculture to changing conditions was not, however, the primary concern of the Irish farmer, and it is to that concern that we must now turn.

The level of rents in Ireland reached its peak in 1880. The best estimate of rent in that year was £12.776 million, or 28 percent above Griffith's valuation (see Chapter 3 above). The increase in rent between 1876 and 1880 was really a nominal increase and cannot reflect rents actually paid. Between these years abatements were being granted; in any case, rents were being withheld. But expert testimony insisted that rental contracts in 1880 amounted to more than they had in 1876: Ball Greene testified that the bad seasons of the late 1870's were not taken into account in his estimates. In other words nominal rents did not fall in the late 1870's and the downturn was treated as temporary and reversible.

By some time in the 1890's, rents had fallen back to the

level of Griffith's valuation.[3] Expert opinion put the date variously at 1891, 1894, 1897, or 1898; but the consensus was clear that by some time in the decade rents had fallen sharply enough to bring them down to the level of the valuation. Stamp merely observes that the decline in rents was "very rapid," and draws a smooth curve connecting the peak and assumed trough, but it should be possible to chart the rate of decline more accurately than that. The course of judicial rents is known, and with some assumptions about rents in the uncovered sector of the economy we can form a better idea of the path of decline.

"We all value on different bases," a landlords' valuer blandly told the Cairns Commission in 1882.[4] Even one of the subcommissioners (Thomas Baldwin) testified that it was "a serious matter . . . to let loose upon the country, upon tenants and landlords, the whole of us without any instructions." [5] If the subcommissioners had no explicit idea of a fair rent, on what implicit notions were they acting? The key seems to be the concept of the "live and thrive" rent. From the gross product of the farm, nonrent costs were deducted, and that rent would be set which enabled a tenant to "live and thrive." Landlords' income was a residual. Some such notion, of what an average tenant could pay without lowering appreciably his standard of living, was probably in the minds of the subcommissioners.

Table 15 shows the percentage reductions granted by the various rent-fixing methods for the first fifteen years after passage of the act. Reductions for the first five years are similar, generally below 20 percent and clustering at around 18 or 19 percent. After 1886 a clearly marked difference is evident. Reductions are almost invariably above 20 percent, in many cases above 25 percent. For various reasons, the working of the Land Commission was not instantaneous, and we can consider that the first five years represent the adaptation of rents to the income level achieved and maintained for a while after 1881.

The total number of cases disposed of by the Land Commission in the five years ending August 21, 1886, was 211,-

Table 15. First-Term Rent Reductions Reported by Land Commission (in percents)

Year Ending Aug. 21	Fixed by Land Comm.	Lease-holders Fixed by Land Comm.	Fixed by Civil Bill Courts	Lease-holders Fixed by Civil Bill Courts	Agreements Lodged with Land Comm.
1882	20.5	—	22.0	—	18.7
1883	19.5	—	22.0	—	17.5
1884	18.7	—	20.1	—	15.5
1885	18.1	—	18.6	—	13.7
1886	24.1	—	22.5	—	15.4
1887	31.3	—	28.1	—	17.4
1888	28.3	29.6	27.8	33.1	22.4
1889	22.7	25.8	26.1	27.4	20.5
1890	21.2	23.5	24.9	25.7	19.9
1891	21.8	23.1	24.1	25.4	20.1
Aug. 22, 1891 to Mar. 31, 1893	23.0	21.9	24.5	26.0	18.6
Year ending Mar. 31, 1894	22.5	21.3	27.0	27.8	18.8
1895	23.7	23.0	26.5	28.1	17.9
1896	25.6	24.3	24.5	31.0	17.3

SOURCE: Compiled from the *Annual Reports* of the Irish Land Commission.

980. This includes 35,053 dismissed or withdrawn, so that 176,927 rents were fixed. This means that over half of those eligible for rent reduction in fact applied, but nothing like half the total value of Irish rents was covered. The reduction of the total rental dealt with was 18 percent, from £3.2 million to £2.6 million.

What can we say about rents in the rest of the economy?

According to the 1881 census, there were 499,108 agricultural holders in Ireland. An estimated 150,000 leaseholders were exempt from the act, as were holders of pasture and town parks (residential districts). Landlords reduced rents voluntarily in all of these categories, according to one of the subcommissioners who testified before the Cowper Commission in 1886.[6] One witness estimated that as many as 50,000 leaseholders may have been affected,[7] but, considering the hue and cry among leaseholders in 1886, this number seems excessive. In view of price movements, the inclusion of leaseholders and pasture tenants probably came to be important after, or at the very end of, the period we are now considering. The best guess would seem to be that, although there was some voluntary rent reduction outside the act, it was moderate in amount and extent, and the decrease in agricultural rents over the whole island from 1881 to 1886 probably amounted to no more than 10 percent: from the peak level of £12.776 million in 1881 to £11.498 million after five years' operation of the act.

In 1886 it became apparent that a serious new economic situation had developed. There was a fresh fall in prices, possibly induced by decreased demand due to depression in England, and now the dry cattle industry began for the first time to feel the blows. There spread over Ireland the conviction that the downturn of the late 1870's was not a temporary phenomenon resulting from bad seasons but a harbinger of a new order, and the prosperous days of 1876 would never return again.

The response of the rent commissioners was sharply to increase rent reductions (see Table 15). But the early comers now complained that their rents deserved to be renegotiated, and leaseholders and pasture holders now clamored to be admitted to the benefits of the 1881 act. On

September 29, 1886, the Cowper Commission was appointed to inquire into the workings of the existing act, and at another important juncture in Irish history we can hear the voices of more than 300 contemporary witnesses representing every county in Ireland: commissioners, landlords, agents, tenants, experts, officials, and clergymen.

For our present purposes, it is the Cowper Commission's recommendations on judicial rents that are relevant. The majority report, signed by three of the five commission members, urged that the duration of first-term rents be reduced from fifteen to five years and that rents be renegotiated on the sole ground of price changes. The *Report* also supported the inclusion of leaseholders in the act and recommended changes that would admit some holders of pasture and town parks. The result of all the discussion was the Land Act of 1887, which received royal assent on August 23, 1887, faithful to the spirit of the Cowper Commission *Report*. Leaseholders were permitted to apply for rent reductions, and 25,521 did so within the year. Although the 1887 Act kept up a fiction of not tampering with judicial rents, all rents fixed before 1886 were in fact lowered. This was done in the following way: each year (beginning December 18, 1888) the Land Commission issued an order for additional rent reductions for tenants whose rents had been fixed in the years 1881–1885. The abatements were based on price movements and differed for each Poor Law union. Thus, in 1888, a tenant in Abbeyleix Poor Law Union whose rent had been reduced in 1881 received for 1888 a further abatement of 5¾ percent; a tenant there whose rent had been reduced in 1882 got a 6½ percent abatement for 1888; in 1883 a 7 percent abatement; in 1884 a 9½ percent abatement; but an Abbeyleix tenant whose rent had been set in 1885 received no further abatements for 1888. If Abbeyleix tenants had received anything like average reductions in 1881–1885, then without the new law they would have been paying in 1888 from 18–24 percent below their old (pre-fixed) rents. The result of the new legislation would have been to lower these rents further by between 5¾ and 9½ percent.

The leaseholders who flooded the courts in 1888 received rent reductions of 29.6 percent from the Land Commission, 33.1 percent from the Civil Bill Courts (Table 15). It was in the years after 1886 that voluntary rent reductions must have been important.

Thus, after 1886, the inclusion of leaseholders and the abatements on earlier judicial rents combined to drive the rent level down toward the Griffith valuation. The year in which it reached that level will be a matter of conjecture, but there is general agreement that it did fall that low. It may have taken five years, possibly more, for rents to respond to the new downturn in 1886. My own preference is for the earlier date, but in any case by sometime in the early 1890's rents must have fallen by 28 percent from their 1881 level (which was, as we recall, 28 percent above the Griffith valuation). They would have amounted to £9,198,-720.

Did the 1881 act and its successors lower rents more than they would otherwise have fallen? After all, if product prices fall, rents will fall, and if the supply of agricultural land is inelastic, landlords will have to bear the brunt. I have suggested that, if the demand for rental land is inelastic, then compared with a country with more elastic demand —as England may well have been—the Irish tenant would be worse off than his counterpart. But this hardly establishes anything very definite. The acts did lower rents with promptness and certainty, and it can be argued that this is the negligible matter. Moreover, to the extent that rents had previously been below competitive values (as I have argued), the rent-setting acts signaled a permanent ceiling on landlords' shares. For no one really believed that (land-lord) rents would be allowed to rise if conditions improved. Indeed the free sale provisions insured that any increases in land values in the future would become the property of tenants if they chose to realize them. The lowering of rents by legislation thus had a significance for the future, inde-pendent of the answer we give to the question of whether rents would have fallen as much "by themselves."

Rents, prices, incomes, all were falling in the 1880's. Without some notion of their relative movements, we are unable to interpret what was happening. Table 16 sets out

Table 16. Ratio of Rent to Total Agricultural Income, before and after Rent Reductions

Year	Rent	Agricultural Income	Ratio (percent)
1876	12,482,000	49,554,000	25+
1881 before reduction	12,776,000		31.6
		40,374,000	
1881 after reduction	11,498,000		28.5
1886 before reduction	11,498,000		36.0
		31,921,000	
1886 after reduction	9,198,720		28.8

the estimates of agricultural income for 1876, 1881, and 1896. Against them are set out the rent for 1876, for 1881 without reductions, for 1881 after reductions, for 1886 without further reductions, for 1886 with further reduc-tions. Then the ratio of rent to agricultural income may be readily calculated.

The story told by Table 16 goes something like this. In 1876 at the peak of prosperity, the ratio of rent to income was 25 percent. Because 1876 was alike a peak year for yields and prices, and income was abnormally high, this 25 percent may be too low to be taken as normal. Rents continued to rise until 1881, but income had plummeted. It is probably correct to be skeptical about the amount of the rise, but it corresponds to the best contemporary estimates. Then if those 1881 rents had been paid out of the 1881 income, the ratio of rent to income would have risen to 31.6 percent. But they were not paid. The Land Act of 1881 was passed, and, allowing some time for its effects to work out, rents fell by 10 percent. If we assume the income level steady at its 1881 figure, the rent/income ratio would be lowered back down to 28.5 percent, something much nearer its 1876 level. Then, in 1886, income fell again. Had rents continued without fresh reductions, the rent/income ratio would have shot up to 36 percent. But further reductions were forthcoming and in an amount that tended to reestablish the old rent/income ratio. After the new reductions had worked themselves through the economy, the relation of rent to the 1886 income level fell back to 28.8 percent.

The probable course of rents and income, then, was such that the ratio of rent to income tended to remain fairly stable at a few points above the 1876 level. With some notion of movements in the price level, we can get an idea of the absolute magnitudes involved. The only available price index for Ireland for this period is the Statist-Sauerbeck index of general (wholesale) prices.[8] Putting 1876 = 100, the Sauerbeck index gives 1881 as 89 and 1886 as 73. Thus the fall in the wholesale price index is estimated to be 11 percent from 1876 to 1881, and 27 percent from 1876–1886, or almost exactly the percentage declines in rents in these two periods.

While it would be nice to believe that the Sauerbeck index was calculated with a precision so sharp as to render it correct even to two decimal places, perhaps the most that can be said is that the rent decline and price level decline were sufficiently close so that rents were approximately maintained in real terms. While it would not be strictly correct to identify value added in agriculture minus rents as the income of the tenants,[9] if we are willing to make the identification, then it is apparent that tenant income was also fairly well maintained in real terms, declining from £37 million in 1876 to £33 million in 1881 (in constant pounds) and remaining at £33 million (in constant pounds) in 1886.

While it might appear that in the course of the decade nothing much had changed in real terms—that prices, and landlord and tenant income all declined together in similar proportions—in fact, a very great change had been wrought: the great bulk of tenants' fixed costs (rent) had been lowered pari passu with the price level, but the great bulk of landlords' fixed costs remained fixed and payable in 1876 pounds. And landlords fixed costs were formidable.

It is a commonplace that falling price levels are disastrous for agricultural interests. Farmers are debtors. Falling prices mean mortgages foreclosed, leases thrown up, farms abandoned. In Ireland in the 1880's, the landlord class bore the brunt of the blows. Rents, traditionally lagging and sticky, were rapidly readjusted to the falling price level under the influence of the Land Acts. The landlords were left to be squeezed between their inflexible costs and their declining rent rolls.

"There is scarcely an estate in Ireland that has not more or less of encumbrance, some very heavy and some comparatively light; but I think, generally speaking, a great number of estates in Ireland are encumbered," a Carlow magistrate told the Cairns Commission.[10] Another witness estimated that commonly the landlords' margin amounted to 25 percent of the total rent.[11] If this were true, and other testimony suggests that it may well be, then a 25 percent rent reduction would sweep away the landlords' profit altogether.

The nature and extent of these charges varied greatly from estate to estate. There were various forms of family settlement. In Ireland the fee simple was sometimes divided among the children like personal property, but in the general case the land went to the eldest, and he had to pay the charges of the younger children. There would also have been widows', and perhaps other, jointures. In English settlements very often there was a provision that only a specified amount of the estate could be so charged, but this was not so in Ireland.

The mortgage burdens on Irish land were numerous. Not only were mortgages taken out in the usual way—English and Scottish insurance companies were the principal lenders —but, owing to a difference between English and Irish law, all unpaid judgments against landowners could be registered as mortgages.[12] Any creditor of a person owning land in Ireland had only to swear an affidavit that he had an unsatisfied judgment and the judgment was registered as a mortgage.

Much of Irish land was subject to head rents. Murrough O'Brien, who was Chief Agent in the Land Commissioners Court and superintended all land purchase under the 1881 act, estimated that a third of Ireland was subject to head rents.[13] There were many varieties of head rents: the property of the Irish Church had largely consisted of the ownership of head rents, and after disestablishment these rents became payable to the Church Temporalities Commission; Trinity College continued to hold its property that way; and many private individuals owned head rents, arising from very old renewable leases. (There were also quit rents payable to the Crown.) In these cases the landlord received rent from his tenants and paid a fixed sum to the owner of the head rent. Head rents might be large or small, relative to the value of the property. There was a market in head rents, although some were part of property settlements and thus not salable, the holder of the head rent having only a limited interest in it.

In addition to family charges, mortgages, head rents, and quit rents, landlords were also burdened with tithe rent charges. The tithe rent charge of the late Irish Church was vested in the Church Temporalities Act at the disestablishment. By 1881 some of it had been redeemed for cash, some converted to annuities, some remained outstanding and was payable to the Land Commission, which superseded the Church Temporalities Commission. Although the amount of tithe rent charge was not great, amounting to £410,000 per annum in 1869 and was payable by 36,000 persons, it was heavier in some localities than in others.

A few specific examples will illustrate the plight of encumbered landlords. The Earl of Belmore held an estate in Fermanagh. It was subject to a widow's jointure, some head rents, and tithe rent charge. After these charges and rates and taxes were paid, the earl estimated that he received less than a fifth of the rental. A 25 percent rent reduction would have made it impossible for the earl to meet his charges.[14] A Kerry landlord with a rental of £1,200 a year had a head rent of £100, tithe rent charge of £30, a jointure of £120, taxes and management costs of £400, interest on mortgages of £400, making total charges of £1,050. The rents were reduced by a third by the Land Commission.[15] Captain Newton's estate in Carlow, in the family for generations, produced a total annual rental of £1,668. Of fixed charges there were £67 17s. 11d. in head rents, £75 11s. 8d. in tithe rent charge, £83 11s. 8d. for life insurance premiums connected with loans, £804 15s. in interest on the loans, £100 7s. 8d. in annuities, and about £200 for taxes and agent's fees. The total outgoing amount was £1,374 8s. 11d. or £294 more than the rental. The rental was reduced by 30 percent, leaving less than nothing to Captain Newton.

Not all the landlords in Ireland were in such positions in the 1880's. Some of them may have found ways of decreasing their fixed costs, and not all of them were as encumbered as our examples. But there is ample testimony that many of them, especially the small landlords, faced the disappearance of a large part of their income.

The Irish tenant weathered the storms of the 1880's fairly well. His money income fell greatly, but so did the prices of the things he bought, and so did the value of his contractual obligations. He too had debts, but his real income was reasonably well maintained. It is often said that the Land Act of 1881 gave the tenant something of what he wanted but not his final demand, which was a land purchase program. This is quite wrong; it is borne out neither by the data on land purchase nor by tenant testimony. In fact, the Land Acts of 1881 and 1887 gave the tenants so much that the question arose whether the advantages of land ownership amounted to anything at all. When tenants acquired fixed rent for fifteen years, guaranteed tenure, and the confidence that political pressure would prevent rents from rising at the end of fifteen years, they had little to gain by purchasing their holdings. "I do not mind whom I give the money to," a tenant told the Cowper Commission.[16] When tenants were asked if they wanted to purchase their holdings a typical reply was "Yes, if I could reduce my pay-

ments substantially," or "Well, I would not like to pay from
year to year more than two-thirds of what I pay at the present time." [17] Some tenants still felt (still!) that in the event
of bad seasons or temporary difficulties they would rather
face a landlord, who would be lenient, than a government
notice to pay installments promptly. As owners, tenants
would be liable for rates and taxes; as tenants, they would
see any increases in these borne by the landlord. There is
persuasive evidence that the Land League discouraged tenants from purchasing holdings, in the interest of getting
better terms later, but the importance of such intervention
is hard to evaluate. Only 731 tenants bought their holdings
under the terms of the Land Act of 1881 (25 percent down,
the balance repayable at 5 percent for thirty-five years),
and the evidence tends to show that tenants were content
to stand pat unless their annual repayments plus interest
and taxes could be brought below their judicial rents.

The Irish landlord was in a far worse position. His revenue had fallen with the price level but his fixed costs had
not. For some, these fixed costs exceeded revenues. Mortgages were called in "in every direction," [18] and it was impossible to borrow money on the security of Irish land.
Landlords, indeed, had nowhere to turn. In 1888 the Irish
Landowners' Convention presented a statement to the government begging for relief. They sought state loans to pay
off mortgage and family charges, reduction in tithe rent
charges, reduction in the interest payments on Board of
Works loans, renegotiation of succession duties on estates
whose rents had fallen, rearrangement of the incidence of
the poor rate and other local rates and taxes. But relief was
not forthcoming in this form.

To the heavily encumbered Irish landlord, there was no
alternative but to sell. But to whom? "I cannot conceive of
any person buying an estate in Ireland now," Uniacke

Townshend told the Cairns Commission.[19] No one wanted
an estate with the prospect of rent-fixing ahead: "They will
not buy lawsuits." [20] "Land is absolutely unsaleable," Lord
Leconfield's agent testified.[21] On this there was general
agreement. It will be immediately objected that, if landlords had lowered their prices sufficiently, they would have
found buyers. But the block in the Irish land market after
1881 did not merely reflect landlords' unwillingness to
recognize that land values had declined. There continued to
be a market in untenanted land and land in tenants' possession; there was still profit to be made in Irish land, but
landlords were prevented from realizing it. When Lord
Leconfield's agent said land was unsalable, presumably he
meant that it was unsalable at anything near the value he
felt it could produce. No one wanted to become an Irish
landlord after 1881, except for a presumably very large
premium to cover risks.

"All the landlords have to look to is to the tenants, and
I do not think the tenants will buy," a witness prophesied
to the Cairns Commission in 1882.[22] He was right. The
land market was paralyzed between tenants who wanted to
reduce current payments and landlords who were unwilling
to accept such prices as reduced current payments would
imply. The tenants could hope that their current payments
might be reduced by judicial rent-setting but this was no
way out for landlords. The solution was plain for all to see:
if the government would lend the tenants purchase money
at an interest rate so low, and a repayment term so long,
that they could buy the land for smaller annual repayment
than their current rents, then the landlord could get his
price and the tenant his payment reduction at the same
time. The British taxpayer would cut the Gordian knot by
subsidizing the whole operation. Agricultural income fell in
money terms; the tenant by getting his rent reduced avoided

a decline in his real income; the landlord, on account of his fixed charges, suffered a decline; but in the end the British taxpayer picked up the bill. (To the extent that the landlords were English, the subsidy was being paid by the non-landed classes in England and the landed classes whose estates were in the home island to those English landowners whose estates were in Ireland.) The subsidy provided finally effected an intersection between the tenants' demand curve and the landlords' supply curve.

This is not the place to launch a detailed discussion of Irish land purchase, and only a superficial glance is offered here. The early history of that subject is more full of words than deeds. Only 877 tenants purchased their holdings under the Bright clauses of the Land Act of 1870, only 731 under the Land Act of 1881. But as the effects of the latter act worked themselves out, it became clear to prescient people that the easing of the purchase clause would be the salvation of the landlord class. "Is it not the only hope for landlords who have mortgages on their property that the purchase clauses should be improved?" Lord Tyrone had asked in 1882.[23] The witness agreed. As time passed, this view spread. In 1888 the Irish Landowners' Convention was petitioning to have their fixed costs readjusted; by 1895 the Irish Landowners' Convention affirmed that the ultimate solution to the Irish Land Question lay " 'not in any amendment of the Act of 1881, but rather in promoting the more rapid and effective working of the Land Purchase Acts' . . . the policy indicated in these words [the words are Gerald Balfour's] will command the sympathy and approval of a large proportion of the landlords and tenants of Ireland." [24]

The first important land purchase bill had been passed by the Conservatives during Lord Salisbury's Caretaker Government in 1885. This bill, the Ashbourne Act, received the royal assent on August 14, 1885. The entire purchase price was advanced to the tenant, repayable in an annuity at 4 percent for forty-nine years, but 20 percent of the price had to be deposited by the landlord with the Land Commission as a guarantee of repayment. Once a certain amount had been repaid on the loan, the landlord would receive this 20 percent (with interest at 3 percent). By August 21, 1888, 14,002 applications to purchase had been made under the Ashbourne Act for advances of £5,800,-369.[25] Only £5 million had been provided by the act, so an amending act was passed, granting a further £5 million. This act received the royal assent on December 24, 1888.

The terms of the Ashbourne Act were considerably more favorable to the tenant than the purchase clauses under the 1881 Act. Under the latter he had to raise a quarter of the purchase money himself and could borrow the rest from the government. It was repayable in equal installments of 5 percent for thirty-five years. Under these terms a tenant paying £50 rent, who bought his holding at twenty years' purchase, would be repaying the government and the lender of his down payment at 5 percent £50—to which would have to be added poor rate and county cess, which were estimated on an average at £5.[26] On these assumptions, a tenant would be paying £5 a year more than his rent, and this was not a sufficient inducement to tenants to buy. They apparently preferred the extra £5 a year to the certainty that in thirty-five years they would own their farms outright. Under the terms of Ashbourne Act, on the other hand, the same tenant would be making annual repayments of £40, which, adding the same £5 of poor rate and county cess, would bring him £5 under the original rent. A tenant could not only become owner of his land eventually, but he would be paying for it in annual installments that were less than his rent.

For the first time, land purchase figures appear in the thousands instead of hundreds; in the six years of the Ashburton Act, 16,788 tenants bought their holdings. The number is divided about equally between Ulster and the rest of Ireland. Considering that these were the years of the first Home Rule Bill, the Plan of Campaign, and moreover of pressure by the National League against purchase, this is a good record indeed. There were other factors that kept the number of sales down. From the landlord side, the 20 percent of the purchase price held on deposit was a real bar. If the landlord agreed to accept twenty years' purchase of the rent as his price, his income upon reinvestment would be severely curtailed. The landlords were really gambling that they could get better terms from legislation. Once the possibility of such subsidies arose, landlords did not need to take their losses immediately. Accordingly, landlords were unwilling to sell unless the price was higher than twenty years' purchase, but at such a price it was unprofitable for tenants to buy. Justice O'Hagan and Associate Commissioner O'Shaughnessy both testified before the Cowper Commission to the seriousness of this provision in discouraging purchase. The entanglements of Irish landlords among head rents, middlemen, and annuitants could also present insuperable problems, even when landlord and tenant could agree on a price. If head rents were small, they could be settled on one or two properties, from which the owner of the head rent could collect his revenue and which would stand as his security. If head rents were large and many tenants were involved, it could be a very real problem; unless the Land Commission had some kind of compulsory power to apportion all these charges, satisfactory purchase arrangements were hard to envisage. For all its promise, the Ashbourne Act was not an adequate vehicle to effect land purchase on a really grand scale.

Arthur Balfour himself undertook the next step in land purchase. Instead of improving and amending the Ashbourne Act, which was perhaps a natural step, he decided to strike out in a new direction. L. P. Curtis suggests that Balfour disliked the Ashbourne Act "partly because it was Ashbourne's," a very likely explanation since Balfour feared and disliked Ashbourne.[27] If it was this animus that explains the Land Purchase Act of 1891, it was not a fruitful one.

Under the Land Purchase Act of 1891, which received the royal assent on August 5, 1891, the Land Commission was empowered to advance to the tenants in Guaranteed Land Stock the nominal amount of the purchase price. With this stock the tenant paid the landlord. The stock was issued through the Bank of Ireland, carrying interest at 2¾ percent payable half-yearly and irredeemable for thirty years from August 1891. There were limits on what each county could obtain, and it was estimated that the total sum available for all Ireland would be £30 million. (This would remain a revolving credit.) The holders of the Land Stock could exchange it for consols, thus insuring that the value of the stock could not go below the value of consols. If the price of the holding were equivalent to, or more than, twenty years' purchase (or when the advance did not exceed ¾ of the purchase money), the tenants' repayment terms remained those of the Ashbourne Act: 4 percent for forty-nine years. For a lower price, provision was made for higher payments in the first five years to set up an insurance fund; if not needed for this purpose, the excess moneys collected would go to reduce the amount or duration of the payment subsequently. In addition to these insurance provisions, a Guarantee Fund was established. If tenants' repayments were insufficient, the deficit was to be made up from funds ordinarily made available to Ireland by Parliament, which funds would have to be paid by local taxation. The amount of money available to each county was limited to twenty-five times the share of the county in the Guarantee Fund.

The 1891 Act, larger in scope and not less liberal to both parties in its terms, was not a success. In the four years of the Ashbourne Act ended August 22, 1889, over 19,000 loans had been applied for; in the three years eight months ending March 31, 1895, only 6,686 applications were received under the 1891 Act. Applications dwindled further after that. Although the complexities of the act are frequently blamed for its failure, there are other possible reasons as well. Shortly after the passage of the act, it became known that a general election would take place, and that Mr. Gladstone would make a second attempt at Home Rule. Tenants waited in expectation, or at least hopes, of what they would receive under Home Rule. In the years that followed the collapse of these hopes, and the collapse of the Irish party after the fall of Parnell, it was the landlords' turn to stiffen. Peace was generally restored to the countryside in the 1890's and prices recovered from the levels of the late 1880's. The Land War had spent itself. There was thus less panic selling; it even began to be possible to borrow again on security of Irish land. With the Conservatives safely in power, the landlords began to hope for better terms.

With interest at 2¾ percent on the Land Stock of the 1891 Act, the income to a landlord from twenty years' purchase of a £50 rent would amount only to £27 10s. 10d. Allowing some deduction for management and other expenses, his income loss would amount to a little under 40 percent, at seventeen years' purchase to nearly 50 percent. An encumbered landlord paying 5 percent on his mortgage would be the gainer by such a transaction, but not an unencumbered landlord. Although the 1891 Act was improved somewhat by an 1896 Act abolishing the annoying provisions on county percentages and purchasers' insurance money and guarantees, and providing for decadal reductions in annuities, the number of landlords willing to sell under the existing law (at a price at which tenants were willing to buy) gradually dwindled to a few.

Both political parties were firmly committed to land purchase; after 1885 the tenants' terms were so favorable that they could scarcely afford not to buy; it remained to place the landlords in an analogous position if the large-scale transfer of Irish land were to be effected. It was perfectly clear how this could be done. "If the government and Parliament mean business in this matter," announced the Landowners' Convention, "they must deal with it in a businesslike manner, by a more liberal use of the great asset at their disposal—the credit of the British Exchequer." [28] If the British wanted land purchase, they would have to pay—neither the Irish tenant nor the Irish landlord was willing to suffer an income loss.

The bill that brought this about bears the name of George Wyndham, that romantic quintessential Edwardian figure who succeeded Gerald Balfour as Chief Secretary. The summer after Wyndham's first undistinguished effort at land purchase legislation in 1902, Lindsay Talbot-Crosbie (and others) began to urge a landlord-tenant conference to settle the problem once and for all. The story of the conference is best told by its chairman, Lord Dunraven, and need not concern us here,[29] but the recommendations of the Conference became, except for a few minor details, the basis of Wyndham's Land Act of 1903. For the tenants the Wyndham Act assured that the repayments would stay below the rents; advances were made when the agreed prices were such that the annuity amounted to 10–30 percent below the

second term rents (set after 1896) or 20–40 percent below first term rents. The rate of repayment was reduced to
3.25 percent and the term lengthened to 68.5 years. For
landlords there was a 12 percent cash bonus, in addition
to the price of the holding. All payments were made in
cash, not in stock. Landlords also got the right to sell their
own demesnes to the Estate Commissioners and then repur-
chase them on the same easy terms that tenants were paying—thus, for some, replacing high mortgage rates by a
3.25 percent repayment rate. Total Treasury advances were
limited to £150 million, to be raised by an issue of Guaranteed Stock at 2.75 percent. The inducements to both
parties and the funds required were both large enough to
move the market. At last, neither tenant nor landlord could
afford not to enter the transaction. Under the Wyndham
Act and its successor, passed in 1909 when Augustine Bir-
rell served as an equally decorative Chief Secretary, the
transfer of Irish land to the tenants finally took place. Instead of sales of individual holdings, entire estates changed
hands in one transaction. Such arrangements, possible under the previous acts, had never occurred in any important
quantity before. In 1870, 3 percent of Irish holdings were
tenant occupied, by 1908, 46 percent.[30] The Wyndham Act
made by far the greatest contribution: under the 1870 and
1881 Acts there were only 1,600 sales in fifteen years; the
Ashbourne Act realized about 25,000 sales, the 1891 and
1896 Acts about 35,000 (with some additional sales under
variants of these Acts), and the Wyndham Act over 200,-
000 sales in all—1906–1908 were the peak years when
nearly 100,000 purchased.

As the last act in the history of the Irish Land Question
was being played out, the tragic irrelevance of the drama
was plain to see. Thirty years of land tenure legislation—
and in the West there were still tenants living as they had

in 1870, huddled in a hovel, clothed in rags, on a diet of potatoes, with the great hope of meat once a year, at Christmas. Thirty years of land tenure legislation—and instead of being at the end of the Irish economic problem, a beginning had yet to be made. Under Arthur Balfour it was made. The poor districts of the West were finally singled out for special treatment, and the Congested Districts Board was set up with broad discretionary powers to assist in their development. With the limited funds available, work was pushed ahead in fisheries, cottage industries, and communications: harbors and piers constructed, steamship lines and telegraph subsidized. Loans and grants were made available under the Light Railways Act. A Department of Agricultural and Technical Instruction was set up, and programs for improved livestock breeding and poultry programs began. Animating it all was the restless figure of Horace Plunkett, organizing, inspiring, scheming; serving on the Congested District Board, as vice-president of the Department of Agricultural and Technical Instruction, founding of the Irish Agricultural Organization Society, fathering the cooperative movement in Ireland. It all came, too little and too late, to a hopelessly divided land. "Rathkeale is a Nationalist town—" they told him when he tried to get a cooperative creamery started there—"Nationalist to the backbone—and every pound of butter made in this creamery must be made upon Nationalist principles or it shan't be made at all." [31]

Thirty years of land agitation and Home Rule, which had been an impossible fantasy in 1870, passed the House of Commons in 1892. Thirty years of land agitation and the power of the landlord class was broken forever. The prize was great. So was the cost.

8.
Some Reflections

A most peculiar thing! I had quite for-
gotten the incident, it's so many years
ago. I was driving with my uncle in one
of those old-fashioned high dog-carts. We
were coming back from duck-shooting and
a rabbit ran across the road directly in
front of us. I remember it distinctly now.
My uncle rose from his seat, took a care-
ful aim, and shot the horse through the
head. It was a most surprising incident at
the time.

Denis Johnston

If by the Irish Land Question we mean the problem of reforming the legal institutions governing the tenure of land to prevent their seriously restraining economic progress, then there was no such thing as the Irish Land Question. We must look elsewhere to understand the principal factors in the economic development of nineteenth-century Ireland. But the belief in the Irish Land Question resulted in important legislative acts and had a profound effect on Irish history.

The Ireland that emerges from Connell's pages appears to provide perhaps as good a fit of an economic model—the Ricardian-Malthusian model—to an historical situation as the real world is able to afford. The traces of the outlines of tiny cabins on the bleak sands of the western shores of Ireland are the eloquent embodiment of the notion "margin of cultivation." It cannot be seriously supposed that any change in tenure laws would have provided a flow of capital investment in 1845, and if it had, there remains the Malthusian point that population increase would probably have eaten up the increment.

If pre-Famine Ireland was a case study in Ricardian and Malthusian economics, the Famine and its aftermath were case studies of the application of classical remedies. The decline in population and the emigration and consolidation the classical economists preached all occurred. By important legislative enactments—the Encumbered Estates Acts and the Deasy Act—barriers to the freer movement of capital were removed, and free trade in land was facilitated. The overpopulation spectre had departed and the feudal aspects of the law had been replaced: in the classical scheme, economic growth ought now to take place.

What occurred? In fact, economic growth did take place, partly in the way envisaged. In places where the population had thinned out and farms of moderate size were the rule, progress was marked, although it was probably due as much to changed demand conditions as to the mere change in population. But progress was limited in two ways. First, in important parts of the country the overpopulation problem was not solved; pre-Famine conditions still persisted and population pressed on subsistence in the old way. Secondly, the tenure customs limited the working of the classical mechanisms. We have seen that evictions were rare and rent was sticky in Ireland all through the post-Famine years. There must indeed have been Encumbered Estates landlords who came in and raised rents and did nothing else. But a careful search of the literature has supported those who claim their number was small. More important was the limitation on landlords' investment because of tenants' customary tenure rights. There was profit to be made in Irish agriculture and there was English capital ready to exploit it, but not on terms the Irish tenant would accept. Holdings would have to be rearranged, techniques altered, and there was no place in this scheme for all the Irish tenants to remain on their tiny old family farms. The Irish tenant prevailed, and indeed did much better after the Famine; landlords like Pollock, Talbot Crosbie, and Bence Jones did what they could. How many like them were prevented from investing in Irish land at all?

This is not to say that the laissez-faire policy of the classical economists was the best economic policy for Ireland. If we consider the pre-Famine conditions of the West, it would have been tragically inadequate economically; for all of Ireland it would have been inhuman socially. Laissez-faire was not, however, the only alternative to land legislation. However inadequate laissez-faire would have been as an economic policy, it ought to be said in defense of the classical economists (and their followers) that their analysis and diagnosis of the Irish question were much closer to the truth than alternative theories.

By 1870 an observer could point to the West and say the classical system had been tried and failed. Or to other parts of the country—or, indeed, to the many available statistical series reflecting economic progress—and say the classical system had been tried and succeeded. Certainly, the success of the policy was only partial, whether because of deficiencies in the policy or obstructions in its application; its continuance promised no political advantages, to say the least. Mr. Gladstone turned his hand to tenure legislation.

Perhaps too much has been made of the Land Act of 1870 as a pioneering instance of government interference in property rights. Property rights, after all, do not grow on trees; they are defined by the legal code, and the 1870 act was a change in that code. In a way, the act was in the same laissez-faire tradition as the free-trade-in-land legislation. It assumed that, if the institutional framework provided no restraints on the mobility of factors, investment would be automatically forthcoming.

The act was a reasonably good remedy for the defect in the land law, but since this defect had only a minor effect on economic development (as we have argued), the remedy produced no startling improvement. On the contrary, the effect of the Land Act of 1870 was severely to curtail (landlord) investment in Irish agriculture. The prosperous years of the early 1870's should have been a time for investment and modernization in Irish agriculture. Instead, the Land Act of 1870 signaled the end of landlord investment. The number of agricultural machines of all types eventually declined, though forces other than the Land Act were certainly at work as well; the introduction of modern techniques, especially in dairying, never occurred at all. The economy that faced the subsequent downturn was more ill-prepared than it should have been.

The downturn came with such severity that there was no question of a leisurely initial reexamination of policy. As occasionally happens, when an inadequate policy fails to produce results, it is applied in even stronger doses. The Land Act of 1881 was really less a considered policy than a wholesale income-maintenance program, a relief program, at the expense not of the government but the landlords. Morley and Ensor have viewed the 1881 act as great statesmanship, but it is hard to go along with this view. True, the failure of the 1881 act made land purchase inevitable, but it is hard to attribute greatness to an act whose failure led to an entirely different approach.

The period from 1870 until the early 1890's forms a coherent episode in Irish economic history, during which policy was made on the assumptions of the tenure theory.

Tenants associated themselves with this theory in a way, but what tenants really cared about was their income. Their attacks on rent were not in the service of any theoretical mechanism whereby increased investment would eventually result; they attacked rent because it was a way directly to increase their income in the short run. To them it may have seemed the only way to increase income. Davitt wanted them to attack rent because he foresaw that success in the attack would eventually drive the landlords out of Ireland. He explicitly felt that economic progress would not automatically result; in fact, he looked to land nationalization schemes as the eventual solution. Up to a point, the course of events was a brilliant vindication of Davitt's revolutionary strategy, until in the end it was overwhelmed by the realities of Irish life. But as an economic policy the attack on the "land question" was not successful. The Land Act of 1870 had had small positive effect, some negative effect; nothing else was attempted. In the prosperous years of the period, investment might have been expected, but the 1870 act discouraged it. When the downturn came, there was nothing to do but continue to wrangle over rent in a worse way.

The great success story of the downturn was Denmark, and to a lesser extent, Holland and Switzerland. A modern historian writes that, although "the impact of the trans-Atlantic cereal flood was no less severe . . . all levels of agricultural opinion, from the leaders of the Danish Royal Agricultural Society down to the peasant farmer, saw the crisis coming and were preparing to meet it when it came." [1] The readjustment was a "textbook answer." Between 1871 and 1903 (almost the exact period we are concerned with), butter production trebled, milk more than doubled, pig meat tonnage increased over fourfold. Eventually, one butter cooperative was available to every two parishes and every pig keeper found a producer-owned bacon factory nearby.

There were 370 societies for promoting the production and marketing of eggs.

Could Ireland have done something like this? It is a question that cannot be answered. To some extent readjustments were made: poultry and egg production, for example, increased notably. But what if the energies of the people and the policies of the government had been harnessed together in a direct attempt at economic improvement? At the very least, it was worth a try. One of the obvious difficulties was that the English Liberals could be got to care about Ireland sooner than they could be got to spend; the Tories might be got to spend but not to care. Still, Irish political leverage in this period was considerable. But all the political power of the Irish and of Mr. Gladstone on their behalf was spent on land reform and Home Rule. The tenants' energies went into the same battle. "The primary object [of the Cork Farmers' Club]—the object with which it was established— was with the view of teaching farmers an improved system of agriculture, by giving prizes for roots and for good farming in every way. Afterwards, when it became better known its objects were extended. To protect farmers who were badly treated by their landlords, by mentioning cases at the club, and by bringing public opinion to bear upon them." [2] In view of the modest but very real accomplishments of the Congested District Board, the A.I.O.S., and others, it is legitimate to ask whether this approach might not have shown good results if attempted earlier, with more energy and resources, in a less embittered atmosphere. Certainly, the economic developments after land purchase were not a success. The physical output of Irish agriculture did not rise, and no fundamental changes in Irish agriculture took place. In the century after the Famine, gross physical output rose by about 25 percent or 30 percent—the peak had occurred in about 1909–1910, and this peak was probably not much better than the peak of 1876. (Rural population decreased 58 percent from 1851 to 1951, so that the output per worker rose by about 200 percent. This is low by European standards.) It is ironic to view land purchase as a solution to anything.

The conventional views of the relationship of economic development to the mainstream of Irish political and constitutional history in the nineteenth century need to be revised. Ruthless economic exploitation of the Irish tenant by the English landlord cannot play a starring role.

The mainspring of nineteenth-century Irish Nationalism —not eighteenth-century Nationalism, which is different— may perhaps be found in those earlier developments that made the British decide to maintain Ireland as a fully segregated society. The Penal Laws were a concrete embodiment of this policy. In addition to the usual civil and religious disabilities, they imposed on the Roman Catholic Irish severe restrictions on the ownership of property, the right to bear arms, and the right to education—it was illegal for Catholics to go abroad for education and forbidden to keep public schools in Ireland. Relief and relaxation of these restrictions commenced in the last quarter of the eighteenth century, and there was genuine progress and many important landmarks, of which the Catholic Emancipation of 1829 is the most famous. We shall never know whether by this kind of gradual liberalization Ireland could have been changed to an integrated society, not only in the sense of maintenance of the Union or some form of Home Rule or Devolution, but in the sense that positions of power and prestige in the government and society as a whole would be equally open to both Roman Catholic and Protestant. Cer-

tainly it took a long time before local government was re-
formed and before a Roman Catholic had an important
position in Dublin Castle.

It seems clear that this kind of gradual integration would
have had a better chance of success in a prosperous setting.
The Famine ended that possibility. Nor is the great recovery
afterward a contradiction: the importance of the Famine
may lie less in its immediate effects than in its influence on
the historical imagination of the Irish people. A subjugated
people will probably always blame their rulers for whatever
befalls them, regardless of what the impartial judgment of
historians might be. (And the importance of the Famine in
the historical imagination of those who emigrated can hardly
be overestimated, though one has the suspicion that if the
Yankees in Boston had been more hospitable to the immi-
grants, the English in Ireland might have had an easier time
of it.) Possibly, the Famine and the renewed hard years of
the 1880's made any reconciliation impossible. Still, in
1870, at the beginning of our period, only a handful of people in Ireland were adamantly opposed to it. From that date
on, Irish political history is concerned with the eventual triumph of those who opposed an integrated Ireland. (The
word "integrated" is not out of place: *Sinn Fein* is Gaelic for
Black Nationalism.) To the eventual triumph of separatism land legislation made several contributions: it did not
ameliorate economic conditions, and at a critical time it pre-
empted the field of economic policy; and in the course of
this, its working exacerbated landlord-tenant relations by
focusing on a point of conflict of interests; finally, the greatest contribution of land legislation was that it eventually
resulted in the end of landlordism in Ireland. Once the garri-
son was gone, the island became much less important to the
English, as Algeria would have been to the French had there
been no colonists.

The eventual triumph of Irish separatism depended on many complex factors, and in the long struggle, stories of eviction and rack-renting were pressed into service as economic myths. As economic myths they did yeoman service. The importance of these stories is not to be found in the pages of the *Agricultural Statistics,* but in Sorel. It may be suspected that some at least of the Irish Nationalists would have agreed. Sam Hussey used to twit the Nationalist politician McCarthy Downing " 'Why is it in these land attacks we only hear of the Harenc estate?' And he used to laugh at me and say, 'that is the most handy one we have.' I think it was the only one they had." [3]

Perhaps it was. Perhaps in terms of prices and acres and rents and evictions the Irish landlord did nothing seriously to restrain economic development in Ireland. Perhaps Sam Hussey, who was one of Kerry's largest land agents, behaved that way, too. But the arrogance and condescension that illumine nearly every page of Sam Hussey's reminiscences are reason enough why he was the most shot-at agent in Ireland. Lord Fingall told his wife, who told Horace Plunkett, "You should never give the Irish anything they have not asked for. If the people want anything I can give them, they know the way to my study door." [4] Martin Ross writes of the election of a Home Ruler in Galway in 1872, the first occasion on which the Ross tenants voted against their landlord: "it was a priest from another part of the diocese who gave forth the mandate, with an extraordinary fury of hatred against the landlord side; one need not blame the sheep who passed in a frightened huddle from one fold to another. When my father came home that afternoon, even the youngest child of the house could see how great had been the blow. It was not the political defeat, severe as that was, it was the personal wound and it was incurable."

An election petition and trial followed, in which intimidation by the priest was an issue, "but these things could not soothe the wounded spirit of the men who had trusted in their tenants." [5] Trusted in them how? To render unquestioned obedience like frightened sheep? To line up at Lord Fingall's study door? When Martin Ross, that cultivated and charming girl, returned to Ross in 1888, she met an old family retainer " 'whom Carlie and I used to beat with sticks til he was "near dead," as he himself says proudly.' " Eventually, one supposes, he stopped being proud of being beaten with sticks.

If the Irish sacrificed economic progress on the altar of Irish nationalism, who can say it was the wrong choice?

Appendixes
Notes
Bibliography
Index

Appendix A.
Statistical Sources and Methods for Density and Size of Median Holding

For every Poor Law union in 1876 I calculated the density of population and the size of the median agricultural holding. The relevant density pertains to the rural population only, and the relevant area will be the improved area. For 1876 the population of each Poor Law union was taken as the 1871 census figure.[1] This is preferable to using an average of the 1871 and 1881 censuses, because it excludes the effects of the renewed emigrations, which come after 1876. I first calculated the density per square mile of improved area (defined as area in crops and grass, excluding fallow, weeds, waste, bog, and water). I concluded that it would be impossible to segregate the agricultural from the other population in seventeen unions, because the unions contained either large cities or concentrations of small industrial towns within their borders.[2] For the remaining 145 unions, it was possible to exclude civic population.

Civic districts in Ireland are defined as places containing over 2,000 inhabitants, but the 1871 census clearly states that population figures for townships "comprise in each case a rural district surrounding the town." Thus when we learn that 3,568 people live in the township of Clonakilty in County Cork, we know first that some of them are living in rural areas surrounding the town proper. Second, we know (from the census and other sources) that a great many people living in the town of Clonakilty proper hold land in the rural district and are in fact farmers, either full time or part time. Third, it is clear that, if we exclude the 3,568 people from the dividend in the calculation of rural density in Clonakilty Poor Law Union, we ought also to exclude some unknown acres of improved land from our divisor. If we were to exclude all the Clonakilty population without excluding this land, we should be underestimating the density of population. In view of these factors, I arbitrarily raised the definition of a civic district from 2,000 to 3,000. Of the 145 Poor Law unions, about 50 contained civic areas, by my definition; I subtracted the civic population in each case in calculating the density figures. I made no effort to correct the decreased area of improved land, hoping that wherever the civic population of the Poor Law union was large, the surrounding rural area within the union borders might be small. There remain some 95 Poor Law unions whose population is totally rural; they contained in 1871 no borough, town, or township with 3,000 or more inhabitants.

If one excludes the big cities and the few industrial areas in Ulster, one would be pretty well justified in calling *all* the rest of Ireland rural. Aside from the omitted unions, only nine adjustments had to be made in Ulster, and nine in Connaught. In a great many cases the excluded civic population bore a modest relation to the total population in the union, so the adjustment did not change density greatly. Even in Munster and Leinster, there were only eighteen and fourteen corrections needed, respectively, many resulting in negligible changes (Clonakilty is one).

The calculation of the median holding in each Poor Law union is perfectly straightforward, resting on breakdowns by size of holding given in the *Agricultural Statistics* for 1876. The holdings of less than an acre are included. For all Ireland only 9 percent of total agricultural holdings were under an acre in 1876. Belfast Poor Law Union had 20.5 percent of its holdings in that category, Dublin North 47.7 percent. Probably one would not want to consider these real agricultural holdings. If we agree to ignore the Poor Law unions containing large cities, we shall probably not go far wrong by including these small holdings elsewhere. When we calculate medians for rural Ireland, there is no particular reason to exclude them.

DISTRIBUTION OF LAND

The *Agricultural Statistics* provide data on acres in crops; grass; fallow; woods and plantations; and bog, waste, and water for each Poor Law union. In the Irish agricultural statistics, meadow is counted as a crop, though not, I believe, in the English. Pasture is defined as permanent grass, while meadow is temporary grass, that is, included in the crop rotation. The distinction between them is arbitrary to a large extent: "meadow" may be in a long rotation; "permanent grass" may have to be reestablished.[3] For purposes of reflecting the dependence of the economy on livestock production as compared with tillage, we shall want to exclude meadow from the definition of crops. For these reasons I have subtracted "meadow" from "crops" and added it to "pasture," so that we can see the distribution of land in each union between tillage crops on the one hand and pasture plus meadow on the other. I have neglected fallow land, and woods and plantations (they are negligible), but I included bog, waste, and water as a third category.

TYPES OF CROP

The types of crop that can be grown in various regions of Ireland are limited by topography and climate. The country's mountains rim the coasts, and the interior is essentially a gently rolling lowland plain, with the result that Ireland is often described as being shaped like a saucer.

The rainfall in the west of Ireland is excessive by any standard. Whether in the Northwest, Connaught and Clare, or the Southwest, 40–60 inches of rain fall each year. In the mountains, annual rainfalls of 60–100 inches are the rule. The East, on the other hand, has much less rain, least on the central lowlands, and generally 30–40 inches per year on lowlands throughout the East. The winds in the West are an important element of the climate and reach the force of gales of awesome velocities. The gale warnings that the U.S. Weather Bureau issues for small craft are in the West of Ireland issued to railways.[4] The natural tree limit in the West is held down practically to sea level near the coast. Not only does the West have more mountains, but the limits of cultivation are much lower; the high winds and rain tend to produce leached and gleyed soils.

Only the Southeast and a favored part of the Northeast have sunshine enough to provide good ripening conditions for wheat and barley. Potatoes, oats, and grass withstand wetness much better. Oats grow best with heavy rainfall and a cloud cover, being ripened by a minimum of sun and of value even when not fully ripe. In addition, oats are a particularly versatile crop. Not only can they be fed to all livestock, but the straw is useful fodder as well.

The temperature of Ireland is generally mild, and cattle can be left outdoors all year round in the South and West, and even up to ten months in the North and East. The mildness and the rainfall combined with favorable soil conditions make the central lowlands a favorable environment for rich grassland.[5]

This sketch of geographical conditions provides a notion of the limits within which economic adjustments can be made.

To see what crops actually were grown in 1876, I calculated for each Poor Law union the share of corn crops, green (root) crops, and flax in the total area of the union. These are given in the *Agricultural Statistics*. These may total less than 100 percent, owing to the elimination of mangels, beet root, carrots, parsnips, cabbage, vetches, other green crops, and rape, but these minor crops never come to more than 2 or 3 percent of the total area. I considered it unsatisfactory to use green crops as an aggregate, because potatoes and turnips, the two crops of any importance in the category, do not share the same characteristics. Accordingly, the crop shares were calculated for corn (wheat, oats, barley, and minor crops); potatoes; turnips; and flax.

LIVESTOCK DISTRIBUTION

Livestock distribution by age and type of livestock for each Poor Law union is given in the *Agricultural Statistics*. Without going into detail, it is possible to get an idea of the distribution of livestock population in 1876 by inspection. The cattle population of 4 million (4,117,440) was made up of 1.5 million milch cows, nearly 1 million dry cattle, two years old and up (928,912), slightly less between one and two years (778,465) and under a year (877,089). If we look at the unions with milch cow population of over 20,000, we shall find them all in the Southwest, except one. Limerick and Kerry and the parts of Tipperary and Cork that lie near Limerick and Kerry contained a significant share of the milch cows of Ireland. There were large numbers of milch cows in Ulster, too, and Leitrim and Sligo unions also had some concentration.

Cattle two years old and up were still more concentrated. Of the 900,000 cattle this age in Ireland, the unions of County Meath alone contained almost 100,000. Adding in the other Poor Law unions with dense herds of this category of cattle—Celbridge and Naas unions in Kildare, Edenderry and Parsontown in King's, Mullingar in Westmeath, Drogheda in Louth, and Balrothery in County Dublin—we find a sizable percentage of dry cattle two years old and up concentrated in a small geographic area.

The sheep population was also concentrated. Of the dozen or so unions with the most sheep, six were in Galway. Some of the regions high in cattle two years old and over were also high in sheep: unions in Kildare, King's, Louth, Meath, and Westmeath. There was also an important amount of sheep-raising in unions in Wicklow and Wexford.

The pig population did not show the same marked regional character. There is reason to expect an association between dairy herds and pig population, and we did in fact find large numbers of pigs in unions in Limerick and Kerry; Wexford had a large pig population, too.

Appendix B.
Calculation of Value Added in Irish Agriculture, 1876, 1881, and 1886

1. CROPS

The derivation of the crop figures is perfectly straight-forward. The values for wheat, oats, barley, flax, potatoes, and hay were derived by multiplying production by price and subtracting that portion of each crop retained for seed or fed to livestock on the farm. Production figures were available from the annual *Agricultural Statistics*. Price figures for 1881 and 1886 were taken from official figures; for 1876 from *Thom's Almanac,* which in turn were derived from the *Farmer's Gazette.* The proportion of each crop retained as input for further agricultural production was assumed to be the same as in 1908. These proportions are given in *Agricultural Output of Ireland 1908.*

To account for other crops besides those named, it was assumed that the latter represented 95 percent of the value added from crop production in Ireland. This figure is higher than its 1908 counterpart because the production of minor crops, like grass seed and fruit, developed later.

2. LIVESTOCK

There were formidable difficulties in estimating values in the livestock sector, since output figures are not available. Only the population of the animals is given in the *Agricultural Statistics,* with breakdowns by age. The use of relationships between population and annual output developed for

1908 solved many problems, but it was impossible to utilize the 1908 methods for the dry cattle industry, the principal source of livestock income, so that a method was developed of deducing annual marketings directly from population statistics for dry cattle.

Dry Cattle

To obtain an estimate of dry cattle marketed in any given year, we assume that the mortality from natural causes is known, that no cattle are slaughtered under a year old, but that yearlings and two-year-olds are the cattle marketed. All these assumptions appear reasonable in the light of what is known of the Irish dry cattle industry. As the period progressed, however, there was a trend to holding cattle for a third year. One indication that the marketing of three-year-olds became commoner after our period is that price and quantity data on older cattle are not given until 1887. Nevertheless, to the extent to which cattle older than two years are marketed, the present method underestimates the value of dry cattle marketed.

Income from cattle in any given year *t* will equal the quantity of two-year-olds marketed times the price of two-year-olds, plus the quantity of one-year-olds marketed times the price of one-year-olds, allowance being made for natural mortality. Two-year-olds marketed in any given year will be equal to last year's two-year-olds plus last year's one-year-olds minus this year's two-year-olds. In other words, the difference between the older cattle held over from the previous year and the older cattle counted in the census of the present year must have been marketed (allowance being made for natural mortality). Similarly, the number of one-year-olds marketed will be equal to last year's less-than-a-year-old cattle minus this year's one-year-olds. Thus (always allowing for mortality):

$$I_t = [(Q_{2t-1} + Q_{1t-1}) - Q_{2t}]P_{2t} + (Q_{0t-1} - Q_{1t})P_{1t}$$

It would also be possible, though ostentatious, to include with income the capital gain (or loss) incurred every year by changes in the stock of cattle. The calculation of cattle values is now possible, since annual data on dry cattle population by age (less-than-one-year, one-to-two, two and over) are available from the *Agricultural Statistics*, and price series for one-year-olds and two-year-olds are available from official sources for 1881 and 1886 and *Farmer's Gazette*, reprinted in *Thom's Almanac* for 1876. Mortality assumptions were adopted from those made for dry cattle in *Agricultural Output of Ireland 1908*.

Butter and Milk

The number of milch cows (given in annual *Agricultural Statistics*) was multiplied by the average yield of milk (400 gallons, given in *Agricultural Output 1908*), then deductions were made for (1) mortality, suckling cows, dry cows, (2) milk fed to young calves, (3) milk fed to young pigs, and (4) milk consumed by the human population. The first deduction was assumed to be 10 percent; the second was made by multiplying the number of young calves each year by an assumed consumption of 35 gallons; the third, by multiplying the number of young pigs each year by an assumed consumption of 5 gallons; the fourth, by multiplying the population of Ireland in each year by an assumed consumption of 20 gallons. The last-mentioned was then multiplied by a conventional price (8d.) for milk, and is taken as the estimated value of milk output.

After the four deductions listed above, the remaining milk was assumed to go into butter production. Cheese and other milk products were assumed negligible at this period. Butter prices were available from official sources for 1881 and 1886, from *Thom's Almanac* for 1876. The method of calculation and the coefficients were taken from *Agricultural Output 1908*.

Pigs

The proportion of sows to the total pig population was estimated on the basis of figures that begin to appear in the *Agricultural Statistics* in 1907 (annually thereafter). It was assumed that each sow produced 14 marketable pigs, and a deduction was made for mortality. Again *Agricultural Output 1908* was the source of the assumptions. Pork prices are given per hundred weight, not per pig, but a series was fortunately available on the basis of single animals.[1] The implied average weight of a pig did not seem unreasonable.

Sheep and Wool

The output/ewes ratio of sheep was taken from the figure implicit in *Agricultural Output 1908*. Some ambiguity exists between the calculations there presented and the textual description, and the calculations were followed. Price data as before are from official sources for 1881 and 1886, from *Thom's Almanac* for 1876.

The wool estimate is crude. For *Agricultural Output 1908,* a special census of different breeds of sheep was taken and an estimate made of the weight of fleece obtainable from each breed. For our purposes, the best that could be done was to preserve the average yield of fleece per sheep at the 1908 level. We have no information on the changing composition of the sheep population by breed. Prices sources are as before.

Eggs

The number of grown turkeys, geese, duck, and fowl (as opposed to newly hatched) are available from the annual *Agricultural Statistics*. Assuming that 95 percent of the grown birds were female, we find that the total number of eggs can be calculated by multiplying the average number of eggs laid by each type of poultry. These numbers are given in *Agricultural Output 1908*. By far most of the production came from ordinary fowl. Since turkey and geese eggs cost a little less, and duck eggs a little more than ordinary hen eggs, it was not considered too misleading to use hen eggs as the price multiplier.

Other

The principal items included are poultry, horses, and hides, and minor animals such as mules, jennets, and asses. The estimates for earlier years were made with reference to the estimated values for 1908.

Notes

1. INTRODUCTION

1. Alexander G. Richey, *The Irish Land Laws*. I also owe a heavy debt to A. D. Hargreaves, *Introduction to Land Law*. I am grateful to Professor K. M. Wedderburn of the London School of Economics for the second reference.

2. Richey, *Irish Land Laws*, p. 36. The incidents of yearly tenancies were altered in 1876 in important ways.

3. Hargreaves, *Introduction to Land Law*, p. 180.

4. The fascination of the history of English law is exemplified by the fact that the discussion of distress in Pollock and Maitland is quite relevant to the present discussion: the legal theory and its difficulties remain practically unchanged from the reign of Henry III (Frederick Pollock and Frederic William Maitland, *The History of English Law before the Time of Edward I*, 1:353–355).

5. The Deasy Act of 1860 made changes in the state of the land laws as described here, not more favorable to landlords than to tenants, and in general brought Irish law closer to the French code. This was not by design but rather in consequence of establishing land tenure as a contractual relationship. Much of the Deasy Act is concerned with reversions and remainders and what rights do or do not "run with the land"; it is unnecessary to describe the complicated provisions of the act here.

6. James A. Froude, "Romanism and the Irish Race," *North American Review* (January, 1880), p. 38, quoted in R. Barry O'Brien, *The Parliamentary History of the Irish Land Question*, p. 8.

7. O'Brien, *Parliamentary History*, p. 68.

8. Ibid., pp. 69–70.

9. Ibid., p. 71.

10. Robert Blake, *Disraeli*, p. 496.

11. G. Kitson Clark, *The Making of Victorian England*, pp. 75–76.

2. MR. GLADSTONE AND THE LAND ACT OF 1870

1. Dr. Kitson Clark has emphasized the importance in this period of the breakup of the Church of Scotland and the introduction there of free churches, the growth of Calvinist Congregationalism in Wales, and the introduction of American techniques of religious revivals into England and Northern Ireland. For these matters, and for the general view of mid-Victorian England sketched out here, I am indebted to Kitson Clark's lectures on Victorian history which I was privileged to attend in Cambridge, 1963–64.

2. John Morley, *The Life of William Ewart Gladstone,* 1:886.

3. For the relation of the Irish in America to the Fenian movement, see Charles Callan Tansill, *America and the Fight for Irish Freedom: 1866–1922,* pp. 27–40.

4. Algar Labouchere Thorold, *The Life of Henry Labouchere,* p. x. Recall also that the Reform Act of 1867 enfranchised a large number of Roman Catholic voters.

5. Morley, *Life of Gladstone,* 1:893–894.

6. Gladstone Papers, esp. British Museum, Additional Manuscripts, 44758, 44235, 44121, and 44122. For a full account of the cabinet discussions on the bill, see E. D. Steele, "The Irish Land Act of 1870 and the Liberal Party."

7. The paradox is, of course, only apparent and not real. Only a man of enormous moral and religious fervor could have elevated a few dry theoretical results into something like a holy political crusade. The results of Mr. Gladstone's spectacular success along these lines continued to plague us into the twentieth century.

8. Gladstone Papers, 44758.

9. There are, of course, aspects of Mr. Gladstone's career to which this description simply does not correspond: his attitude on parliamentary reform is obviously one.

10. Gladstone Papers, Memorandum of December 11, 1869, 44758.

11. Steele, "Irish Land Act," p. 353.

12. Ibid., p. 245.

13. Ibid., p. 341.

14. Lord Dufferin conceptualized the tenant's property right exactly this way: as an unacknowledged lease (Steele, "Irish Land Act," p. 256).

15. Brian A. Kennedy, "Tenant Right," in *Ulster Since 1800: A*

Political and Economic Survey, ed. T. W. Moody and J. C. Beckett, pp. 40–41. For a collection of early opinions, see R. Barry O'Brien, *The Parliamentary History of the Irish Land Question,* e.g., Leslie Foster, Ulster landlord: "I attribute the great difference between the province of Ulster and the other counties of Ireland to the settlement of James I . . . Wherever the tenants have a beneficial and substantial interest, there are no disturbances. They have such an interest in Ulster" (p. 173). Also Mr. Handcock, agent: "Much of Ulster's prosperity has been the result of this extraordinary matter (namely, tenant right)" (ibid., p. 176). Handcock's evidence before the Devon Commission was quoted by Daniel O'Connell in the House of Commons, according to Barry O'Brien.

Similar opinions can be cited by the dozen.

16. Arthur Young, *A Tour in Ireland,* ed. Constantia Maxwell, p. 38.

17. Ibid., p. 52.

18. Ibid. This is perhaps the place to recall that the casual observations of untrained travelers are untrustworthy guides to economic conditions. Arthur Young's wide experience and our knowledge of his biases entitle him to more serious consideration than most. "Mr. Young's pictures of Ireland, in his tour through that country," wrote Maria Edgeworth in *Castle Rackrent* (1798), "was the first faithful portrait of its inhabitants." There is a particular point about travelers' reminiscences in Ireland, however. From the time of Arthur Young to the time of Sir Horace Plunkett, the Irishman was not known for pride in the appearance of his home or indeed for fastidiousness of any kind. Arthur Young observed that there were men in Ireland of £5,000 who lived in habitations a man in England of £700 would disdain (p. 204). Harriet Martineau, in *Letters from Ireland* (1852), observed that "the fearful apparent wretchedness of the people is no necessary indication of poverty. The five pigs wallowing near the bed's head is an instance. At the present value of pigs here . . . these must be worth many pounds. Elsewhere we have seen a very fine cow, or perhaps two, belonging to a hovel so wretched that you would suppose the people had no prospect of another meal" (quoted in K. H. Connell, *The Population of Ireland, 1750–1845,* p. 87). Horace Plunkett was still scolding the Southern Irish for their lack of neatness at the beginning of the twentieth century, long after Ulster farmers had mended their ways.

19. Here is Arthur Young again: "Change the scene [from Nor-

folk] and view the North of Ireland; you there behold a whole province peopled by weavers. It is they who cultivate, or rather beggar, the soil as well as work the looms. Agriculture is there in ruins; annihilated; the whole region is the disgrace of the kingdom; all the crops you see are contemptible; are nothing but filth and weeds. No other part of Ireland can exhibit the soil in such a state of poverty and desolation."

20. Conrad Gill, in the standard work on the Irish linen industry, *The Rise of the Irish Linen Industry,* believes that the land system accounts for the persistence of weavers in Ulster and their absence in the South. It is striking that in a book of modern scholarship he only asserts, never demonstrates, the importance of the land issue. No historical data on rents or evictions are offered. While Gill convincingly shows that the failure of the industry in the South was due to the premature introduction of a capitalistically organized industry, he fails to show that the absence of weaving was due to the land system.

21. It is perhaps superfluous to mention the simplest and most obvious counterexample to the proposition that Ulster Custom was responsible for prosperity, namely, the condition of Donegal, in which Ulster Custom was well established and which contained some of the most poverty-stricken districts in Ireland throughout the nineteenth century.

22. The evidence for this statement in the post-Famine period is developed in detail in Chap. 3. Connell, *Population of Ireland,* chap. 6, contains much similar evidence for the pre-Famine years (1815–1845).

23. The Marquis of Lansdowne, *Glanerought and the Petty-Fitzmaurices,* p. 60. The leases on the Kerry property dated from 1696/7. Lord Shelburne, the great politician of the Georgian era, was a direct descendant (great-grandson) of Sir William Petty, who obtained possession of lands in Ireland in the course of the Cromwellian settlement. Petty's daughter married Thomas Fitzmaurice, afterward first Earl of Kerry. Lord Shelburne's father was the second son of this marriage. Shelburne was created first Marquis of Lansdowne and this title, as well as the Kerry title, has continued in a direct line to the present day.

24. Ibid., pp. 61–62.

25. Ibid., pp. 66–67.

26. Cf. the interesting letter written to Francis Horner in 1805

by Lord Henry Petty when he first came into possession of the Kerry estates. Lord Henry Petty became the third Marquis of Lansdowne. "[The Irish middleman] expends neither capital nor industry, unless that activity can be called industry which he exerts driving for rents, and goading the tenantcy to over-work the land and over-work themselves. It is more easy to do the former than the latter, and the farm, in which he has of course no permanent interest, comes out of his hands with a diminished value" (ibid., p. 116).

27. Connell, *Population of Ireland*, pp. 181, 169.

28. W. Bence Jones, *A Life's Work in Ireland by a Landlord Who Tried to Do His Duty*, p. 39. Bence Jones argues that the abysmal level of agricultural technique practiced by Irish tenants is evidence that it is not landlords who are the effective bar to investment.

3. THE ASSUMPTIONS OF THE LAND ACT: EVICTIONS, RENTS, AND IMPROVEMENTS

1. For holdings of less that £50 per year, not held under a written agreement. The procedure differs slightly for higher rents.

2. A good case can be made for assuming that the effects of the Famine on eviction and emigration were not completely worked out until 1854. Evictions usually occur after some years of arrears have accrued. S. H. Cousens, in his "Emigration and Demographic Change in Ireland, 1851–1861," identifies emigration up to this date as Famine-connected. He attributes the lag to lack of funds on the part of some would-be emigrants during the worst Famine years. "More than 55 percent of total emigrants leaving Ireland between 1851 and 1861 had left the country by the end of 1854" (p. 275).

3. A refined estimate would have to consider not only turnover, but also multiple holdings and the possibility of one person's suffering more than one eviction.

4. M. Cochran Davys, Bessborough Commission, 14288ff.

5. Cf. *Twenty-eighth Report of H. M. Inland Revenue Commissioners, P.P.* 1884–1885 (4474), XXII, p. 80: "The 'annual value' for purposes of the income tax may, in popular language, be described as the best rent that can be obtained when the landlord and tenant, respectively, bear their own burdens." "Rent" and "value" are used as equivalents in this connection, e.g., "it is the duty of the occupier . . . to render a return to the assessor of the rent or value of the lands . . . in his occupation."

6. "Except in Ireland, the income tax, Sch. A. figures undoubtedly represent most closely the real facts, but in revaluation years far more closely than at other times" (Josiah Stamp, *British Incomes and Property*, p. 31). Stamp's book is an indispensable guide to the income tax figures and provides a valuable study of the Irish figures, as well as a full bibliography on them.

7. Ibid., p. 161.

8. Sir Richard Griffith, a distinguished and colorful civil servant, had undertaken the earlier tenement valuations, as well as the one that goes by his name. Sir Richard was succeeded by John Ball Greene, who had been his principal assistant for fifteen or sixteen years. Ball Greene in turn was succeeded by Sir J. G. Barton in 1892. Barton was still serving in the office up to World War I. Because each of these men had such long service and intimate knowledge of the Valuation Office, we can rely with some confidence on their verbal testimony and impressions to supplement the meager quantitative data available.

9. Houses were valued separately on the basis of the actual rent paid. About half of the total value of rural houses was accounted for by landlords' demesnes, the other half by tenants' cottages. The latter were valued, for the most part, on a nominal basis, at £1 apiece.

10. The counties completed in each year are given below (*Report from the Select Committee on General Valuation &c [Ireland], P.P.* 1868–1869 (362) IX, Appendix 2; also given in Appendix 8). Sufficient data were apparently available to enable the valuers to convert the six counties done under the 1846 act to the basis of the 1852 act without further field work.

1853 Carlow, Cork, Dublin, Kerry, Kilkenny, Limerick, Queen's, Tipperary, Waterford
1854 Kildare, Wexford, Wicklow
1855 King's, Longford, Louth, Meath, Westmeath
1856 Clare
1857 Cavan, Galway, Leitrim, Mayo
1858 Donegal, Roscommon, Sligo
1859 Londonderry
1860 Tyrone
1861 Monaghan
1862 Antrim
1863 Fermanagh

1864 Down

1865 Armagh

11. One estimate gives the highest annual expenditure on poor rates during the Famine as £2 million (C. U. Townshend, Bessborough Commission, 1576).

12. Ball Greene, Bessborough Commission, 676: "We found things so much better, and so much improved, that we took into account the improved state of things in the north of Ireland."

13. Thomas Carlyle, *Reminiscences of My Irish Journey in 1847*, pp. 158, 135. Recall that six of the counties valued under the Act of 1852 had been surveyed in 1848–1852.

14. The only countervailing factor is the increase in the cost of labor. Ball Greene estimated the cost of labor on cereal production rose by 50 percent from the original price scale to 1880. This was accompanied by a great shift away from cereal production over the period, as well as by some introduction of machinery on large- and medium-sized holdings.

15. *Royal Commission on the Depressed Condition of the Agricultural Interest: Preliminary Report*, P.P. 1881 (2778) XV, Q28235.

16. *Royal Commission on Local Taxation*, P.P. 1898 (c. 8673), XLI, Q3321.

17. *Report from the Select Committee on General Valuation &c (Ireland)*, P.P. 1868–1869 (362) IX, Q702.

18. Ibid., Q5282.

19. Ibid.

20. Ibid., Q5279.

21. Stamp, *British Incomes*, p. 151.

22. Ibid., p. 130.

23. *Royal Commission on Financial Relations*, Q5671. The quotation comes from the questioner, Sexton. The answer was "Exactly."

24. Ball Greene gives 30 percent for 1876. My guess is that the higher estimates of Ball Greene may occur in the later years because he sometimes slips in his testimony from the valuation of *agricultural* Ireland to the valuation of *all* Ireland.

25. Bessborough Commission, 34106.

26. Compare, e.g., ibid., 19943; 21063.

27. Ibid., 8939.

28. Ibid., 8991.

29. Ibid., 38821ff.

30. Ibid., 8476.

31. E.g., see R. Barry O'Brien, *The Parliamentary History of the Irish Land Question*, pp. 73–74.

32. For a full discussion of compensation for improvements in England, see A. H. H. Matthews, *Fifty Years of Agricultural Politics*, chap. 6.

33. Bessborough Commission, 40137.

34. *Reports from Poor Law Inspectors in Ireland as to the Existing Relations between Landlord and Tenant in Respect of Improvements on Farms*, P.P. 1870 (c. 31) XIV.

35. This, of course, was widely realized at the time. In the autumn of 1869 Lord Castlerosse told Gladstone that tenant improvements "generally had to be undone (i.e., partially) for the tenants' habit was to reclaim very small bits, putting up a large fence around each, which became incumbrances and had to be leveled by the landlord" (Gladstone Papers, British Museum, Additional Manuscripts, 44758).

36. Bessborough Commission, 16521.

37. Ibid., 14028.

38. Ibid., 23012.

39. Ibid., 3925.

40. Ibid., 1137; 1145.

41. Ibid., 32090. The exchange continues: 32091. "I should think the tenant would call that a man who left them alone.—No."

42. Ibid., 26859.

43. W. Bence Jones, *A Life's Work in Ireland by a Landlord Who Tried to Do His Duty*, p. 110.

44. Bessborough Commission, 26906.

45. Ibid., 26240.

46. In connection with the squaring of some farms, Talbot Crosbie was the object of virulent attacks in the Nationalist newspapers over a period of years in the 1870's.

47. Bessborough Commission, 3294.

48. This is abundantly clear from the testimony before the Bessborough Commission. See, for example, Atkinson, 7294; Young, 5942; Forde, 7048; Blakiston-Houston, 7193; Brush, 6652; Hewson, 23045. The index lists thirty-three witnesses who said that the Land Act had checked landlord improvements, as against three or four who said it had no effect.

4. REAL FACTORS IN THE DEVELOPMENT OF THE IRISH AGRICULTURAL ECONOMY TO 1876

1. P. M. Austin Bourke, "The Agricultural Statistics of the 1841 Census of Ireland." In this useful article Bourke offers amended versions of some important statistics. The accuracy of post-Famine agricultural statistics has never been questioned, and Bourke agreed with Hooper in viewing them as "free from major error." We have used Bourke's pre-Famine holdings figure (his table 4, p. 380) and official figures thereafter. The official figures are given annually in the *Agricultural Statistics*.

2. James Caird, *The Landed Interest and the Supply of Food*, pp. 28–29.

3. Thomas Barrington, "A Review of Irish Agricultural Prices."

4. Barrington, "Review of Prices," p. 259, quoting a table in Department of Agriculture, *Agricultural Output of Ireland 1908*. Other figures in this section on the disposition of total crop come from this table.

5. Hans Staehle, "Statistical Notes on the Economic History of Irish Agriculture, 1847–1913." Staehle's figures are not for all Ireland; they exclude the six counties of Northern Ireland. Not the least of the horrors of the Partition is the exclusion of these counties from the historical statistics published by the government of Ireland.

6. These data are all taken from Thomas W. Grimshaw, "A Statistical Survey of Ireland from 1840 to 1888." I came across this article after I had taken 1876 as the culminating year of the adjustment process. Grimshaw was the registrar general of Ireland; his work can probably be considered as reasonably authoritative.

7. It may be unnecessary to observe here that this does not mean that the largest farms in Ireland were found in Cork. Belmullet in County Mayo, e.g., contained 46 farms of over 500 acres in extent; the median holding in Belmullet was nevertheless 9 acres. Macroom in County Cork had 4 farms of over 500 acres; the median holding in Macroom was 62 acres.

8. Saorstát Eireann, *Agricultural Statistics 1847 to 1926* with an introductory essay by John Hooper, Director of Statistics, Department of Industry and Commerce.

9. Hooper, Introductory essay, p. xxxii.

10. *Land Use in Northern Ireland*, Leslie Symons, ed., pp. 38–39.

11. *Agricultural Statistics for Ireland 1871, P.P.* 1873 (c. 762) LXIX. Within the total area devoted to crops, the tendency for the share of meadow to increase with size is marked. Cereal area as a share of crops shows no consistent variation with size. The larger the farm, the larger the share of green crops, *excluding* potatoes; the *smaller* the farm, the larger the share of green crops, *including* potatoes.

12. Hooper, Introductory essay, p. vii.

13. Hooper, Introductory essay, p. xliii.

14. In the words of a contemporary, Charles Uniacke Townshend: "You have in Ulster the flax culture, which, when judiciously carried on, is a most paying crop; £50 an acre I have known to be made from flax. You have there the flax manipulation for the young hands. You have the after treatment of flax all tending to give employment, and to thrift. There is an amount produced out of the soil there that, in my judgment, is not produced in the South. There is more tillage, I would say, in Ulster than in the other provinces." Bessborough Commission, 1588.

15. J. M. Synge, *The Aran Islands,* p. 66. Synge first visited the islands in 1898.

16. Ibid., p. 149. Yield differentials do not show up strikingly in the *Agricultural Statistics.* Instead of finding high yields in Carlow and low yields in Mayo, for example, we find that yields are similar but that very little tillage is attempted in Mayo.

17. Quoted in Barrington, "Review of Prices," p. 263.

18. Hooper, Introductory essay, table 8, p. xxxi.

19. *Agricultural Statistics of Ireland for the Year 1882,* table 3, p. 9.

20. J. H. Clapham, *Economic History of Modern Britain,* 2:296.

21. Bessborough Commission, 16882, 16884.

22. S. H. Cousens, "Emigration and Demographic Change in Ireland, 1851–1861," *Economic History Review,* 2nd ser., 14 (1961): 275–288; "The Regional Variations in Population Changes in Ireland, 1861–1881," ibid., 2nd ser., 17 (1964): 301–321. See also his "The Regional Pattern of Emigration during the Great Irish Famine, 1846–1851," *Institute of British Geographers, Transactions and Papers,* no. 28 (1960), pp. 126–129.

23. S. H. Cousens "Regional Variations in Population Changes in Ireland, 1861–1881," pp. 320–321. More work remains to be done

along these lines, but it will not, I think, alter Cousens's main conclusions. The major contrast between East and West has naturally received most attention, but differences between the Southeast and Eastern Ulster remain to be explored.

24. The change in the West is illustrated in Sean O'Faolain's autobiographical novel, *A Nest of Simple Folk,* which is full of interest to an economic historian. The older generation in the West (Co. Limerick) is a large family; the succeeding generation shows late marriage and fewer children.

25. S. H. Cousens, "Emigration and Demographic Change in Ireland, 1851–1861," pp. 284, 285.

5. THE DOWNTURN IN IRISH AGRICULTURE, 1877–1879

1. Data on weather and crop yields are given in the *Agricultural Statistics of Ireland* for 1877, *P.P.* 1878 (c. 1938) LXXVII; for 1878, *P.P.* 1878–1899 (c. 2347) LXXV; and for 1879, *P.P.* 1880 (c. 2534) LXXVI.

2. By province, the 1879 potato yields were Leinster 1.5 tons per acre, Munster 1.6, Ulster 1.1, and Connaught 1.3.

3. James Caird, *The Landed Interest and the Supply of Food,* pp. 159, 169.

4. *Thom's Almanac,* annually. This figure contains all crops, tillage and green, and a large proportion is not final output but is consumed within the agricultural sector. The magnitude of the 1879 disaster can be gauged in some rough way, but nothing more can be claimed for the comparison. Much refinement would be necessary before the income decline could be estimated (see Chap. 7 below).

5. Henry Robinson, *Memories: Wise and Otherwise,* pp. 9–10. As a result of this experience, Sir Henry wrote the Undersecretary at Dublin. His letter came beneath the notice of Lord Randolph Churchill, who arranged Robinson's appointment to the Local Government Board. Sir Henry remained at the Local Government Board until it passed out of existence, rising to vice president. He was a knowledgeable though narrow civil servant; he believed the Irish should be assisted in the event of above-average destitution and starvation, but that a merely *average* rate of destitution ought to be borne cheerfully.

6. Bessborough Commission, 13192.

7. Robinson, *Memories,* pp. 22–24.

8. Biggar's first obstructionist speech was delivered on April 22, 1875, the very day that Parnell took his seat. See John E. Pomfret, *The Struggle for Land in Ireland 1800–1923,* p. 114.

9. The Fenian organization was by no means pleased with the prospect of cooperation with the parliamentary party. Biggar and Power were expelled from the Supreme Council in August 1877 (the date is given differently in different sources, but August 1877 makes most sense). John Barry and Patrick Egan resigned from the council in protest (see T. W. Moody, "The New Departure in Irish Politics, 1878–1879," p. 310).

The following month, however (September 1877), Fenian support enabled Parnell to win his first victory over Isaac Butt when Butt lost to him the presidency of the Home Rule Confederation of Great Britain. John Barry was instrumental in Butt's defeat; he was to be instrumental in Parnell's downfall, too, an irony that Parnell did not fail to comment on in the nearly hysterical scenes in Committee Room Fifteen in 1890. He called Barry, though not by name, "the leader-killer who sharpens his poniard to stab me as he stabbed the old lion Isaac Butt, in the days gone by" (F. S. L. Lyons, *The Fall of Parnell, 1890–1891,* p. 128). Butt died in May 1879. He was succeeded as leader of the Irish parliamentary party by William Shaw, a Protestant banker who had once been a Nonconformist minister.

10. Moody, "New Departure in Irish Politics," p. 313. Pomfret's version of the meeting is much more romantic. He believed that Parnell met Davitt at the deathbed of one of the latter's fellow prisoners who was dying from the effects of the prison confinement (Pomfret, *Struggle for Land,* p. 109).

11. Letter in the *Irish Felon,* quoted in Michael Davitt, *The Fall of Feudalism in Ireland,* p. 59.

12. L. Fogarty, ed., *James Fintan Lalor, Patriot and Political Essayist* (1918), pp. 57–60. Quoted in Moody, "New Departure in Irish Politics," p. 306.

13. T. P. O'Connor, *Memoirs of an Old Parliamentarian,* 1:45.

14. A recent biography is Donald McCormick, *The Incredible Mr. Kavanagh.* The Kavanaghs date back to the eleventh century. Of course they are descended from kings.

15. The market for tenant right was limited by the establishment

of office rules reserving to the landlord a veto power over particular bidders, or giving adjoining tenants first rights, or limiting the sum per acre that could be paid.

16. "4505. The O'Conor Don. Do you have more sales in a bad year or a good year?—Mr. McElroy [an auctioneer, and representative of the County Antrim Central Tenants' Right Association comprising six local associations]—In a good year.

"4506. Would you not find that in a bad year the tenant got into difficulty, and was obliged to sell?—But we cannot sell then. I had only two sales in 1880, although I had the usual number of orders."

Some witnesses, however, testified that tenant-right prices had not fallen very much (Bessborough Commission, 11419).

17. Ibid., 9447.

18. Ibid., 14047.

19. This is not the Lord Leitrim who was assassinated, allegedly "a victim, it is said, to the revenge of a farmer's son whose sister had suffered an unforgiveable wrong." (The words are Michael Davitt's, *Fall of Feudalism*, p. 143.)

20. The fall in the price of kelp was important to many tenants at this time. This is especially true of the islands, but even some mainland communities were practically dependent upon the kelp trade. Camus, a townland near Ballinrobe, is one example.

21. Bessborough Commission, 11565.

22. The exchange continued (ibid.): "11310. [Shaw] It [Ulster Custom] is no loss to you?—It is indirectly, you don't get your land farmed so well, and you don't have the same security for your money.

"11311. If the man pays a certain sum he creates an interest in it for himself?—Yes, and he pays it how? Sometimes never. The losses on my estate are very large every year, sometimes they never pay, and sometimes they may be a long time in arrears, other times the rent may not be collected for three years. I have got three or four years' rent due in many—I should say most of the holdings on my estate."

23. Of course, not all Donegal landlords were of the philanthropic kind—they were the exception—but even the best were powerless. Arthur Brooke, a land agent to Murray Stewart, a Donegal landlord, testified (Bessborough Commission, 11594ff.) that Murray Stewart had spent between £20,000 and £30,000 on his estate on roads, tenant housing, nine schools, and a corn mill. The rents

were raised £1,389 from 1847 to 1880; there were 1,320 tenants. Tenant right was sold at seventeen years' purchase. Yet the smallest tenants, who held a potato patch and depended on the fishing, were by 1880 on relief. The agent realized that nothing but emigration or the provision of alternative employment would help.

24. Ibid., unnumbered; follows 17265.

25. Ibid., 16748.

26. Ibid., 16719.

27. Quoted in Davitt, *Fall of Feudalism*, p. 168.

28. Testimony of Charles C. Boycott, Bessborough Commission, 18467ff.

6. THE LAND ACT OF 1881

1. This is authenticated by one of Morley's anecdotes: "One day in 1880 when Lord Beaconsfield was finally quitting the official house in Downing Street, one who had been the ablest and most zealous supporters of his policy in the press, called to bid him goodbye. The visitor talked gloomily of the national prospect; of difficulties with Austria, with Russia, with the Turk; of the confusions to come upon Europe from the doctrines of Midlothian. The fallen minister listened. Then looking at his friend, he uttered in deep tones a single word. *'Ireland!'* he said" (John Morley, *The Life of William Ewart Gladstone*, 2:287).

Gladstone was so out of touch with Ireland at this time that he gave in a speech at Edinburgh the incredible reply to Disraeli's election address that there was "an absence of crime and outrage, with a general feeling of comfort and satisfaction, such as was unknown in the previous history of that country" (quoted in Bernard Holland, *Life of the Duke of Devonshire*, 1:264). I myself find the remark so incredible that I hesitate to quote it. But it is well established that Mr. Gladstone minimized the Irish problem in 1880.

2. *Royal Commission on the Depressed Condition of the Agricultural Interest*, P.P. 1881 (c. 2778) XV, XVI (hereafter cited as Richmond Commission).

3. Richmond Commission, 2797.

4. Ibid., 3619.

5. Richmond Commission, 3446.

6. John O'Donovan, *The Economic History of Live Stock in Ireland*, chap. 16.

7. Richmond Commission, 9991ff. See also the testimony of Mahony (Richmond Commission, 28,932) who also shipped his butter to London. Bence Jones's story is more fully told in the Appendix to his *A Life's Work in Ireland by a Landlord Who Tried to Do His Duty.* Bence Jones attributed the success of French butter in London partly to superior marketing arrangements.

8. Richmond Commission, 23,104.

9. Richmond Commission, 20,988ff.

10. Holland, *Life of Devonshire,* 1:330.

11. "As it happened, I called on Mr. Gladstone one morning early in 1881, 'You have heard,' I asked, 'that the Bessborough Commission are to report for the Three F's?' 'I have not heard,' he said, 'it is incredible!' " (Holland, *Life of Devonshire,* 1:333–334). The conversation probably took place not in early 1881 but in December 1880, since Lord Hartington was informed of the news by Mr. Gladstone in that month.

12. Bessborough Commission, *Report,* p. 19.

13. "The condition of society, in which the land suitable for tillage can be regarded as a mere commodity, the subject of trade, and can be let to the highest bidder in an open market, has never, except under special circumstances, existed in Ireland . . . It was of little use to the landlord, who thought of rent raising, that there were hundreds of applicants for a farm of his, when a tenant, or a swarm of tenants, already occupied it, whom the law itself was frequently not able to eject" ibid., p. 4.

14. Ibid., p. 36.

15. Ibid., p. 37.

16. Ibid., p. 11.

17. Ibid., p. 51.

18. Hansard, April 21, 1893.

19. Morley, *Life of Gladstone,* 2:296.

20. First Cairns Commission, 1505.

21. Ibid., 4236–37.

22. Ibid., 3707.

23. Cf. ibid., 1483. There are examples also of valuers who are unwilling to be quoted publicly.

24. Ibid., 1561–63.

25. Davitt, *The Fall of Feudalism in Ireland,* pp. 317, 321.

7. RENT AND INCOME IN THE 1880'S

1. Quoted in L. P. Curtis, Jr., *Coercion and Conciliation in Ireland 1880–1892,* p. 409.

2. Department of Agriculture and Technical Instruction for Ireland, *The Agricultural Output of Ireland 1908.*

3. A collection of opinions may be found in Josiah Stamp, *British Incomes and Property,* pp. 152–153.

4. Second Cairns Commission, 6742.

5. Third Cairns Commission, 1072.

6. Cowper Commission, 722. I use the words Cowper Commission to refer to the *Report of the Royal Commission on the Land Law (Ireland) Act, 1881, and the Purchase of Land (Ireland) Act, 1885, P.P.* 1887 (c. 5015) XXVI.

7. Ibid., 595.

8. Thomas Barrington, "A Review of Irish Agricultural Prices," table 1.

9. Depreciation and interest would have to be deducted, possibly some other minor items. I think the principal item would be depreciation on the stock of animals. Buildings and agricultural implements were not of great value in nineteenth-century Ireland. Buildings added perhaps 10s. to the value of a small holding and were estimated to add £8, £10, or £12 to a holding as large as 350 acres.

10. Second Cairns Commission, 5789.

11. First Cairns Commission, 1312.

12. First Cairns Commission, 1309.

13. First Cairns Commission, 2041. The same estimate is given by George Fottrell, solicitor to the Land Commission, ibid., Appendix E, p. 141. Possibly these are not independent estimates.

14. Ibid., 4909.

15. Ibid., 5562.

16. Cowper Commission, 8047.

17. Ibid., 8022.

18. First Cairns Commission, 896.

19. Ibid., 1787.

20. Ibid., 810.

21. Ibid., 2913.

22. Ibid., 1583.

23. Ibid., 1574.

24. *Irish Land Purchase Legislation: A Memorandum as to the*

Amendments to the Land Purchase Acts Submitted for the Consideration of Her Majesty's Government by the Executive Committee of the Irish Landowners' Convention, p. 1.

25. *Land Commission Report,* August 22, 1887, to August 21, 1888, *P.P.* 1888 (c. 5586) XXXIII.

26. First Cairns Commission, *Report,* vi.

27. Curtis, *Coercion and Conciliation,* p. 349.

28. *Resolutions and Statement on the Irish Land Question Adopted by the Irish Landowners' Convention on the 10th October 1902.*

29. The Earl of Dunraven, *Past Times and Pastimes,* vol. 2, chap. 1. The report of the Land Conference is printed in full in Appendix II.

30. Elizabeth R. Hooker, *Readjustments of Agricultural Tenure in Ireland,* p. 82.

31. Margaret Digby, *Horace Plunkett,* p. 55.

8. SOME REFLECTIONS

1. Robert Trow Smith, *Life from the Land,* pp. 163ff. The data in the paragraph are also from the same source. The great spurt in Danish agriculture probably should be dated from 1865, the end of the Danish-Prussian War, but its development continued all through our period.

2. Richmond Commission, 13,414.

3. Richmond Commission, 18,876.

4. Margaret Digby, *Horace Plunkett,* p. 44.

5. Edith Œ. Somerville and Martin Ross, *Irish Memories,* pp. 27–28.

APPENDIX A

1. *Census of Ireland, 1871, P.P.* 1871 (c. 375) LIX, 801. The population of each Poor Law union for the most recent census date is also given in the *Agricultural Statistics* of Ireland each year.

2. Banbridge, Belfast, Carrick on Suir, Clonmel, Cork, Drogheda, Dundalk, Galway, Larne, Limerick, Lisburn, Londonderry, Lurgan, Newtownards, Newry, Waterford, and Wexford.

3. For a full discussion of the problems involved in classifying

pasture and meadow, see Leslie Symons, ed., *Land Use in Northern Ireland,* pp. 127–129.

4. Sean O'Faolain in his autobiography, *Vive Moi!,* recalls in his youth the light railways in Clare taking on *ballast.*

5. The standard geography of Ireland is T. W. Freeman's *Ireland.* I have taken my information from this source.

APPENDIX B

1. Richard M. Barrington, "The Prices of Some Agricultural Produce and the Cost of Farm Labour for the Past Fifty Years," a paper read before the Statistical and Social Inquiry Society of Ireland, December 14, 1886, p. 7.

Bibliography

PRIMARY SOURCES

Parliamentary Papers

Account of the Irish Land Commissioners for the Period from 22nd August 1881 to 31st March 1882, with the Report of the Comptroller and Auditor General Thereon, 1882 (393) XXXVII. To 1883, 1884 (53) XXII. To 1884, 1884–1885 (8) XX. To 1885, 1886 (53–Sess. I) XIX. To 1886, 1887 (17) XXV. To 1887, 1888 (57) XXXIII. To 1888, 1889 (47) XXVII.

Agricultural Statistics for Ireland for 1876, 1877 (c. 1749) LXXXV. For 1877, 1878 (c. 1938) LXXVII. For 1878, 1878–1879 (c. 2347) LXXV. For 1879, 1880 (c. 2534) LXXVI. For 1880, 1881 (c. 2932) XCIII. For 1881, 1883 (c. 3332) LXXIV. For 1882, 1883 (c. 3677) LXXVI. For 1883, 1884 (c. 4069) LXXXV. For 1884, 1884–1885 (c. 4489) LXXXV. For 1885, 1886 (c. 4802) LXXI. For 1886, 1887 (c. 5084) LXXXIX.

> *General Abstract, Showing the Acreage under Crops; Also the Number and Description of Live Stock in Each County and Province, for 1876,* 1876 (c. 1567) LXXVIII. For 1876–77, 1877 (c. 1841) LXXXV. For 1877–78, 1878 (c. 2146) LXXVII. For 1878–79, 1878–79 (c. 2409) LXXV. For 1879–80, 1880 (c. 2652) LXXVI. For 1880–81, 1881 (c. 3071) XCIII. For 1881–82, 1882 (c. 3366) LXXIV. For 1882–83, 1883 (c. 3768) LXXVI. For 1883–84, 1884 (c. 4151) LXXXV. For 1884–85, 1884–85 (c. 4501) LXXXV. For 1885–86, 1886 (c. 4805) LXXI. For 1886–87, 1887 (c. 5186) LXXXIX.

> *Tables Showing the Extent in Statute Acres and the Produce of the Crops, with Observations of the Royal Irish Constabu-*

lary and Metropolitan Police Who Acted as Superintendents of the Agricultural Statistics for 1881, 1881 (c. 3048) XCIII. For 1882, 1882 (c. 3359) LXXIV. For 1883, 1883 (c. 3809) LXXVI. For 1884, 1884–1885 (c. 4258) LXXXV. For 1885, 1884–1885 (c. 4602) LXXXV. For 1886, 1886 (c. 4902) LXXI.

Census of Ireland, 1871: Abstract of the enumerators' returns showing by provinces, counties, cities and certain corporate towns: I, Number of Inhabitants in 1841, 1851, 1861, and 1871; II, Religious Profession in 1861 and 1871; III, Number of Houses in 1841, 1851, 1861, and 1871; IV, Number of Families in 1841, 1851, 1861, and 1871; 1871 (c. 375) LIX.

First Report from the Select Committee of the House of Lords on Land Law (Ireland); with the Proceedings, Evidence, Appendix, and Index; 1882 (249) XI. *Second Report, with the Proceedings, Evidence, Appendix, and Index*; 1882 (379) XI. *Third Report, with the Proceedings, Evidence, Appendix, and Index*; 1883 (204) XIII. *Fourth Report, with the Proceedings, Evidence, Appendix, and Index*; 1883 (279) XIII. [Cairns Commission.]

Report from the Select Committee on General Valuation &c (Ireland), 1868–69 (362) IX.

Report of the Commission of Inquiry into the Working of the Landlord and Tenant (Ireland) Act, 1870, and the Amending Acts, with Evidence, Appendices, and Index; 1881 (c. 2779) XVIII, XIX. [Bessborough Commission.]

Report of the Royal Commission on the Land Law (Ireland) Act, 1881, and the Purchase of Land (Ireland) Act, 1885; with Evidence, Appendices, and Index; 1887 (c. 4969) XXVI. Separate report by Mr. Thomas Knipe; 1887 (c. 5015) XXVI. [Cowper Commission.]

Reports from Poor Law Inspectors in Ireland as to the Existing Relations between Landlord and Tenant in Respect of Improvement on Farms, 1870 (c. 31) XIV.

Return by Provinces and Counties, of Cases of Evictions Which Have Come to the Knowledge of the Constabulary in Each Year, 1849 to 1880; P.P. 1881 (c. 185) LXXVII.

Returns of Cases of Evictions in Ireland in Each Quarter in Each Year, Showing the Number of Families and Persons Evicted in Each County, and the Number Readmitted as Tenants and as

Caretakers, for 1880, 1881 (2) LXXVII; *for 1881;* 1881 (285)
LXXVII and 1881 (320) LXXVII.

*Royal Commission on the Depressed Condition of the Agricultural
Interest: Preliminary Report,* P.P. 1881 (c. 2778) XV. Final
Report, 1882 (c. 3309) XIV. Assistant Commissioners' Reports, 1880 (c. 2678) XVIII. 1881 (c. 2778–II) XVI. 1881
(c. 2951) XVI. 1882 (c. 3375–I to VI). Minutes of evidence;
1881 (c. 2778–I) XV. 1881 (c. 3096) XVII. 1882 (c.
3309–I.) XIV. Digest of evidence; 1881 (c. 2778–II) XVI.
1882 (c. 3309–II) XIV. Appendices; 1881 (c. 2778–II) XVI.
1882 (c. 3309–II) XIV. [Richmond Commission.]

*Royal Commission on the Financial Relations between Great Britain
and Ireland,* 1895 (c. 7720–I), XXXVI.

Royal Commission on Local Taxation, 1898 (c. 8673) XLI.

*Twenty-eighth Report of H[er] M[ajesty's] Inland Revenue Commis-
sioners,* 1884–1885 (c. 4474) XXII.

Contemporary Printed Sources

Bailey, William F. *The Irish Land Acts: A Short Sketch of Their
History and Development.* Dublin, 1917.

Barrington, Richard M. *The Prices of Some Agricultural Produce
and the Cost of Farm Labour for the Past Fifty Years.* Paper
read before the Statistical and Social Inquiry Society of Ireland, December 14, 1886. Dublin, 1887.

Caird, James. *The Landed Interest and the Supply of Food.* London,
1880.

Campbell, George. *The Irish Land.* Dublin, 1869.

Carlyle, Thomas. *Reminiscences of My Irish Journey in 1849.*
London, 1882.

Cecil, Lady Gwendolen. *Life of Robert, Marquis of Salisbury,* 2
vols. London: Hodder and Stoughton, 1921.

Davitt, Michael. *The Fall of Feudalism in Ireland.* London and
New York: Harpers, 1904.

Dugdale, Blanche E. C. *Arthur James Balfour, First Earl of Balfour,
K.G., O.M., F.R.S., etc.* 2 vols. London: Hutchinson, 1936.

Dunraven, The Earl of. *Past Times and Pastimes.* 2 vols. London,
undated.

Grimshaw, Thomas W. "A Statistical Survey of Ireland from 1840 to 1880." *Journal of the Statistical and Social Inquiry Society of Ireland,* vol. 9 (December 1888).

Healy, Timothy. *Letters and Leaders of My Day.* 2 vols. London: Butterworth, 1928.

Holland, Bernard. *Life of the Duke of Devonshire.* 2 vols. London: Longmans, Green, 1911.

Hussey, S. M. (with Home Gordon). *The Reminiscences of an Irish Land Agent.* London: Duckworth, 1904.

Jones, W. Bence. *A Life's Work in Ireland by a Landlord Who Tried to Do His Duty.* London, 1880.

Mackail, J. W., and Wyndham, Guy. *Life and Letters of George Wyndham.* 2 vols. London, undated.

Mill, John Stuart. *Chapters and Speeches on the Irish Land Question Reprinted from "Principles of Political Economy" and Hansard's Debates.* London, 1870.

Monypenny, William Flavelle, and Buckle, George Earle. *The Life of Benjamin Disraeli, Earl of Beaconsfield.* 2 vols., rev. ed. London: John Murray, 1929.

Morley, John. *The Life of William Ewart Gladstone.* 2 vols. London: Macmillan, 1905.

———— [Viscount]. *Recollections.* 2 vols. New York: Macmillan, 1917.

O'Brien, R. Barry. *The Parliamentary History of the Irish Land Question.* London, 1880.

O'Connor, T. P. *Memoirs of an Old Parliamentarian.* 2 vols. New York: Appleton, 1929.

Richey, Alexander G. *The Irish Land Laws.* London, 1880.

Robinson, Henry. *Memories, Wise and Otherwise.* New York: Dodd, Mead, undated (1923?).

Somerville, Edith Œ., and Ross, Martin. *Irish Memories.* New York: Longmans, Green, 1918.

Synge, J. M. *The Aran Islands.* Boston: J. W. Luce, 1911.

Thorold, Alger Labouchere. *The Life of Henry Labouchere.* New York: Putnam, 1913.

Young, Arthur. *A Tour in Ireland,* ed. Constantia Maxwell.

Miscellaneous

Department of Agriculture and Technical Instruction for Ireland. *The Agricultural Output of Ireland 1908.* London: H.M.S.O., 1912.

Gladstone Papers. British Museum, Additional Manuscripts, 44758, 44235, 44121, 44122.

Irish Landowners' Convention. *Irish Land Purchase Legislation: A Memorandum as to the Amendments to the Land Purchase Acts Submitted for the Consideration of Her Majesty's Government by the Executive Committee of the Irish Landowners' Convention.* Dublin, 1895.

——— *Resolutions and Statement on the Irish Land Question Adopted by the Irish Landowners' Convention on the 10th October 1902.* Dublin, 1902.

Saorstát Eireann. *Agricultural Statistics 1847 to 1926,* with an introductory essay by John Hooper, Director of Statistics, Department of Industry and Commerce, Dublin, 1930.

Thom's Almanac and Official Directory of the United Kingdom and Ireland. Dublin, annually.

SECONDARY SOURCES

Barrington, Thomas. "A Review of Irish Agricultural Prices." *Journal of the Statistical and Social Inquiry Society of Ireland,* vol. 15 (1927), 249–280.

Blake, Robert. *Disraeli.* New York: St. Martin's, 1967.

Bourke, P. M. Austin. "The Agricultural Statistics of the 1841 Census of Ireland: A Critical Review." *Economic History Review,* 2nd ser., vol. 18 (1965).

Clapham, J. H. *Economic History of Modern Britain,* 2 vols. New York, 1938.

Clark, G. Kitson. See Kitson Clark, G.

Connell, K. H. *The Population of Ireland, 1750–1845.* Oxford: Oxford University Press, 1950.

Cousens, S. H. "Emigration and Demographic Change in Ireland, 1851–1861." *Economic History Review,* 2nd ser., 14 (1961): 275–288.

——— "The Regional Variations in Population Changes in Ireland, 1861–1881." *Economic History Review,* 2nd ser., 17 (1964): 301–321.

——— "The Regional Pattern of Emigration during the Great Irish Famine, 1846–1851." *Institute of British Geographers, Transactions and Papers,* no. 28 (1960): 126–129.

Curtis, L. P., Jr. *Coercion and Conciliation in Ireland 1880–1892; A Study in Conservative Unionism.* Princeton: Princeton University Press, 1963.

Digby, Margaret. *Horace Plunkett: An Anglo-American Irishman.* Oxford: Macmillan, 1949.

Ernle, Rowland Edmund Prothero. *English Farming, Past and Present.* 6th ed. Chicago: Quadrangle Books, 1961.

Freeman, T. W. *Ireland.* 2nd ed. London: Methuen, 1960.

Gill, Conrad. *The Rise of the Irish Linen Industry.* Oxford: Oxford University Press, 1964.

Hargreaves, A. D. *An Introduction to the Principles of Land Law.* 3rd ed. London: Sweet and Maxwell, 1952.

Hooker, Elizabeth R. *Readjustments of Agricultural Tenure in Ireland.* Chapel Hill: University of North Carolina Press, 1938.

Kennedy, Brian A. "Tenant Right." In *Ulster Since 1800: A Political and Economic Survey,* ed. T. W. Moody and J. C. Beckett. London: British Broadcasting Corporation, 1957.

Kitson Clark, G. *The Making of Victorian England, Being the Ford Lectures before the University of Oxford.* London: Methuen, 1962.

Lansdowne, The Marquis of. *Glanerought and the Petty-Fitzmaurices.* London: Oxford University Press, 1937.

Lyons, F. S. L. *The Fall of Parnell, 1890–91.* Toronto: Toronto University Press, 1960.

McCormick, Donald. *The Incredible Mr. Kavanagh.* London: Putnam, 1960.

McDowell, R. B. *The Irish Administration, 1801–1914.* London and Toronto: Routledge and Kegan Paul, 1964.

Matthews, A. H. H. *Fifty Years of Agricultural Politics: Being the History of the Central Chamber of Agriculture, 1865–1915.* London: P. S. King & Son, 1915.

Moody, T. W. "The New Departure in Irish Politics, 1878–1879." In *Essays in British and Irish History in Honour of James Eadie Todd,* ed. H. A. Cronne, T. W. Moody, and D. B. Quinn. London: Mueller, 1949.

Moody, T. W., and Beckett, J. C., eds. *Ulster Since 1800: A Political and Economic Survey.* London: British Broadcasting Corporation, 1957.

——— *Ulster Since 1800, Second Series, A Social Survey.* London: British Broadcasting Corporation, 1958.

O'Brien, Conor Cruise. *Parnell and His Party, 1800–1890*. Oxford: Oxford University Press, 1957.

O'Donovan, John. *The Economic History of Live Stock in Ireland*. Cork and Dublin: Cork University Press, 1940.

Palmer, Norman D. *The Irish Land League Crisis*. New Haven: Yale University Press, 1940.

Pollock, Sir Frederick, and Maitland, Frederic William. *The History of English Law before the Time of Edward I*. 2 vols. 2nd ed. Cambridge: Cambridge University Press, 1952.

Pomfret, John E. *The Struggle for Land in Ireland, 1800–1923*. Princeton: Princeton University Press, 1930.

Staehle, Hans. "Statistical Notes on the Economic History of Irish Agriculture, 1847–1913." *Journal of the Statistical and Social Inquiry Society of Ireland*, 18 (1950–51): 444–47.

Stamp, Josiah. *British Incomes and Property*. London: P. S. King & Son, 1927.

Steele, E. D. "The Irish Land Act of 1870 and the Liberal Party." Ph.D. diss. Cambridge University, Cambridge, England, 1963.

Symons, Leslie, ed. *Land Use in Northern Ireland: The General Report of the Land Utilisation Survey of Northern Ireland*. London: University of London Press, 1963.

Tansill, Charles Callan. *America and the Fight for Irish Freedom: 1866–1922*. New York: Devin-Adair, 1957.

Trow Smith, Robert. *Life from the Land: The Growth of Farming in Western Europe*. London: Longmans, 1967.

Index